JOURNALISM AND DEMOCRACY

JOURNALISM AND DEMOCRACY

Rajesh Kumar

SUMIT ENTERPRISES
New Delhi-110 002 (India)

First Published 2011

ISBN 978-81-8420-276-2

Published by:

SUMIT ENTERPRISES
4649B/21, Ansari Road, Darya Ganj
New Delhi-110 002
Phone: 011-23279353, 9810217567
E-mail: sumit_enterprises2007@yahoo.co.in

PRINTED IN INDIA

Published by Sri Lokesh Kumar for Sumit Enterprises, New Delhi-110002, Typeset by Abhijeet Typesetters, Printed at Nev Prabhat Printing Press, Tronicacity (UP)

Contents

	Preface	*(vii)*
1.	Role of Journalism in Democracy	1
2.	Communication Deficit in Democracy and Development	18
3.	Public Sphere and Media Democracy	42
4.	Human Rights and Journalistic Ethics	72
5.	Freedom of Press and Responsible Journalism	93
6.	An Analysis of Parliamentary Privileges in India	110
7.	Media Culture in Globalization	139
8.	Public Broadcasting and Digital Media	159
9.	Investigative and Political Journalism	204
10.	Weblogs and Journalism	222
11.	Forms of Participatory Journalism	240
12.	Broadcasting Laws in India	266
	Bibliography	283
	Index	287

Preface

Journalism is the practice of investigation and reporting of events, issues, and trends to a broad audience. Although there is much variation within journalism, the ideal is to inform the citizenry. Besides covering organizations and institutions such as government and business, journalism also covers cultural aspects of society such as arts and entertainment. The field includes jobs such as editing, photojournalism, and documentary. Democracy is a form of government in which all citizens have an equal say in the decisions that affect their lives. Ideally, this includes equal participation in the proposal, development and passage of legislation into law. It can also encompass social, economic and cultural conditions that enable the free and equal practice of political self-determination.

At present, a few transnational media corporations in the more developed countries dominate the commercial media system. Government media monopolies together with foreign economic interests control the flow of information and news in most of the less developed countries. In both authoritarian and democratic structures, domestic order and national security are claimed to determine the main ethical imperative. Commercial systems gravitate towards an ethics of freedom, i.e. rights to property and maximum profits. Public media systems have developed a notion of public service originally defined in terms of elitist cultural concepts but increasingly eroded by the competition from the commercial media. Community media systems such as those belonging to religious or labour organizations serve their own constituencies. Finally, "independent media" activists, including zine-publishers and bloggers have been spreading the free blogosphere media gospel, but the digital divide and other constraints still limit its worldwide adoption at present. A mixed media system, combining channels of all five models could provide better service. It would encourage media ethics and professional standards to activate pluralism of content and checks and balances in news coverage. This would allow for honest representation of all voices in given societies, for the development of policies and projects beneficial to their "developed", "developing", and "underdeveloped" sectors and for better representation of peace in the media.

Journalism is necessary because direct democracy is obsolete. People do not really have a say in modern democracy, aside from their vote, unless they are a politician themselves. Journalism serves as a window; however it could be rose coloured glass, to the bureaucracy that is democratic process. From there you can see what policies and philosophies you buy into. Journalism, relating to the politicians, is the glass display counter that lets the audience see what kind of watches there are to buy. Some are fake, some are real. You buy the one you like, but in an eerie "twilight zone" plot twist, the appreciated watches stay under the display, and the underappreciated watches disappear. The average man is discreetly unconnected in a democracy, his opinions and beliefs have no real influence on anything. The only real reason there is journalism in a democracy is so the average man is aware that there is an election, so he can vote! And to vote for whom, largely depends on which newspaper and journalist you subscribe to. While politics might make up less than a quarter of a newspaper, make no mistake, journalism is the advertising agency of politicians. The rest is simply marketable brain fodder.

This book provides a lively and authoritative introduction to journalism in all its forms. The focus of the book is to show how journalists do their job, not only by explaining the process but also by hearing from those who do it on a daily basis.

—*Editor*

1

Role of Journalism in Democracy

In the 1920s, as modern journalism was just taking form, writer Walter Lippmann and American philosopher John Dewey debated over the role of journalism in a democracy. Their differing philosophies still characterize a debate about the role of journalism in society and the nation-state.

Lippmann understood that journalism's role at the time was to act as a mediator or translator between the public and policy making elites. The journalist became the middleman. When elites spoke, journalists listened and recorded the information, distilled it, and passed it on to the public for their consumption. His reasoning behind this was that the public was not in a position to deconstruct the growing and complex flurry of information present in modern society, and so an intermediary was needed to filter news for the masses. Lippman put it this way: The public is not smart enough to understand complicated, political issues. Furthermore, the public was too consumed with their daily lives to care about complex public policy. Therefore the public needed someone to interpret the decisions or concerns of the elite to make the information plain and simple.

That was the role of journalists. Lippmann believed that the public would affect the decision-making of the elite with their vote. In the meantime, the elite (i.e. politicians, policy makers, bureaucrats, scientists, etc.) would keep the business of power running. In Lippman's world, the journalist's role was to inform the public of what the elites were doing. It was also to act as a watchdog over the elites, as the public had the final say with their votes. Effectively that kept the public at the bottom of the power chain, catching the flow of information that is handed down from experts/elites.

Dewey, on the other hand, believed the public was not only capable of understanding the issues created or responded to by the elite, it was in the public forum that decisions should be made after discussion and debate. When issues were thoroughly vetted, then the best ideas would bubble to the surface. Dewey believed journalists should do more than simply pass on information. He believed they should weigh the consequences of the policies being enacted. Over time, his idea has been implemented in various degrees, and is more commonly known as "community journalism."

This concept of *community journalism* is at the centre of new developments in journalism. In this new paradigm, journalists are able to engage citizens and the experts/elites in the proposition and generation of content. It's important to note that while there is an assumption of equality, Dewey still celebrates expertise. Dewey believes the shared knowledge of many is far superior to a single individual's knowledge. Experts and scholars are welcome in Dewey's framework, but there is not the hierarchical structure present in Lippman's understanding of journalism and society. According to Dewey, conversation, debate, and dialogue lie at the heart of a democracy.

While Lippman's journalistic philosophy might be more acceptable to government leaders, Dewey's approach is a better description of how many journalists see their role in society, and, in turn, how much of society expects journalists to function. Americans, for example, may criticize some of the excesses committed by journalists, but they tend to expect journalists to serve as watchdogs on government, businesses and other actors, enabling people to make informed decisions on the issues of the time.

The Elements of Journalism

According to *The Elements of Journalism*, a book by Bill Kovach and Tom Rosenstiel, there are nine elements of journalism. In order for a journalist to fulfil their duty of providing the people with the information they need to be free and self-governing. They must follow these guidelines:

1. Journalism's first obligation is to the truth.
2. Its first loyalty is to the citizens.
3. Its essence is discipline of verification.
4. Its practitioners must maintain an independence from those they cover.
5. It must serve as an independent monitor of power.
6. It must provide a forum for public criticism and compromise.
7. It must strive to make the significant interesting, and relevant.
8. It must keep the news comprehensive and proportional.
9. Its practitioners must be allowed to exercise their personal conscience.

In the April 2007 edition of the book, they have added one additional element, *the rights and responsibilities of citizens* to make it a total of ten elements of journalism.

Professional and Ethical Standards

In the UK, all newspapers are bound by the Code of Practice of the Press Complaints Commission. This includes points like respecting people's privacy and ensuring accuracy. However, the Media Standards Trust has criticised the PCC, claiming it needs to be radically changed to secure public trust of newspapers.

This is in stark contrast to the media climate prior to the 20th Century, where the media market was dominated by smaller newspapers and pamphleteers who usually had an overt and often radical agenda, with no presumption of balance or objectivity.

Recognition of Excellence in Journalism

There are several professional organizations, universities and foundations that recognize excellence in journalism in the USA. The Pulitzer Prize, administered by Columbia University in New York City, is awarded to newspapers, magazines and broadcast media for excellence in various kinds of journalism.

The Columbia University Graduate School of Journalism gives the Alfred I. duPont-Columbia University Awards for excellence in radio and television journalism, and the Scripps Howard Foundation gives the National Journalism Awards in 17 categories. The Society of Professional Journalists gives the Sigma Delta Chi Award for journalism excellence. In the television industry, the National Academy of Television Arts & Sciences gives awards for excellence in television journalism.

Failing to Uphold Standards

Such a code of conduct can, in the real world, be difficult to uphold consistently. Journalists who believe they are being fair or objective may give biased accounts—by reporting selectively, trusting too much to anecdote, or giving a partial explanation of actions. Even in routine reporting, bias can creep into a story through a reporter's choice of facts to summarize, or through failure to check enough sources, hear and report dissenting voices, or seek fresh perspectives.

A news organization's budget inevitably reflects decision-making about what news to cover, for what audience, and in what depth. Those decisions may reflect conscious or unconscious bias. When budgets are cut, editors may sacrifice reporters in distant news bureaus, reduce the number of staff assigned to low-income areas, or wipe entire communities from the publication's zone of interest.

Publishers, owners and other corporate executives, especially advertising sales executives, can try to use their powers over journalists to influence how news is reported and published. Journalists usually rely on top management to create and maintain a "firewall" between the news and other departments in a news organization to prevent undue influence on the news department. One journalism magazine, Columbia Journalism Review, has made it a practice to reveal examples of executives who try to influence news coverage, of executives who do not abuse their powers over journalists, and of journalists who resist such pressures.

Self-censorship is a growing problem in journalism, particularly in covering countries that sharply restrict press freedom. As commercial pressure in the media marketplace grows, media organizations are loath to lose access to high-profile countries by producing unflattering stories. For example, CNN admitted that it had practiced self-censorship in covering the Saddam Hussein regime in Iraq in order to ensure continued access after the regime had thrown out other media. CNN correspondent Christiane Amanpour also complained of self-censorship during the invasion of Iraq due to the fear of alienating key audiences in the US. There are claims that the media are also avoiding covering stories about repression and human rights violations by the Israeli and Iranian regimes in order to maintain a presence in those countries.

Reporting Versus Editorializing

Generally, publishers and consumers of journalism draw a distinction between reporting — "just the facts" — and opinion writing, often by restricting opinion columns to the editorial page and its facing or "op-ed" (opposite the editorials) page. Unsigned editorials are traditionally the official opinions of the paper's editorial board, while op-ed pages may be a mixture of syndicated columns and other contributions, frequently with some attempt to balance the voices across some political or social spectrum.

The distinction between reporting and opinion can break down. In the UK, the Press Complaints Commission states that "the Press, whilst free to be partisan, must distinguish clearly between comment, conjecture and fact but some commentators have suggested there can sometimes be a blurring of opinion and fact Complex stories often require summarizing and interpretation of facts, especially if there is limited time or space for a story. Stories involving great amounts of interpretation are often labelled "news analysis," but still run in a paper's news columns. The limited time for each story in a broadcast report rarely allows for such distinctions.

Legal Status

Journalists around the world often write about the governments in their nations, and those governments have widely varying policies and practices towards journalists, which control what they can research and write, and what press organizations can publish. Many Western governments guarantee the freedom of the press, and do relatively little to restrict press rights and freedoms, while other nations severely restrict what journalists can research and/or publish. Journalists in many nations have enjoyed some privileges not enjoyed by members of the general public, including better access to public events, crime scenes and press conferences, and to extended interviews with public officials, celebrities and others in the public eye. These privileges are available because of the perceived power of the press to turn public opinion for or against governments, their officials and policies, as well as the perception that the press often represents their consumers. These privileges extend from the legal rights of journalists but are not guaranteed by those rights. Sometimes government officials may attempt to punish individual journalists who irk them by denying them some of these privileges extended to other journalists.

Nations or jurisdictions that formally license journalists may confer special privileges and responsibilities along with those licenses, but in the United States the tradition of an independent press has avoided any imposition of government-controlled examinations or licensing. Some of the states have explicit shield laws that protect journalists from some forms of government inquiry, but those statutes' definitions of "journalist" were often based on access to printing presses and broadcast towers. A national shield law has been proposed.

In some nations, journalists are directly employed, controlled or censored by their governments. In other nations, governments who may claim to guarantee press rights actually intimidate journalists with threats of arrest, destruction or seizure of property (especially the means of production and dissemination of news content), torture or murder.

Journalists who elect to cover conflicts, whether wars between nations or insurgencies within nations, often give up any expectation of protection by government, if not giving up their rights to protection by government. Journalists who are captured or detained during a conflict are expected to be treated as civilians and to be released to their national government.

Right to Protect Confidentiality of Sources

Journalists' interaction with sources sometimes involves confidentiality, an extension of freedom of the press giving journalists a legal protection to keep the identity of a source private even when demanded by police or prosecutors; withholding sources can land journalists in contempt of court, or in jail. The scope of rights granted to journalists varies from nation to nation; in the United Kingdom, for example, the government has had more legal rights to protect what it considers sensitive information, and to force journalists to reveal the sources of leaked information, than the United States. Other nations, particularly Zimbabwe and the People's Republic of China, have a reputation of persecuting journalists, both domestic and foreign.

In the United States, there has never been a right to protect sources in a federal court. Some states provide varying degrees of such protection. However, federal courts will refuse to force journalists to reveal sources, unless the information the court seeks is highly relevant to the case, and there's no other way to get it. Journalists, like all citizens, who refuse to testify even when ordered to can be found in contempt of court and fined or jailed.

Right of Access

Journalists often depend on freedom of information legislation to access information held by the government. These rights also vary from nation to nation.

United States

In the United States, the Freedom of Information Act guarantees journalists the right to obtain copies of government documents, although the government has the right to black out some information from these documents. Other federal legislation also controls access to information. Some states have more open policies for making information available, and some states have acted in the last decade to broaden those rights. New Jersey has updated and broadened its freedom of information legislation to better define what kinds of government documents can be withheld from public inquiry.

Journalists in the state of Michigan have access to information based on the latest provisions from the state amended in 1996 PA 553 Office of the Michigan Attorney General. Michigan's defined basic intent for the Freedom of Information Act (FIOA) is that it is an act that regulates and sets requirements for the disclosure of public records by all "public bodies" in the state.

The definition of a public body is any state officer, employee, agency, department, division, bureau, board, commission, council, authority, or other body in the executive branch of the state government (it does not however include the governor, or lieutenant governor. Other bodies included are school boards, or bodies created or funded by state or local authority. A public record is something that is written regarding the performance of a official function held by any of the previously named bodies.

Accessing information in the state of Michigan is available for records that are made public, which includes all records held by those named previously, but not those specifically marked as exceptions. Items that are commonly held as public record include meeting notes, voting records, and written statements. Records can be found and kept in a number of manners; anywhere from typewritten to handwritten, to printed, photographed, or even audio recording. Items as such are also allowed to be kept as public record in a combination of mediums per type of information.

Some information however, is not allowed to be public knowledge and is not available to look up as a public record. A public body may (but is not required to) withhold information from the public. Some items are exempt from the FOIA such as personal information about an individual that may be a clear invasion of privacy. Other information includes that which may impair an individual of having a fair trial, disclose the identity of a confidential source, information gathered during an investigation, or that which may put law enforcement personnel in danger. Accessing public records in the state of Michigan is made possible via a request in writing to the FOIA coordinator of the public body. One may ask to inspect, copy, or receive a copy of a public record. An individual of any age can request this type of information. The only individuals not entitled to making requests as such are prisoners in state, county, or federal correctional facilities. It is also the responsibility of the public body to respond within five days of the request. There may be charges associated with copying, or providing the information requested. A denial may also be made by the public body in writing within the five day period, or within 15 business days if an extension is granted. If denied, the public body must provide a full explanation of the reason why the denial was made. A person does have the option to appeal a denial, or may take the request for disclosure to a circuit court.

If a court decides that a public body has violated the FOIA, it may grant the person looking for information, on top of providing the person with the information, hold the public body responsible for paying a $500 award to the individual looking for the information illegally denied. Journalists can take this information in the State of Michigan and use it when looking up information that is pertinent to the topic under report or research and do so without violating privacy in order to justify stories or provide sources to enhance journalistic integrity.

India

In India, the Right to Information Act was passed in 2005, giving citizens the right to access state and national records.

France

In France, the freedom of press Act was passed in 1881, giving citizens the right to read and create any newspaper of his choice. In 1935, a new act was passed to protect the right of the journalist to work in good conditions, responding to the demand of the main journalist's Union, the 'Syndicat national des journalists. *In 1971, two other unions, the* Syndicat national des journalists CGT, *and* Union syndicale des journalists CFDT *signed the* charte de Munich, *a stylebook dedicated to protect the deontology and spirit of journalism on a broadbased attempt to boost it all over the world.*

Media Development Organizations

There exist several organizations that use journalism as a form of media development. Such organizations include Search for Common Ground, BBC World Service Trust, and Journalists for Human Rights.

Current State

In 2008, journalism came under heavy fire. The decline of print newspapers has led to a sharp increase in job cuts for journalists. In 2008 alone, approximately 16,000 journalists were terminated – a budgetary response to declining subscription dollars and the inability to adapt to a free-news-driven society. With advertising revenues taking a harsh rapping from the transitional shift of a subscription-based/advertising model to online ad placements, the discrepancy in advertising revenue is making it difficult for traditional newspapers to survive. The Rocky Mountain News (one of the country's oldest newspapers) closed its doors after 150 years of business; The Christian Science Monitor transitioned from its daily newspaper edition to online distribution; 120 newspapers closed their doors in the first three months of 2009; newspaper circulation is down 7% in the first six months of 2009.

Newspapers are forced to maximize their current staff in a response to declining advertising and circulation revenue. As formerly relied upon revenues shore-up, newspapers are exploring radically new ways of reaching readers. The New York Times has partnered with Amazon's Kindle DX to bring current subscribers and Kindle users NYT content. This, along with other social media properties, are ways in which traditional media are fighting to stay relevant in the digital age.

Crime

Crime is the breach of rules or laws for which some governing authority (via mechanisms such as police power) may ultimately prescribe a conviction. While every crime violates the law, not every violation of the law counts as a crime; for example: breaches of contract and of other civil law may rank as "offences" or as "infractions". When informal relationships and sanctions prove insufficient to establish and maintain a desired social order, a government or a sovereign state may impose more formalized or stricter systems of social control. With institutional and legal machinery at their disposal, agents of the State can compel populations to conform to codes, and can opt to punish or to attempt to reform those who do not conform.

Authorities employ various mechanisms to regulate (encouraging or discouraging) certain behaviours in general. Governing or administering agencies may for example codify rules into laws, police people to ensure they comply with those laws, and implement other policies and practices designed to prevent crime. In addition, authorities provide remedies and sanctions, and collectively these constitute a criminal justice system. Legal sanctions vary widely in their severity, they may include incarceration of temporary character aimed at reforming the convict. Some jurisdictions have penal codes written to inflict permanent harsh punishments: legal mutilation, capital punishment or life without parole.

The label of "crime" and the accompanying social stigma normally confine their scope to those activities seen as injurious to the general population or to the State, including some that cause serious loss or damage to individuals. Those who apply the labels of "crime" or "criminal" intend to assert the hegemony of a dominant population, or to reflect a consensus of condemnation for the identified behaviour and to justify any punishments prescribed by the State (in the event that standard processing tries and convicts an accused person of a crime).

Often a natural person perpetrates a crime, but legal persons may also commit crimes.

Definition

A normative definition views crime as deviant behaviour that violates prevailing norms – cultural standards prescribing how humans ought to behave normally. This approach considers the complex realities surrounding the concept of crime and seeks to understand how changing social, political, psychological, and economic conditions may affect changing definitions of crime and the form of the legal, law-enforcement, and penal responses made by society. These structural realities remain fluid and often contentious. For example: as cultures change and the political environment shifts, societies may criminalise or decriminalise certain behaviours, which will directly affect the statistical crime rates, influence the allocation of resources for the enforcement of laws, and (re-)influence the general public opinion.

Similarly, changes in the collection and/or calculation of data on crime may affect the public perceptions of the extent of any given "crime problem". All such adjustments to crime statistics, allied with the experience of people in their everyday lives, shape attitudes on the extent to which the State should use law or social engineering to enforce/encourage any particular social norm. One can control/influence behaviour in many ways without having to resort to the criminal justice system. Indeed, in those cases where no clear consensus exists on a given norm, the drafting of criminal law by the group in power to prohibit the behaviour of another group may seem to some observers an improper limitation of the second group's freedom, and the ordinary members of society have less respect for the law or laws in general — whether the authorities actually enforce the disputed law or not. Legislatures pass laws (called *mala prohibita*) that define crimes which violate social norms. These laws vary from time to time and from place to place: note variations in gambling laws, for example, and the prohibition or encouragement of duelling in history. Other crimes, called *mala in se*, count as outlawed in almost all societies.

THE MEDIA AND DEMOCRACY

No-one was in any doubt about the weight of pressures on the traditional media. Media companies were businesses, and journalism was a profession, harder hit by twenty-first century change than almost any other. Newspapers and their advertising were in financial crisis; blogs, Facebook and other modern phenomena turned any member of the public into a potential journalist; and virtually free access to information on the internet under such pervasive instruments as Google affected advertising choices and therefore business models. Some participants believed that the house was on fire.

So Ditchley entered yet another of its ping-pong games between optimists and pessimists. The optimists pointed to the huge opportunities created by change and new technology. Society was increasingly creative and there was innovation everywhere. If there was a risk of market failure for some businesses, others would grow up to take their place. So long as there was diversity, plurality and engagement, there would be plenty of sunshine breaking through the clouds. Greater transparency made governments more accountable, whether or not they favoured transparency. This did not put the pessimists to bed. Business models were failing too rapidly. Most of what was new tended to be of lower quality. If the media industry had to consolidate, diversity would be affected. Commercialisation of the media was driving out responsibility for reporting the facts. If good journalism meant poor business, the trend would be appalling for the health of democracy. The current picture did not mean a lack of interest in serious reporting or a lack of demand for quality, but supplying it without subsidy was becoming increasingly difficult. Some participants saw this as a gap opening up between the collapse of the old model and the arrival of a new audience/readership who would pay for quality. But no-one was clear on how this transition would be managed.

We tried to analyse how these trends might be affecting the health of society itself. Was an increase in sensationalism and popularism amounting to a death of culture? Were audiences becoming so fragmented by diversity that serious mainstream journalism was being crowded out? If trust in politicians and journalists was equally low in public esteem, did this mean that democracy itself was beginning to suffer?

Plenty of people thought these questions needed to be answered. Greater freedom, diversity and personal security produced a greater focus on the individual, with less respect and apparent need for government. This empowerment of the individual might not yet have settled on a balance which gave state structures and the macro-needs of society enough of a place. Political parties seemed to be behind the times, at least until the Obama campaign phenomenon showed that there was another way of doing it. Politicians found that, in creating laws for the freedom of information, they had not succeeded in building greater trust. Parliament and other traditional, formal institutions seemed to be losing out. Yet, even against this gloomy background, there were arguments against excessive pessimism. This was a "creation" society and was well capable of setting its own rules. Young people were innovative, engaged and perfectly capable of the right kind of adjustment. The British, perhaps over-represented in this company, were more inclined to see the dark side because they expected top-down solutions to problems such as these. The United States, on the other hand, had a more vibrant bottom-up society which was more likely to find the answers. As for the rest of the world, whose voices intervened at regular intervals in this discussion with gentle mockery at the state the Anglo-Saxons were getting themselves into, they sounded all too pleased to swap their problems with ours in most respects.

In other words, few wished to suggest that democracy was seriously sick. We could still agree that good journalism mattered and that ways could be found of preserving it. Public service broadcasting was a key issue in this context. Democracy was rather more vulnerable to the rise of extremism, against which the media could play a vital role in pursuing intelligent analysis and establishing sensible norms: indeed, local media needed the support of the international media in the fight against fanaticism. There were nevertheless some problems which needed attention. The sometimes rancid relationship between government and the media, especially in the UK, had been taken too far. Representative democracy was changing its character if individuals believed that they could now participate directly; and yet the way in which they were doing this was not strengthening the fabric of society. The themes of quality and "media literacy" came into our discussion, suggesting that government, the private sector and individual members of society alike ought to take more trouble to understand the context of modern trends and set in hand or support policies which built a more responsible society.

Rather than adding complexity to the subject matter, our discussion of the media and democracy in the developing world gave a sense of proportion to our discussion so far of the developed world. Different countries and different media experiences in Africa and Asia of course presented a mixed picture. But, at its best, the media was capable of generating huge interest and dynamism in countries with younger or only partial democratic systems. Even where the institutions of the state were weak and financial investment was inadequate, the media were showing how government could be called to account and the interests of society served. There were still too many places where the heavy hand of the state caused severe difficulties, where – as one participant put it – subjection had replaced citizenship because independence made only the political elite true citizens. But there were advances in freedom of expression and freedom of the media which were supporting accountability and individual rights.

Even where the state media dominated, governments were finding that they could not afford financial support for public service broadcasting. The resulting commercialisation of state media, while opening up opportunities on some fronts, was also producing noticeable distortions. With internet access too low across many parts of the developing world, radio remained the most available medium. Its power in local politics was well illustrated in Kenya in early 2008 when violence erupted over languages selected for radio. Gradually, however, use of the web was emerging and micro-public spheres were being created. This trend might accelerate quite fast. In addition, as journalism and the diversity of instruments improved, the power of narrative was making itself felt in the developing world, perhaps more so than in the developed world. But this power would not be enough to countervail poor governance unless financial and institutional backing for a free media also made progress. In this context, we were warned that some important countries with a history of state control of the media were increasingly resisting multilateral efforts to promote free media.

We were asked to remember that, outside the advanced democracies, different countries were at different stages of development towards sophisticated systems and that the lessons we were trying to learn from the US and UK experiences did not necessarily yet apply elsewhere. In Russia, for example, for all the talk of democratic practice being on hold, there was a vibrant media debate in Moscow which could be regarded as providing a more lively political opposition to the groups in power than, say, in the United States. The form which the expression of opinion took did not necessarily matter when it came to its effectiveness.

While this discussion did not easily lead to any firm policy conclusions or recommendations, there were areas of focus which emerged as valuable or as needing further concentrated effort. One of these was public service broadcasting, which we covered in some depth. The British system was seen as almost unique in its characteristics, including the nature of the licence fee and the maintenance of the (usually) high quality of the BBC. But there was nervousness about the costs of preserving this quality if the public service broadcaster was also required to reach large audiences and maintain a commercial approach for at least a part of its output. In the United States the role of public service broadcasting was less central because the success of commercial business models was higher. But that did not mean that a debate about quality was irrelevant. In both environments, and perhaps elsewhere as well, the credibility and the innovation of the media was best represented by the news sector, in which public service broadcasting had to play a role. But there was a long argument to be played out in a number of different jurisdictions about the right public service broadcasting model and it was hard to predict at this stage what the outcome would be.

Another strong theme, perhaps in the end the most significant one for policy focus over the next period, was education. We interpreted "media literacy" as meaning not so much the literary quality of journalism itself as the capacity of the public to receive the media's product with discernment and to judge what was healthy for their own interests beyond the short term. It was felt that there was a need to insert a stronger sense of civic responsibility into the education curriculum. Throughout the conference participants constantly returned to the need for young people, and perhaps older generations as well, to understand better the modern context for a healthy democracy. With communications technology racing ahead as it was, public participation in the media was the only modern guarantor of a healthy media sector and the exercising of public judgement by a "literate" society was a necessary requirement for securely-based democracy. Not just schools and universities, but also business management training and government accountability processes, should build in an approach that served these needs.

These thoughts tied in with the theme of quality in journalism and in the use of instruments of modern communication. If the public understood the benefits of having the best true picture of the world presented to them, then good journalism had a prospect of again becoming good business. Transparency needed to be more overtly linked with responsibility and the building of trust. If the government was not able to manage this through policy direction, in other words through a top-down approach, then the relevant parts of the private sector should be encouraged to fill the gap. We wondered whether philanthropic foundations could help, for example by building on models of 'citizen journalism', or whether companies like Google might be persuaded to take an altruistic approach on behalf of society. Neither of these thoughts, especially the latter one, generated much confidence. But we were clear that both the power of innovation and the funding that resulted from commercial success ought to play a part in constructing a system where diversity and openness were accompanied by social responsibility.

In short, we found ourselves concluding that there were still huge strengths in the media industry, though more in the modern than in the traditional forms of it, and there was still dynamism in the evolution of democracy. It was politics that had not yet found the right balance: between government and individual, between plurality and democratic security, between freedom of choice and education on the constraints. That, we felt, was where the next concentration of effort should lie.

There was plenty of hard-bitten media experience around this table and yet the sharing of different perspectives, geographical or professional, threw up a conversation of great freshness and interest. Ditchley owes a great deal for this to the spirit of the participants, and especially to our chairman, who steered between a free-for-all and an over-disciplined discussion with great judgement. As for the optimists and the pessimists, each individual will have to add up his own score. But we all felt we had learnt a lot from these two days.

2

Communication Deficit in Democracy and Development

At the beginning of the 21st century a communication deficit can be identified in the areas of democracy and development. It is expressed in the fact that despite the growth in democratic media spaces in many parts of the world, particularly after the end of the Cold War, an increasing gap exists between mainstream 'official speak', consumer-oriented media and credible communication. A more democratic media structure – including older and newer communication technologies could seek to achieve a better balance between private and public social interests. This would lead to recognition of, first, the equal legitimacy of private economic considerations and of the need for public activities that do not promise immediate profit; second, the need for democratic interaction, through various media, of governments, opposition groups and other organizations, including NGOs and civil society institutions; third, the needs of the public for information and context, beyond private interests; and fourth, the need for a decrease of institutional control over communication among groups and individuals.

At present, a few transnational media corporations in the more developed countries dominate the commercial media system. Government media monopolies together with foreign economic interests control the flow of information and news in most of the less developed countries. In both authoritarian and democratic structures, domestic order and national security are claimed to determine the main ethical imperative.

Commercial systems gravitate towards an ethics of freedom, i.e. rights to property and maximum profits. Public media systems have developed a notion of public service originally defined in terms of elitist cultural concepts but increasingly eroded by the competition from the commercial media (Andersen and Strate, 2000). Community media systems such as those belonging to religious or labour organizations serve their own constituencies (Howley, 2005). Finally, "independent media" activists, including zine-publishers and bloggers have been spreading the free blogosphere media gospel, but the digital divide and other constraints still limit its worldwide adoption at present. A mixed media system, combining channels of all five models could provide better service. It would encourage media ethics and professional standards to activate pluralism of content and checks and balances in news coverage. This would allow for honest representation of all voices in given societies, for the development of policies and projects beneficial to their "developed", "developing", and "underdeveloped" sectors and for better representation of peace in the media.

CONFLICTS AND PEACE IN THE MEDIA: DEFICIT AND BALANCE

Most post-Cold War conflicts have had a global impact, regardless of their nature as sporadic eruptions of regional violence or worldwide "democratic anti-terror crusades". Local, regional, and global interests, loyalties, and power plays have been interacting, propelled by the development of communication technologies, and by increasing media usage. Some striking findings show that the media can help enhance both "peace deficits" and "peace-balanced performances". Thus:

a. The media can contribute to war, genocide, terrorism, oppression, and repression as well as to security, dignity, growth, and decision-making by citizens on the basis of accurate, credible, and manageable information.
b. The media are stakeholders of democracy together with inter-governmental organizations, global civil organizations, and transnational financial and industrial corporations.
c. In concert with the premise that the interests of world peace and security create an urgent need to devise

effective ways of handling conflict, there is need to explore mediating mechanisms that may assist in developing better understanding of conflict and better ability to reduce its impact.

d. Media structures and ethics can be adapted to the needs of democracy, peace and human development, by:
    1. Uplifting professional standards and social awareness of journalists, and their organizations;
    2. Encouraging a transition in the working logic of the media from hierarchical, hegemonic, and mobilized transmission practices to better-balanced and negotiated (with the public) transmission-reception processes;
    3. Recognizing the added value that can be contributed by newer technologies, such as web logs, to the media repertoire;
    4. Presenting honest, reliable, and autonomous representations of reality, in terms of each society and culture, rather than having them imposed by outside powers;
    5. Striving to produce human and social change in individuals, groups, collectives and systems, and to develop critical awareness, and a better understanding of self and other.

THE PROMISE OF PEACE COMMUNICATION

Peace-oriented communication is essential for enhancing development policies as well as for encouraging the development of democratic media structures. Expectations have been growing that combinations of democratic media structures and peace communication might increase the effectiveness of development programs; reduce socio economic inequality, corruption, and exploitation, and increase social and self-respect towards the weaker components of societies. The promise of peace communication and its techniques, such as Peace Journalism and peace-oriented strategies of media usage, is based on their integrative and synthesizing roles in bridging gaps of context and linkage of information and interpretation that prevail in both the professional and the consumer end of conventional mainstream journalism. When performed effectively, they might enhance critical awareness, and encourage the change of attitudes and behaviour necessary for both parties of the communication processes to recognize the value of peace-oriented and democratic media for development.

Peace Journalism and peace-oriented strategies of media usage aim at improving both media representations of reality and how they are perception by the public. They propose to frame stories in broader, fairer, and more accurate terms than the ones dictated by the biases of the "ratings culture and structure", and of the interests of governments and movements. They explore and create demands for learning backgrounds and contexts of conflict formation in order to make media sources, processes, and effects more relevant. They provide space for alternative voices and encourage an interest in learning the views of all involved parties while ensuring that conflict – rather than involved parties – is seen as the problem. Also they trace connections between journalists, their sources, the stories they cover, and the consequences of their reporting, including the common interests of media owners and power structures. Successful outcomes of this process might introduce a better-balanced literacy and discourse of nonviolence and creativity into media coverage, and enhance a different media producing and consuming consciousness. Also the adoption of these techniques can call public attention and opinion to the impact and threats of conflicts.

Peace-Oriented Communication Make a Difference

Two relevant types of applications can test the performance of peace-oriented communication against their promise: the first is the introduction and use of new media structures in efforts made at conflict transformation and reconciliation. Such structures have usually followed the end of conflict in less democratic environments moving towards democracy and in less developed regions and countries. The second application is the socialization of journalists, media organizations and the public, to a different working logic. It is expressed in the production of contents and in attitudes different than those inspired by the prevailing ratings culture and structure of the media.

Media Structures

In addition to the creation of peace-oriented media structures out of a major motivation to enhance peace, many such structures have helped to strengthen democratic powers, and have become assets in development processes. The frightening impact of "hate-media" in national wars of the 1990s, such as in Rwanda, Bosnia and Sierra Leone has produced "boomerang reactions". Rwandan Radio-Television Libre des Milles Collines conducted a vicious genocidal campaign inciting the slaughter of more than half a million Tutsi people in less than one hundred days. Bosnian electronic and print media also helped to promote ethnic conflict. While explicit hate messages were broadcast less frequently than in Rwanda, their cumulative impact fuelled hatred over a long period of time (Bratic, 2006).

Perhaps in reaction to this trend, an impressive number of projects have been conducted involving the implant of peace-oriented media. Bratic (2006) reports that in the last decade or so, a total of about forty media projects in 18 countries on four continents were reported as efforts at postwar conflict transformation. In many cases they have become tools of democratization and development. In Cambodia, the success of Radio UNTAC (UN Transitional Authority) set up a model whereby subsequent UN missions (in Sierra Leone, Rwanda, Bosnia, Ethiopia, East Timor, and Kosovo), have included the operation of radio stations in their peace building efforts. Radio UNTAC gave Cambodia, for the first time, a reliable source of nonbiased news and enabled political parties and candidates to access to the media. When the station became popular, it moved forward to perform development functions, adding music, entertainment and information programs.

In East Timor, Studio Moris Hamutuk is a production facility intended to promote reconciliation between East Timor and Indonesia. Set up by Swiss-based Foundation Hirondelle, the studio provides independent and credible information, focusing exclusively on news programs, current affairs, documentaries and interviews. In Africa, the establishment of new peace-oriented media structures has been sponsored mostly by humanitarian NGOs, such as the international SFCG-Search for Common Ground, and Foundation Hirondelle, some in cooperation with UN missions.

These projects focused on the establishment of radio stations, such as UN Radio MINURCA in the Central African Republic, Sierra Leone Radio Ndeke Luka [Bird of luck] and STAR Radio in Liberia as well as on the production of peace oriented radio contents and assistance to local journalists. Studio Jumbo, established in Burundi by SFCG in 1995, in direct response to the production and broadcasting of hate incitement and genocidal propaganda by neighboring Rwandan Radio Television Libre de Mille Collines (RTLM), became a model for the entire continent. Since 2002 Congolese Radio Okapi, a joint venture of Foundation Hirondelle and the UN mission, has been broadcasting from Kinshasa, capital of the Democratic Republic of Congo in local languages to almost one million refugees.

The media have played an equally significant role in European peacemaking and peace-keeping. The use of radio and television as weapons of war led to the development of new media structures in the Bosnian process of reconciliation, supported by international organizations and NGOs. The Free Exchange Radio Network (FERN) was established by OCSE (the Organization for Cooperation and Security in Europe), to provide coverage of the first postwar Bosnian elections. Later, it became a nationwide station, providing news, information and music. Another dimension of the difference made by media organizations is the reform of previous media structures.

In Bosnia, the Independent Media Commission (IMC) was established to prevent the propagation of hate messages. A similar process occurred in Kosovo, where the UN, OSCE and other international organizations helped establish a national television and radio system, and encouraged strict regulation of hate broadcasts. Like in Bosnia, in July 2000 UN media experts encouraged the system to become a public entity, thus moving from its specific peacemaking function into a fully-fledged tool for democracy and development.

SOCIALIZATION OF JOURNALISTS AND AUDIENCES

In Africa, the establishment of peace-oriented media structures has been sponsored mostly by humanitarian NGOs, such as SFCG (in Angola, Rwanda, Burundi, and Sierra Leone), Foundation Hirondelle (in the Central African Republic, Liberia, and the Democratic Republic of Congo). In addition to the establishment of radio stations, these projects focused on the production of peace oriented contents (news, soap operas, programs for women and children and musical shows featuring peace songs) and assistance to local journalists, such as The Hirondelle News Agency, set up to cover the Rwanda genocide trials at the International Criminal Tribunal, in Arusha, Tanzania.

Studio Jumbo in Burundi has produced peace-oriented contents that became a model for the entire continent. Under the slogan "Dialogue is the future", most programs directly address the roots of the regional conflict. Three surveys conducted since 1999 indicate that 80 to 90 percent of the population listens to the local soap opera "Umubanyi Niwe Muryango" regularly. In Latin America, the Colombian organization of journalists "Medias porla Paz" (Media for Peace) has been engaged in training and education, and in helping journalists who have been subject to violence as a result of their reporting. The organization has established archives, information networks and publications for journalists in conflict areas. One of the most prominent projects is the publication of a dictionary that lists 600 words signifying conflict or peace connotations in an attempt to "disarm language".

In the Middle East, most Israeli, Arab, and Palestinian mainstream media have not been investing serious efforts in peace-oriented communication. Some NGOs have been much more effective in this sense. Based on European sponsorship, Keshev, the Israeli Association for the Protection of Democracy, and its Palestinian counterpart Mufti, have been monitoring media coverage of the conflict, and publishing reports that have had considerable impact. In addition, Israeli-Palestinian jointly operated All for Peace Radio, has been successfully engaged in peace journalism. Common Ground News Service (a SFCG project) was established as a news agency to provide information to both sides in the conflict. The service presents coverage of the Israeli-Palestinian conflict, employs local and international experts and provides syndicated articles, analysis and op-ed pieces. Supported by the European Community and UNESCO, the service operates on a non-profit basis. Also journalism-training organizations, such as The Institute for Further Education of Journalists (FOJO), USAID and Internews have offered courses to Palestinian journalists. SFCG has been involved in training and created an award program that recognizes journalism that contributes toward common understanding and dialogue.

Northern Ireland differs from other cases. Unlike most other conflict regions, it enjoys a fairly advanced system of commercial and public media organizations, particularly in broadcasting. Therefore, Northern Ireland has not seen the creation of new media outlets specializing in peace programming or training in peace journalism. Engaging in the socialization of its professionals and audiences, the existing Irish media structures acted as a cornerstone in support of the Stormont Castle peace negotiations and agreements. Finally, SPEAR (Support Programming for Emergency Assistance by Radio) was a project that provided assistance to journalists from warring communities to produce peace and development oriented programs.

Sponsored by Media Action International (MAI), it was originally aimed at the refugees in Macedonia, Kosovo (Serbia) and Albania. Three radio series' were produced in each country. The Kosovo program "In the Name of Humanitarianism" used local broadcasters on both sides of conflict at the time when the need for humanitarian information was at its peak. Also in Macedonia, the success of "Nashe Maalo" (Our Neighborhood), a television series for children, led to its continuation as a street theatre, puppet theatre and magazine, later released as a CD soundtrack.

The show was watched by 76% of the young audience regularly (SFCG, 2002). Additional cases appear in publications such as the Berghof Handbook for Conflict Transformation, featuring proposals for reporting on ethane-political conflicts in a manner that fosters peace. A basic model is offered to explain the impact of media and to discuss NGO-activities and a proposal for reform efforts in Europe. A case study of the role media can play in ethane-political conflict portrays initiatives of the NGO Common Ground (in Greece, Turkey, Macedonia, Sierra Leone, and Burundi), and shares lessons concerning the design, implementation and assessment of projects aimed at cooperating with media, promoting pluralism and fostering ethical standards.

Last but not least, Loretta Hieber's *Lifeline Media* (2001) *Reaching Populations in Crisis: A Guide to Developing Media Projects in Conflict Situations*, is a guide for those involved in setting up media-related projects in conflict and post-conflict settings. Her approach is designed to ensure that affected populations always have access to well-produced humanitarian information in a manner that enhances local media capacity. Also she explores how the skills of professional Western journalists can best be applied in realizing this objective.

DEVELOPMENT JOURNALISM

Development journalism is often a stage of transition from revolutionary journalism to a media engaged in post-colonial national development or as part of marginalised Indigenous media within a main stream society. It involves the 'fleshing out' of the structure of national independence begun in the revolutionary journalism phase. This includes the seeking of answers to the question: What shall we do to become the nation we want to be? Critics of development journalism—mostly from Western countries—criticise a distortion of it—the coopting of this media term by politicians seeking self-interested goals.

A majority of journalists in developing countries, including the South Pacific, work in a communications field essentially dependent on a national government for its existence. Every state press system has an agenda of involvement in society; the selection of news itself is non-objective. Characteristics of government-style development journalism include:

- A communications system that is an integral part of the national government. It is often run by a ministry of information.
- Journalists being asked to take part in major tasks of nationbuilding. These include upholding the new political system and helping critics 'understand' the new nation; trying to overcome poverty and illiteracy; and preserving the cultural heritage.
- A national communications policy or guidelines that are adopted to help achieve the goals of nationhood. These can range from heavy handed control and censorship to consultation.
- Journalists who are often government employees.

- Private enterprise news media being expected to consider 'national interest' above its own private interest.

Important to the success of the media in performing this 'nation building' role is the freedom to be informed and a freedom of expression constitutional framework. Strong protection for free expression, or a free media, needs a range of legislative provisions to be enacted that recognise the obligations of the media and governments to ensure effective freedom of expression. It also needs a rigorous scrutiny of legislation. While all Pacific Island constitutions—other than that of Niue—refer to freedom of expression or speech, only some constitutions specifically refer to the media (Federated States of Micronesia, the state of Pohnpei, Fiji, Kiribati, Palau, Papua New Guinea, Republic of the Marshall Islands, Tonga and Tu valu). However, Pacific Island courts are most likely to interpret constitutional protection for free expression as including protection for media freedom. Examples of pressure by Pacific governments in attempts to muzzle news media in spite of constitutional guarantees are legend. Such an example was in July 1998 when Fiji Television was put under intense pressure from politicians and even its own governance board over coverage of the Monasavu land rights protests in the highlands of Viti Levu.

The Monasavu Dam and catchment fed a generator supplying 80 per cent of the country's electricity, yet at the same time the landowners' village had no power. A 10-year-old grievance spilled over into the public domain with a demand by the landowners for F$35 million in compensation for the national exploitation of the resource. At one stage during the protests on the road access to the dam, a group of landowners 'daubed themselves in warpaint and threatened to 'kill' for their rights in a rather theatrical gesture' (Robie, 2004). 2004a or 2004b A revival of the grievance during the George Speight coup in 2000 saw the power supply to the country sharply reduced or turned off over five weeks. Catchment area compensation for the landowners had been overlooked at the time of the original state purchase and left unresolved. Media coverage at the time of the original threats to the nation was decidedly 'radical' compared with how Australian or New Zealand media might have covered the events.

But Western journalists ought to 'explore ways of combining their privilege of free comment with respect for minorities and the integrity of public discourse', argues Dr. Eric Loo, a Malaysian journalist who became a media educator in Australia. 'One way is to consider the alternative development journalism approach to reporting, in which the social and cultural cohesion of the people takes priority over news commercialism' (Loo, 1994:).

Among successful journalists who have established a reputation for reportage with a development edge that often demonstrates the 'processes' and 'community power' referred to by Loo is Television New Zealand Pacific correspondent Barbara Dreaver, born and raised in Kiribati. Since starting her own newspaper in the Cook Islands, she has managed considerable 'leg work' around the region that has un covered many remarkable stories. In a 2007 interview with the *Listener*, she revealed that her favourite story was a report exposing a US-based baby-smuggling ring in Samoa: 'It was a real punt when I went across but we got the goodies. It was the only time I'd ever cried on a story.' She also talked about the growing global interest in the Pacific.

The US is worried about the Pacific, because it's their border. And in the War on Terror, such as it is, you can see why they're worried—the Pacific is weak in terms of security. And they may be only little countries, but they've each got a vote, as Japan with the whaling knows. I feel sorry for the whales too but it's all very well criticising Tuvalu and Kiribati for supporting Japan, but Japan gave them the money that they really, *really* [original emphasis] needed.

Japan offered aid to small Pacific nations in return for their vote to end a moratorium on commercial whaling. Tongan publisher Kalafi Moala advocates major reform for media systems in the Pacific to address development, saying that to train journalists and then send them to work is like 'sending in soldiers to a war zone without a mission' (Moala, 2005). He has been impressed with Tongan language community broadcasters in San Francisco, where he now lives with his wife, and their contribution to Fourth World development. Moala sees three major media development problems facing the Pacific:

1. An inevitable bias in news coverage because most major media operations in the region have been government-owned or controlled: 'Island journalists sometimes play servant to corrupt policies developed without public participation.'
2. Media business and commercial interests have usurped the traditional role of information: 'They may be entertained, horrified, titillated and stressed—but not informed.'
3. Globalisation has impacted on media to such an extent that less is being done to make media appropriate for Indigenous and local sociocultural contexts: 'Instead, the social-cultural contexts are being progressively adapted to fit the 'one shoe' of a globalized media.'

Development journalism has a critical role to play in the future of the South Pacific region and a new generation of educated journalists has responsibility to their people. Pacific Islanders are no longer people confined to microstates scattered across the vast Pacific Ocean. They are peoples who have migrated around the globe in diaspora (Connew, 2007). Nations such as the Cook Islands, Niue, Samoa, Tonga and Tuvalu have a greater part of their population living as migrants in Australia, New Zealand and the United States or elsewhere. Pacific journalists now have a greater task than ever in encouraging 'democratisation' of the region and informed insights into development issues facing island states.

Some of the region's journalists warn about allowing politicians' slogans such as 'cultural sensitivity' being used as a smokescreen for the abuse of power and violations of human rights. The development journalist seeks to expose the truth and report on alternatives. 'To use the guise of cultural sensitivity as a cover to protect oneself from criticism is an insult to that culture, for the implication is that culture does not condone transparency, honesty, order and proper management of affairs,' argues Kalafi Moala. 'Corrupt and dishonest politicians and bureaucrats have often reacted to media scrutiny by throwing up a pretentious cover of cultural taboos and insensitivities as excuses to avoid being scrutinised' (Moala, 2005). Development journalism also means a tougher scrutiny of the region's institutions and dynamics of governance.

Answers are needed for the questions: Why, how and what now? Journalists need to become part of the solution rather than being part of the problem.

PRACTISING 'DEVELOPMENT JOURNALISM' IN TSUNAMI COVERAGE

When the Asian tsunami hit the six Andaman provinces of southern Thailand, hundreds of Thai journalists were sent from their national bases in Bangkok to work in the field with their provincial colleagues. The assignment was to report aspects of the disaster as best as they could. It was a challenging task for most Thai journalists due to their lack of experience in covering such a large-scale natural disaster. Never before had Thailand been so badly hit by such a natural calamity. Some journalists admitted that the confusing situation in the first few days made them realise they were sent there to work unprepared. There were no specific guidelines for working in such situations, except for the professional principles they had learnt from day-to-day work.

A number of journalists covering the aftermath of the tsunami said that the first two weeks after the disaster struck provided for an extremely confusing scenario for news coverage. Journalists encountered demands different from what they usually faced while covering stories in normal situations. According to Chavapong Mekarakul, editor of *Siangtai Times* newspaper in Phuket, his journalists were asked by relatives of several tsunami victims for help in finding their loved ones. Some victims wanted newspapers to push for relief from the government. Good journalistic skills are much needed in such chaotic situations. Many journalists said identifying and prioritising issues in a situation that involved massive destruction was extremely important and quite challenging. Said Pichet Choorak from the Bangkok-based daily, *Post Today*: 'We need to identify issues here, and this is hard in a situation where everybody is suffering, with many expecting us to help. Then we have to priorities them. We also learnt that new issues emerge every day. This is the biggest challenge in covering tsunami in my opinion.'

Development journalism was applied from the beginning. When relief operations started immediately after the disaster, journalists diverted their focus from disaster to humanitarian issues. The media reported daily on government relief activities. But not long after relief operations arrived, journalists started to hear several complaints. The most important was about the poor system of aid distribution. Media coverage of relief efforts started to provide a critical look on the issue.

Most journalists covering tsunami relief efforts believed that it was their responsibility to report both positive and negative aspects of the development. Mekarakul of the *Siangtai Times* said that his Phuket-based newspaper received several complaints about the problems of aid distribution. The newspaper viewed it as its role to report such complaints.

Journalists reporting government relief efforts encountered the problem of community conflicts as a result of mismanagement in aid distribution. Ms. Supatra Bhumiprabhas of the Bangkok-based *The Nation* said it was one of several important issues regarding government relief operation. 'There were cases of people fighting over aid and that led to conflict in communities. I wrote about it in order to raise a question on the way the government manages its relief operation,' she said. Thai media did a remarkable job in telling the public about the plight of the tsunami victims in southern Thailand. By providing reports on the shortcomings of relief efforts, it conveyed people's opinions to the government as well to relief organisations. Corruptions and mistreatment of tsunami victims in some areas were also reported and led to public investigations in some cases.

RELEVANT DEVELOPMENT JOURNALISM

Does development journalism matter? Do journalists require good journalistic skills to cover development projects? In reality, the two cannot be separated. Good journalism based on ethics, well balanced information, fairness and accuracy lays the foundation for every type of journalism. In certain situations where development is the core issue, there is a need for journalists to apply such principles to highlight it and make sure that the public is served with accurate information to assist with decision-making.

Bad journalism fails to provide accurate and balanced facts, and often leads to public misunderstanding. It often highlights the roles and needs of only certain players while leaving out the rest. Bad journalism can do a lot of harm by providing the public with superficial information. It can distort knowledge and stop society from learning. Development journalism is called 'bad journalism' when it fails to articulate people's needs and how a development process is carried out and affects society. When the media merely promotes government projects, or praises the political elite for their role in the so-called national development without trying to look deeper into its process and impacts, it is called 'propaganda'.

Development journalism is still relevant and useful if it is able to avoid such a trap. Good development journalism does not serve a government. It serves the society as a whole by doing its best in giving information on positive as well as negative aspects of development projects. By doing so, it will help in opening up a democratic space for meaningful public participation in the process of development. Journalists covering development issues need to take into account several factors. These are:

- People: In covering development, journalists are often confused and overwhelmed with details about projects, process, budget and implementation. Many journalists tend to forget the most important element of development—people. A good journalist must be quick to identify the people involved in his or her development story, and try to get their voices into the story as much as possible.
- People's needs: what are the needs of the people identified in the story? Does the development project respond to such needs? Needs in some cases may not be limited only to basic material well being such as food, shelter, health care or education. It may include a need for their identity to be accepted or for freedom to live the way they choose. A good development story cannot ignore the real needs of the people.
- Types of development: Is the project really a 'development' project, or is it only a charity in disguise? When an uncountable number of groups went to the six Andaman provinces of Thailand to work on relief projects, several reports indicated problems from some

fly-by-night groups whose methods in relief operations were short-term and contrary to sustainable goals. In some cases money or materials were repeatedly given to people in some villages without a long-term plan while villagers in other places still faced severe hardship. Such methods did not properly respond to the overall development goal, while stirring up conflicts among aid recipients.

- Identify people's agendas: In some situations economic well-being is not the only answer to people's needs regarding the high level of poverty they encounter. Good development journalism must be able to extract people's inner agenda and put it in context. In many conflict areas in Southeast Asia, including southern Thailand where armed struggles between groups and government, or among groups have become prolonged, the majority of people suffer poverty. Development projects that cost huge sums of money failed to end the violence. In this case, journalists must find answers to what is lacking in the projects and identify the real needs and problems.
- Find out the truth behind economic growth data: Find out if statistics tell the truth about the majority, or if it lies. While economic growth data says the country has reached a certain level of wellbeing, what do the people in the village really think?
- Raise questions beyond national boundaries: To understand sources of underdevelopment in a country, journalists must be able to look beyond a national context and back. For example, while rich countries pressure for free trade, they keep on protecting their own industries. Journalists must find out if there are impacts on the lives of local farmers or industrial workers and what governments of developing countries are doing to solve the problems.
- Does 'development' create a problem itself? Journalists must find out the shortcomings of development as well. For example, a government policy on 'village funds' in Thailand in 2001 allowed a small loan for villagers throughout the country. Several media reports indicated a higher level of bad debts years later. According to the

reports, while the government said the loan was to help villagers in their farming process, proper control of how villagers should spend the loan was lacking. The policy, which was branded 'populist', was in effect a tool to build a political base for the leader.

- Identify people's potential in development: Instead of painting ordinary people merely as 'victims' or 'passive actors' in development processes, journalists should find out more about their aspirations, inspirations and involvement. Instead of seeking opinions only from government officials and experts, space should be given to ordinary people to express their views.
- Use several sources and verify what they say: Journalists must involve sources from as many groups as possible. Villagers, experts, civil servants, politicians, etc., must be given ample coverage. A media organisation should be open to public input, whether in the form of letters, articles or other forms. Information, however, must be verified using journalistic methods in order to prevent mistakes.
- Follow the money: Development projects usually involve huge amounts of money and complicated procedures. Cases in the past have shown that many development schemes ended up mired in corruption scandals. Journalists covering development projects cannot avoid asking questions such as, 'how the money was spent and by whom, whether the project really benefited people in need, and if not, why'?
- Have a clear ethical position: In many issues, journalists must ask themselves if they are getting drawn into organisational agendas or conflicts while covering development projects. When a project involves many stakeholders and millions of dollars, conflicts often arise. Journalists should be on the guard against such situations and make sure that they report without becoming unduly influenced.

DEVELOPMENT AND POVERTY

As far as the challenge of tackling poverty across the region is concerned, we are all aware of the fact that there are hundreds of millions of very poor people across the Asia-Pacific region. The key facts — many of which are truly shocking — have been repeated many times by many people. However shocking though the facts are, it is hard to avoid the impression that — perhaps understandably — many people who hear about poverty in poor countries suffer from a kind of "poverty fatigue". They have heard about the problems so often — and they have heard so much about the problems of poverty in rich countries as well — that they are inclined to take the view that perhaps the sad truth is that little can really be done to eliminate widespread poverty in poor countries.

This view is wrong for two reasons. It is wrong, firstly, because the problems of poverty in poor countries are very different to the problems of poverty in rich countries. And it is wrong, secondly, because it is just not true that little can be done to tackle widespread poverty in poor countries. In fact, there is a great deal that can be done to reduce poverty in the developing world. These are perhaps surprising assertions to make so let me say a little more about each of them. In thinking about issues of global poverty, it is of central importance to understand that the phenomenon of poverty in the developing world is very different to the type of poverty we usually talk about in rich OECD countries. And because the type of poverty is different, then the responses needed are different as well.

In Western countries, deep and persistent poverty is not a widespread phenomenon. Rather, poverty is generally found in certain segments, or pockets, of society. This is usually localized or segmented poverty because it is found in certain groups which can be defined by region, by age, or by social group. In contrast, in many parts of Asia, mass poverty is the main economic problem. That is to say, in many countries in Asia, large parts of the population (sometimes over 40% or 50%, depending on the particular poverty line chosen) live in deep poverty. This type of poverty is, in a number of ways, very different to the type of poverty that exists in rich countries.

One main difference is that the phenomenon of mass poverty across a poor nation affects the society as a whole, and not just individuals or small groups. Thus the social externalities of mass poverty are an extremely important phenomenon and have far-reaching effects. As a result, poor societies affected by mass poverty often operate in quite different ways to rich societies where localized poverty is the problem. Examples of what I have in mind are the loss of production and the sheer waste which occurs when people are employed in dreadful working conditions, and the damage done by widespread insecurity and weak law.

One main difference is that the phenomenon of mass poverty across a poor nation affects the society as a whole, and not just individuals or small groups. Thus the social externalities of mass poverty are an extremely important phenomenon and have far-reaching effects. As a result, poor societies affected by mass poverty often operate in quite different ways to rich societies where localized poverty is the problem. Examples of what I have in mind are the loss of production and the sheer waste which occurs when people are employed in dreadful working conditions, and the damage done by widespread insecurity and weak law.

My second assertion was that there is a great deal that can be done to reduce poverty in the developing world. In fact, in some ways the solution to the problem of mass poverty in developing countries is fairly straightforward — developing countries need to pursue high-growth economic policies so that rates of growth of GDP perhaps 6-7%, or more, are sustained for at least three or four decades, preferably longer. Many people take the view that is a tall order. However, we know from practical experience in quite a few countries that, first, it is quite possible for economic growth of this kind to be achieved in the developing world, and second, the impact of sustained growth of this kind on mass poverty is usually dramatic. In fact, Asia provides some very good examples of how strong and sustained growth has led to dramatic reductions in poverty.

One of the most-well known, of course, is here in Japan. In recent years we have heard a lot about Japan's economic problems but it needs to recalled that following the Meiji Restoration in 1868 Japan rose, as Professor Ichimura has put it, "from the poverty-stricken feudal conditions in the Edo period to the prosperous modern or post-industrial society in only several generations." This was a stunning economic performance. It brought great benefits to the Japanese people.

And it remains a phenomenon of considerable interest to many other Asian nations because they are eager to find out exactly how Japan managed to achieve this economic miracle and whether it is still possible to copy the process today.

More recently, Korea's economic performance in terms of promoting growth and reducing poverty has been outstanding. Korea registered very high rates of economic growth in the three decades to the mid-1990s. The growth was achieved with little increase in economic inequality across the nation. The overall result was that the proportion of the population living in poverty fell from an estimated 40% in the mid-1960s to less than 5% in the mid-1990s. In Thailand, Malaysia, and Indonesia, high and sustained growth in the thirty years up to the late 1990s resulted in sharp falls in measured levels of poverty in these countries.

Current outstanding performers, in terms of growth, are the People's Republic of China, India, and Viet Nam. In all three countries, the evidence is that poverty has been falling markedly in recent years. Just last week the World Bank released a report on the Viet Nam economy that commented on the link between growth and poverty. The report noted that: "Viet Nam's achievements in terms of poverty reduction are one of the greatest success stories in economic development. A decade ago, 58% of the population had an expenditure level that was insufficient to support a healthy life. Five years later, the proportion of the population below this particular poverty line fell to 37%. It had further declined to 29% by 2002. Thus almost a third of the total population, the equivalent of more than 20 million people, were lifted out of poverty in less than 10 years." The same lesson emerges, but unfortunately as a result of negative experience, from recent economic performance in slow growing countries such as PNG, The Philippines, and Indonesia since the 1998 crisis. In each of these countries, growth has been rather slow in recent years. And in each of these countries, poverty has risen or has been very slow to fall. In the Philippines, for example, there has been almost no increase in income per person in close to two decades. As a result, progress in reducing mass poverty has been disappointing. From one point of view the clear lesson that emerges from these various examples is that strong, sustained economic growth in developing countries is needed to tackle the issue of mass poverty. But from another point of view, this lesson immediately gives rise to new questions. Two of the most important of these questions are: How can developing countries achieve high growth rates? And What can be done to ensure that the growth is "good growth" in the sense of ensuring that the economic growth leads to widespread social and environmental improvements as well as just increases in production?

These are difficult questions that raise many controversial issues. The short answer to both of them is: Ensure that good policies are in place— and in particular, ensure that good macro and microeconomic policies are in place that create a sound investment climate and that provide stability. But this answer quickly prompts the question of: What can be done to encourage policy-makers in developing countries to adopt good policies?

ROLE OF THE MEDIA

This question leads me to the second topic that I want to say something about, which is the role that the media can play in responding to the challenge of tackling poverty in developing countries. The media, through supporting high-quality, thoughtful comment and debate on public issues, has a key role to play in supporting good policies and building decent societies. And this is just as true in the area of economic and development policies as in other areas.

The best single example of this that I know of is the debate about trade and the level of tariffs — that is, levels of protection — that took place over the three or four decades to the early 1980s in Australia. Australia, in economic terms, is today a relatively open, low-protection country. But tariff levels used to be much higher, and significant parts of the Australian industrial sector used to be much more protected than is the case today. For decades, through the 1950s, 1960s and 1970s, a long-running national debate was conducted in parliament, in universities, and in business circles about the pros and cons of cutting tariffs and reducing protection.

Throughout this long debate the national media, and especially economic journalists and commentators at the high-quality end of the print media, played a key role in promoting reform. Several of Australia's most well-known economic journalists such as Ross Gittins and Ken Davidson constantly set out the issues clearly and fairly. One well-known Member of Parliament who wrote hundreds of anonymous articles (semi-anonymous, anyway) under the pen name of "The Modest Member" also lent strong support for reform. In the end, starting in the 1970s and continuing through into the early 1980s, there were very marked reductions in the level of protection in Australia.

The results of these and other pro-market supply-side reforms paid off for Australia in the 1990s. They are still paying off today. During the past decade, Australia's economy has performed very well with one of the highest rates of growth across all of the OECD countries. Looking back at the series of supply-side economic reforms that have underpinned good economic performance in Australia, there seems little doubt that the media played a key role in strengthening the environment for reform. Of course, the media plays a similar role elsewhere. In many other countries well-known economic journalists and commentators constantly argue the case for reform. In the United Kingdom, Martin Wolf who writes for The Financial Times, William Keegan from The Observer, and the numerous columnists and invited contributors who write for The Economist constantly outline key economic issues that need attention. In the United States, Paul Krugman has attracted much publicity as a hard-hitting commentator on public policy issues.

Across Asia, too, there are many well-known national journalists and commentators who contribute to the public debate. Here in Japan, people such as Yoichi Funabashi and Akira Kojima frequently contribute articles on national and international issues. In the Philippines, Amando Doranilo is perhaps the doyen of national journalists in his field. In Indonesia, Professor Mohammad Sadli has been an extremely influential voice for good public policy for over 40 years, while younger commentators such as Hadi Soesastro, Mari Pangestu, and Anggito Abimanyu frequently argue case for economic reform. In Thailand, Ammar Siamwalla is a leading commentator, while in India people like Prannoy Roy, Sanjaya

Baru and Krishna Raj are very well-known journalists. These people, and many others like them, play a key role in supporting the process of good governance across the Asia-Pacific region. This is because the good governance of a nation needs to take place at many levels. Of course, the role of the most senior leaders is important. When the top political, bureaucratic, and military leaders are doing a good job, this is a major step forward.

But good governance needs to go well beyond the top people in government and administration. For one thing, it is highly desirable that the performance of top political and administrative leaders is constantly monitored in an open and transparent way. Experience across many countries and across hundreds of years teaches us that the private interests of leaders and the public interests of the community do not always coincide. In the public interest, therefore, there is much to be said for ensuring that decisions about economic policies — and especially decisions about the sectoral impact of economic policies — are discussed in public by well-informed commentators.

For another thing, while there is a need to ensure that decisions taken by government leaders are constantly scrutinized, there is also a need to ensure that when top leaders do take good decisions they get strong support. It is unrealistic to expect government leaders to be able to promote reform by themselves. They need widespread community support to promote social and economic change across a nation. The role of economic journalists and commentators in supporting reform is a very important one. They can play a key role, first, in helping creating constituencies for reform and then later, once reform packages have been introduced, in helping encourage acceptance of the changes across the nation.

In fact, one of Indonesia's most senior economic ministers reminded me of this recently when I asked him what the ADB Institute might do to strengthen support for good policies in Indonesia. He replied that that it was frequently clear enough what policies were needed but that, too often, there was a lack of public support for the policies. "Do what you can to persuade the public, and the parliament, to agree to reforms," he said. "Without their support, it is hard for me to promote the changes we need."

In talking of support, we need to remember that it is not only the top leaders of a nation who need support but journalists as well. Too often, the role that journalists play in the Asia-Pacific region in challenging existing policies and promoting reforms is risky. Across the region there are many instances of journalists taking substantial personal risks, and sometimes paying a heavy price for telling the news like it is.

I have, by the way, a personal interest in this topic. My son has been a foreign correspondent in Indonesia for over four years. He covered the turmoil in Indonesia in 1998 when President Soeharto resigned from office, and later reported on the transition of power in East Timor. He, along with other journalists in Jakarta, has at times been caught up in angry crowds of anti-foreign demonstrators in Indonesia, and has had to duck for cover during military clashes in Dili. I am therefore very aware of the risks that journalists face in covering events in developing countries in Asia, and strongly believe that all journalists in the region need good support from the international community for the important work that they do.

3

Public Sphere and Media Democracy

Most directly, "the public sphere is paradigmatically associated with discussions on democracy and its shortcomings". In this respect, the public sphere is viewed as a resource for growth of democracy, promoting discussions of civil society and public life. The concept of the public sphere appeals to the nature of civil society as it attempts to explain the social foundations of democracy and to introduce a discussion of the specific organization of social and cultural bases within civil society for the development of an effective rational-critical discourse. Habermas (1992) saw the public sphere as a domain of social life in which public opinion could be formed out of rational public debate. Ultimately, informed and logical discussion, could lead to public agreement and decision making, thus representing the best of the democratic tradition.

Blumler and Gurevitch (2001) argue that the new interactive media have a "vulnerable potential" to enhance public communications and enrich democracy. Scholars of political sciences also ask if it is possible to foster democratic development with the help of communication technology. Hagen states that research on the relationship between communication technologies and democracy has turned up ample evidence illustrating that concepts of electronic democracy contribute both to democratic theory and our understanding of the working of a democratic political system in the information age (Newhagen, 2000).

Accordingly, it is the condition of the public sphere that differentiates democratic political systems from non-democratic ones. In the absence of the public sphere, people are deprived from a space through which they can govern themselves by themselves for themselves. "The importance of the public sphere to democratic theory and democratic movements cannot be underestimated. For a functioning and purposeful citizenry to develop, it is argued that they must have a space in which to engage debate and make decisions. This space is thought to exist outside of the governmental sphere and the private sphere. The public sphere is seen to lie between these two other parts of social life in order to develop solutions to social problems. Citizens in the public sphere are meant to leave their personal concerns behind, and transcend their limited subjectivities in pursuit of 'the common good'" (Franko, 2005).

Engagement in the public sphere defines the public, and it is best to envision the public sphere not necessarily as a public space, but as a purposeful interaction towards discussion and democratic decision-making. Habermas tells us that, "a public sphere comes into being in every conversation in which private individuals assemble to form a public body" (Franko, 2005).

To better understand the nature of the public space we need to differentiate it from other types of spaces. A space is private when given individuals are recognized by others as having the right to establish criteria that must be met for anyone else to enter it. Thus, we speak of a private room, a private meeting, and private parts. Such a space is belongs to someone that has the right to establish criteria by which access is allowed or denied. Sacred space is different and similar. Such a space is neither made by human action nor can it be owned. It is the God. The sacred space as identified here reflects the European view which is completely different from that of Islam, as there is no separation between private and public spaces from the Islamic point of view. At the other extreme, a space may be common to human beings. There are no criteria for common space. It is not owned or controlled and is open to everyone. Thus, the sea or forests are (or can be) common space. This is not a space to which one goes to speak with others and therefore, it is not a public realm, and its boundaries are not contestable per se. Public space is a space created by and for humans that is always contestable, and it is open to those who meet the criteria, but it is not owned in the sense of being controlled.

In the tradition of Western thought, the very idea of democracy is inseparable from that of public space. It is perceived as a disposition to open and contradictory debate with the aim of making possible a reasoned understanding between citizens with regard to the matter of the definition of institutions, the formulation of laws, and their enforcement. From this point of view, public means simultaneously: open to all, well known to all, and acknowledged by all. Public space stands in opposition to private space, because it is civic space and it belongs to the citizens. Historically, the public sphere has been associated with revolution. The public gathering of individuals, to make decisions and garner support is critical to most reform movements. Thus, Habermas defines the public sphere as "the scene of a psychological emancipation that corresponded to a political economic one".

The public sphere and democracy should not be considered as inseparable from one another, because the democratic political systems are based on the voice of the people and the rule of the majority that is likely formed through a liberal public sphere in which people freely discuss the critical public issues. In Egypt, the situation is different from that of Western countries, as the separation between public sphere and democracy is the most likely dominant principle in the Egyptian milieu. The government is obliged to allow a partly-free public sphere. However, it restricts the formation of real public opinion and establishes the types of laws and legislations that perpetuate the dominance of the ruling party. Simply speaking, it seems that the government allows people to say whatever they want, while allowing itself to act whatever it wants. In this political atmosphere, it is difficult to find a link between public sphere and democratic transformations. However, a free or partly-free public sphere may eventually lead to formation of public opinion that will govern.

Habermas (1989) first conceived of the public sphere as a physical space that first emerged in coffee houses in England and salons in France in the 17th and 18th centuries with the rise of capitalism and the state. He describes the public sphere as a physical place where propertied, educated men who were members of the bourgeois joined together to engage in rational-critical discourse on public matters and other issues of the day. Even in the early public sphere, newspapers and journals were an enabling technology that helped create a network bringing the forums of the coffee houses and salons together to create the larger public sphere. For Habermas and Alexis de Tocqueville, the public sphere was a place where men gathered to rationally discuss issues of the day. Newspapers played a key role in the public sphere by supplying information, creating interest, and helping set the agenda for participants in the public sphere.

Conversation and action oriented around discussion define what the public sphere should be, according to classic theorists. John Keane describes the public sphere as "a particular type of spatial relationship between two or more people, usually connected by a certain means of communication...in which nonviolent controversies erupt, for a brief or more extended period of time, concerning the power relations operating within their given milieu of interaction and/or with the wider milieus of social and political structures within which the disputants are situated" (Rajagopal, 2004). The linkage between people via means of communication is critical here, whether this communication exists via conversation, in the press or on satellite television. Communication is essential for the public sphere, and in many ways, it is the only constitutive element of that space (Franko, 2005).

At a general level, the concept of the public sphere is defined by many scholars as designating a realm related to democratic political discourse. Here, the notion of "public" as in "public opinion" refers to a collection of politically significant shared common interests impacting ideologically upon the exercise of state of power. Of course not all politics (democratic or otherwise) take place through discussion (public or not). The public sphere, however, is a concept applicable to voluntary and violence-free political behaviour. For this reason, Habermas argues that the public sphere needs institutional guarantees of a constitutional state on the one hand, and on the other, a political culture in the broader society of populace accustomed to freedom. This perception helps explain the importance of a democratic constitution and the rule of law as contextual conditions of media's optimum democratic role.

When Alexis de Tocqueville, a French nobleman and political scientist, visited the United States in 1831, he was so impressed with what he termed the "voluntary associations" of men in the United States; he devoted much study and later description of these associations in his treatise on American life, democracy in America. Although Tocqueville utilizes the term "associations" rather than "public sphere," a thorough reading of both men's writings leaves little doubt that they are talking about the same thing. There are obviously some differences between the European and American public spheres. These differences are both political and cultural, but the similarities are more numerous and profound than are the differences. Tocqueville even surmised that the notion of associations in America was imported from England and that the differences can be attributed to Americans' incorporation of their manners and customs.

There are numerous and profound similarities between the American public sphere of the 19th century as described by Tocqueville and the European public sphere of the 17th and 18th centuries as described by Habermas. Nonetheless, there are also discernible differences between the spheres with the greatest difference resting in the relationships between the spheres and their governments. The American public sphere did not clearly reside in the private realm; it was often tied to government. The stronger relationship between government and the American public sphere is logical when one remembers that the Americans were members of a self-governing democracy who believed they had a duty to take an active role in the official governance of their communities. The public spheres of Europe occurred at times and within countries where political power was still very much vested in monarchs and church leaders.

Another difference between the two public spheres is that within the American associations, people pursuing public interests coexisted with people pursuing private interests. Habermas believed that the pursuit of private interests displaced the pursuit of public interests in the European public spheres.

In Habermas' conceptualization of the public sphere he privileges face-to-face communication, believing the most valuable role for the media is to provide information for intimate exchanges. He accepts that the printed word played a significant role in the development of the bourgeois public sphere, but he did not fully conceive of the key role for media in the public sphere. In his writings he also expresses a distrust for mediated communication, seeing it as an obstacle to "discursive rationality and communicative authenticity".

Taking the aforementioned discussion into account, it is safe to state that public sphere depends to a large extent on the nature of the political system in which it exists. In Europe, the public sphere-which was achieved despite opposition from the state powers, is at odds with what transpired in the United States. Habermas' suggestion that the European public sphere was regulated by its individual members is contradicted by the U.S.'s case, where the media emerge instead as the first and foremost project of nation-building. Starr considers three extended and overlapping "constitutive moments" when political choices and technological developments shaped the media's growth. "America's first information revolution" was the first constitutive" moment," extending from the colonial period to the onset of the civil war" (Rajagopal, 2006). Its distinctive trait was the deliberate development of inexpensive postage, schools, and newspapers through direct and indirect subsidies. The intent was to enable the people of the nascent and geographically dispersed republic to communicate with each other and thereby strengthen their internal ties. The result was a population that actively participated in public and political life. Thus, while European countries discouraged communication by placing taxes on the postal service, the early Post Office in the U.S. saw its goal as promoting intercourse, and reducing the mental distance between town and country. At one point, America's ratio of post offices to people was four times that of England or France.

Starr also notes the government's early realization of the importance of public education, although it was public schools of the North, not the South, that regularly increased enrollment. Starr explains at length the policies that made books and newspapers far less expensive in the United States than in Europe (among these was a disregard for European copyright laws that made windfall profits possible for U.S. publishers). Contemporary observers noted the effects of the early development of the press in the US. The private realm did not arise from a struggle against state absolutism, as in Europe, but as an effect of state formation. Not surprisingly, the constitution and the government are frequently granted cultural sanction to restrict the scope of these customs (Starr, 2004).

On the other hand, Arab political systems have created a politically repressive atmosphere to control the public sphere. The development of media and state in the Arab world confirm the fact that all Arab states controlled the media, especially radio and television, to prevent the establishment of a free public sphere, to restrict the formation of public opinion and to hinder any democratic transformation in the region. "There are several reasons for the predominance of government–owned broadcasting system in the Arab World. However, the most important factor is the intense government interest in the media as political instruments, media reach beyond borders and literary barriers; the government has a much greater interest in controlling them or at least keeping them out of hostile hands" (Rugh, 2004).

In his research on "Arab media and communication systems in the information age", Hamada concludes that democratizing the media and communication system represents a real threat to any undemocratic regime. The majority of Arab governments have never been interested in creating a democratic communication environment in which the citizens can have a voice regarding public issues. Government operated media agencies provide most of the information, and much of the content it supplies is politically biased, incomplete, and of poor quality.

Most Arab governments claim that the issues of development must take priority and that the time is not right for democracy. Therefore, democracy is not a part of most Arab leaders' political agenda.. Although democracy and development represent two distinctly different human endeavours, they are both required, to ensure success, sustainability, adequate levels of information and popular participation. The more objective and the wider the scope of information conveyed, the more likely it will be to sustain democracy and development. Modern communication technology is essential in the speed and efficiency with which data and news are processed and disseminated among different citizens of the society. Another common and related requirement for both democracy and development is an active and public participation (Attiga, 2001).

The bulk of the discussion on media pluralism as a political value continues to be based on the conceptual framework of the public sphere. As a general normative concept against which to assess the media, much of the debate draws upon Habermas's early work (1989) but also, more broadly, the public sphere is understood as a general context of interaction in which deliberation and discussion take place and citizens in general inform and form themselves into the public (Karppinen, 2004). Lippman conceives of public opinion as the aggregate opinion of persons whose individual opinions are pieced together from what they hear, read, see and are able to imagine. He also believes that their exposure to information is manipulated to create a certain opinion that meets the needs of elites. Lippman's idea of public opinion is quite different from Habermas' conception. Habermas believes public opinion is what develops in the public sphere as the result of rational discourse. He views public opinion as the culmination of sharing of information among enlightened individuals operating in the public interest.

The author completely agrees with Hbermas's notion of the priority of public interests as a condition for the public sphere. First, in order for the public sphere to exist, priority has to be given to social issues. If people left public issues behind and concentrate on their private interests, there will never be a space for the common good, common grounds for members of the public to exchange experience, but personal interests that work against the collective mind. In Egypt, the overwhelming majority are poor, illiterate, and unemployed people who spend much of their time trying to save their food. Hence, the majority is handicapped by illiteracy, poverty, ills and unemployment to such a great extent that they lack motivation to engage in the "public sphere". Also complicating the problem is the government's intolerance with the activities of the opposing parties and political movements. Due to this atmosphere, the role of new communication technologies, especially the Internet, in enhancing public sphere is limited.

MASS MEDIA AND PUBLIC SPHERE

As Mansson (1999) points out, many scholars regard the media as the main institution of the contemporary public sphere. However, we have to consider the fact that restricted media will never contribute to public sphere. If the media are state-owned, working under direct supervision of the government officials and suffer from political and economic pressures, the government's voice is the only one that will be heard in the public sphere. For Habermas, the real public is the one that assembles and engages in dialogue. There is no public space without "reciprocal communication". For Regis Debray, the real public is the one that reads and writes, that reasons, as opposed to one that allows itself to be influenced by images. In the author's opinion, the public sphere is the freedom of the public to convene via free media space which is detached from the government, providing marginalized people an arena to speak out about public policies and decisions. As my definition illustrates media ownership, media diversity and freedom of speech are requirements for a true public sphere.

Although we can accept the assumption made by Manuel Castells who asserts that "the media have become the essential space of politics", we have to be careful of whether all types of media have the potential to establish a public sphere or not. For the public sphere to exist, the media have to provide equal opportunities for its users to freely discuss and form their opinions which eventually will form an important mechanism to affect state policies. Thus, any analysis of the contemporary political climate must take into account the interaction between the media and political candidates, issues and citizens. Political participation, citizenship and the media cannot be separated. As Castells points out, "to an overwhelming extent people receive their information, on the basis of which they form their political opinion…through the media. Thus the media space is the space of information, and the sphere citizens depend on to direct them towards relevant issues" (Franko, 2005).

Having said this, it is not acceptable to conclude that entertainment-oriented media or government–owned media will play a significant role in shaping an Egyptian public sphere. Therefore, Habermas' was concerned about modern media and his concerns stem in part from the media's reliance on mass advertising for revenue. Although advertising dates back to ancient times, mass advertising sharply increased following the industrial revolution as manufacturers sought markets for their factory-produced goods. So, much of what appears in media today is not meant to be informative and enlightening for participants in the public sphere. It is merely entertainment and designed to attract audiences that will appeal to advertisers.

Michael Robinson's research demonstrates that voters who rely on television for political campaign information are prone to develop a feeling of political inefficacy, distrust, and cynicism. He coined the term "videomalaise" in order to express that television gives rise to political malaise among the public. Gerbner and his collaborators' research seems to justify the interpretation that television viewing cultivates fear, alienation, and interpersonal mistrust. In Europe, similar concerns became an issue in public debate and an object of study in the late 1970s and early 1980s in the course of deregulating and commercializing the broadcasting sector. European television adopted the American model in the 1980s and conquered the market with programs emphasizing entertainment, crime and violence. It is quite likely that changes of this kind have an impact on the political system and the public sphere.

With the advent of the technologies of modernity, time has become separated from space and space from place, giving rise to ever more "disembedded social systems". Social relations have been lifted out of local contexts of interaction and restructured across "indefinite spans of time-space" (Giddens, 1990). As a result, what can be defined as a global public sphere emerged. The world trend of democratization starting from the mid of 1980s until now should be understood from the link between global mass media and global public sphere. Political observers like Ted Turner to Robert Kaplan have suggested that many of the changes that led to the breakup of the Soviet Union stemmed from the rapid and uncontrolled spread of information, news, sports, and entertainment across political borders. The Soviet Union spent two decades fighting in vain to control broadcasting into their country. Significantly, they sought to place limits on countries and satellite networks that would seek to beam programming across international boundaries. The Soviet Union's attempt failed and it subsequently broke up. Indeed, the power of satellite broadcasting is powerful.

Though Habermas relates public sphere to face-to face conversations and was skeptical about the influence of mass media, theorists posited suggestions as to how the public sphere was consequently being transformed into the new 'information society'. The national control of governments over the information delivered to the national population was eroded. The new ICTs allowed information to traverse borders and individuals to interact with other audiences beyond the reach of the state. Thus they accelerated and intensified a global social transformation which threatened to make national political structures redundant. Writers like Manuel Castells have notably argued that ICTs provide new opportunities, or spaces, for information to accumulate and be exchanged, not least about what governments do. He has suggested that governments will find it increasingly difficult to control interactive access to this information and thus to assert the power of the state in, or over, the public sphere. He has further suggested that this would progressively lead to a more horizontally networked society in place of current top-down forms of communication. The power of the state would be eroded, while the individual citizen's capacity to engage directly with an un-bordered society would be exponentially increased. The capacity of the state to exert its authority over the range of information or modes of political participation available via conventional means is reduced.

Consistent with assumptions about communication technologies and public sphere, it was the 2002 UNDP report that apparently established a link between communication technologies and freedom and democracy. However, it still rejects a cause–effect relationship between the two. The report concludes that the world has more democratic countries and more political participation than ever, with 140 countries holding multiparty elections. Of 147 with data, 121–with 68% of the world people – have some or all of the elements of formal democracy in 2000. This compares with only 54 countries, with 46% of the world's people, in 1980. Since then 81 countries have taken significant steps toward democratization while 6 have regressed.

The impact of communication technologies in fostering democracy is not universal. Satellite television's potential for democratization depends on the overall socioeconomic political context in which it operates. As Noveck comments: it is not technology per se which either fosters or denigrates between communication media and participatory democratic culture. Technology exists within a framework of values and ideals both inherent to it and imposed by the external legal and institutional structures" (2001). Hence, there is no single relationship between ICTs and democracy, and it is safe to suggest that the Internet and satellite television may have different and sometimes contradicting effects on the democratization process in different socioeconomic and political contexts (Hamelink, 1999). The communication revolution has also led several authors to assume that a fragmentation of the public will be the result of a proliferation of channels in an expanding media environment. Fragmentation refers to the process whereby the same amount of audience attention is dispersed over more and more media sources. The public sphere may dissolve into a large number of subcultures and when this occurs, the common experience for all members of society disappears.

DEMOCRACY UNDER FIRE

This essay starts from the premise that corporate interests have colonised the US press – its dominant institutions as well as its professional assumptions, practices and routines. The colonisation of US news media is especially problematic for working journalists. That is, while economic imperatives and commercial interests have long constrained journalistic autonomy, the corporate consolidation of the news industry – with the attendant demands for cost cutting on one hand and profit maximisation on the other – has all but extinguished any semblance of a free press. In the era of corporate colonisation, the US press corps finds it increasingly difficult to maintain its independence from direct and indirect corporate control.

Of course, the field of journalism is not unique in this regard; corporate interests permeate most every facet of daily living – from family and community life, to education, leisure activities and cultural production. Nevertheless, corporate colonisation of the press is especially troublesome inasmuch as this condition has enormous implications for the prospects of democratic self-governance. With this in mind, I begin with an overview of a growing body of academic and practitioner analyses that illustrate the extent to which the US news media serves corporate interests thereby degrading independent journalism and fundamentally undermining democratic values and practices.

The essay proceeds with an analysis of the journalistic philosophy and routines employed by *Democracy Now!* – Pacifica radio's daily news and public affairs program. It is my contention that *Democracy Now!* is at the vanguard of an emerging independent media sector that is revitalising US news media at a decisive moment in American (journalism) history. Further, I maintain that it is *Democracy Now!*'s attentiveness to counter-hegemonic struggles that contribute to its success as the nation's largest public media collaboration. Throughout, I suggest that *Democracy Now!*'s significance is best understood in terms of its relation to both corporate news organisations and grassroots media.

CORPORATE COLONISATION OF THE PRESS

For a quarter century, former journalist Ben Bagdikian has charted the scale and scope of corporate control of the US media system. Bagdikian's analysis reveals the detrimental effects corporate consolidation has had on the American media landscape: the erection of nearly insurmountable barriers of entry into media markets; the precipitous decline of minority owned media outlets; the homogenisation of media form and content; and the economic censorship of public expression (Bagdikian).

One of the most pronounced effects of media consolidation has been on local news and cultural production. In recent years, communities across the United States have seen locally owned and operated media outlets swallowed up by outside interests eager to maximise profits, minimise investment, and reduce overheads. Regulatory changes – most notably the Clinton-era Telecommunications Reform Act of 1996 – combined with synergies realised through new media technologies, have facilitated this latest round of media consolidation. As sociologist Eric Klinenberg notes, while market efficiencies benefit corporate media giants, local communities have lost a great deal:

> The local reporters, veteran TV producers and live DJs who once provided the stories, sights and sounds that made our hometowns feel like home have become endangered species in the age of Big Media, replaced by the same wire copy, digitally voice-tracked radio programs, video news releases and other canned content that runs in every market, coast to coast. (Klinenberg 22)

When we consider the media system in relation to the broader political economy, the significance of the communication industries to corporate ascendancy comes into sharp relief. As communication scholar Stanley Deetz observes, "the institutional relations between mass-media institutions and other corporate institutions contribute to the preeminence of the corporation as a social institution" (Deetz 31). It is the structural alignments within and between various sectors of the economy that have precipitated the crisis of US journalism and which pose the greatest threat to independent journalism and a free press.

The institutional relationship between the media industries and other corporate enterprises is most fully realised through the practice of advertising. Pleasing corporate sponsors is of the utmost concern for the media industries because commercial advertising "pays the bills." Corporate media, therefore, have little incentive to challenge the values, interests or practices associated with corporate institutions. While this logic makes perfect business sense, applying this same rationale to the practice of journalism is a recipe for disaster.

None of this is not to suggest that corporate elites exercise direct editorial control over working journalists. As media scholar Robert McChesney notes, the effects of corporate media ownership on journalism are far more subtle, but no less profound: "The corporate/commercial pressure on news often takes place indirectly, and is therefore less likely to be recognised as such by journalists or the public" ("Problem of Journalism" 311). Yet, these pressures are manifest in the day-to-day practice of US journalism.

Indeed, in the era of corporate colonisation, news

organisations are expected to do more with less. Compelled to generate profits while minimising redundancies, newsrooms across the country are cutting corners with one hand and enhancing the entertainment value of their news product with the other. Typically, this strategy involves eliminating jobs for working journalists, curtailing if not completely eliminating investigative reporting, re-purposing entertainment fare as news content, and having a growing reliance on the public relations industry for "pre-packaged" news items.

In this environment, journalists are left with few good options. Anxious to avoid antagonising commercial interests or government news sources, journalists rarely challenge people in positions of power and authority for fear of losing access to "official sources." Instead, working journalists play it safe by taking a less confrontational stance toward elites, pursuing instead the sensational, the titillating or the trivial news item. Thus, journalists create the illusion of conflict and controversy by covering relatively inconsequential "news items" like celebrity gossip, or the sexual misconduct of politicians, while studiously avoiding substantive public policy issues.

This condition has dire consequences for our politics and culture. When the public good is subordinate to the marketplace in determining news values and priorities, journalism's role in nurturing an egalitarian public sphere is debased. Divorced from its historic role as an incubator for an active and engaged citizenry, the contemporary practice of US journalism undermines democracy by cultivating a profound sense of apathy, cynicism, and powerlessness.

Troubling as all of this is for the prospects of a self-governing society; this situation is equally problematic for the future of journalism. Journalist James Fallows laments the decline in public trust in media organisations and a general disinterest in journalism. While news workers, editors and publishers are quick to blame the American people for the breakdown of civic values and widespread indifference toward public affairs, Fallows argues that it is journalism's acquiescence to the shortsighted, profit-driven demands of corporate media organisations that poses the greatest threat to the future of journalism. The corporate colonisation of US news media is not limited to the structural arrangements between communication industries and other corporate institutions. Corporate ideology likewise shapes and informs the operational standards, assumptions, and practices associated with professional journalism today. In the next section, we will consider how corporate interests have penetrated journalistic culture – and explore the ways in which *Democracy Now!* challenges the hegemony of corporate news organisations, routines and performance.

THE CULTURAL POLITICS OF NEWS

The contemporary crisis in journalism can be traced to an earlier period when commercial interests first overshadowed the democratic aspirations enshrined in the free press clause of the US constitution. During the late nineteenth and early twentieth century, the newspaper industry came under withering attack from a broad cross-section of American society. Not unlike today, charges of fear and favor in the newsroom, crass commercialism, and salacious content were common. To deflect this criticism, newspaper publishers launched a massive public relations campaign designed to assure the public – and, significantly, would-be regulators – that journalism reform was at hand.

Describing these efforts, McChesney notes: "Savvy publishers understood that they needed to have their journalism *appear neutral and unbiased...* or their businesses would be far less profitable. They would sacrifice their explicit political power to lock in their economic position" ("Problem of Journalism" 301, emphasis added). The cornerstone of the professional code of journalism that emerged in response to the press criticism of the early twentieth century was the notion of objectivity.

Since that time, academics and practitioners alike have scrutinised the theory and practice of journalistic objectivity. At the risk of oversimplifying this debate, few would suggest that news production is a value-free activity; and most would agree that journalists routinely make choices about the stories they cover, the sources they quote, and the language they use to frame a particular news event. Still, most observers find value in journalistic objectivity inasmuch as it provides a check on a reporter's personal biases and shields working journalists from overt interference from editors and publishers. Insofar as objectivity allows for competing perspectives to weigh in on important public issues, there is a general consensus that objective journalism has considerable potential in supporting a self-governing society.

Nevertheless, journalistic objectivity, as it is currently practiced, tends to reinforce the status quo and stifle social change. For instance, Hackett and Zhao identify a "conservatising" bias in journalistic objectivity. This tendency is most pronounced in relation to conventional understandings of "politics" as being limited to electoral contests and the strategies and tactics employed by political parties, elected representatives, and government officials. This narrow conceptualisation of politics all but ignores those actors and institutions, such as corporations, that exercise considerable, often unchecked power and authority in public decision making. Moreover, "the conflation of democracy with electoral politics" limits public perceptions of legitimate political activity and effectively marginalises individuals and groups who assume oppositional positions and take up counter-hegemonic struggles (Hackett and Zhao 6). This conservatising bias is perhaps most apparent in objective journalism's uncritical reliance upon "official sources." If we contrast corporate media's use of news sources with those of *Democracy Now!* we can begin to appreciate the cultural politics of news in America today.

GOING WHERE THE SILENCE IS

Throughout the spring of 2006, the subject of immigration reform was everywhere in the news. Journalists eagerly awaited press briefings from the Bush Administration regarding its proposed overhaul of the nation's immigration laws. Congressional leaders on both sides of the aisle were quizzed regarding their positions on the upcoming debate. And the press corps examined competing bills in the US House and Senate with considerable fervor. Moreover, members of the business community – especially those from agriculture, construction, and the food services industries which rely heavily upon immigrant labour – were frequently asked for their opinion on the issue of immigration reform.

With few exceptions, however, were undocumented immigrants – "illegal aliens" in the corporate media lexicon –

asked for their opinion about pending legislation that would directly affect not only their livelihoods but also their whole way of life. Only when thousands marched for immigration rights in cities and towns across the US – taking much of the corporate news media by surprise – did journalists begin to take stock of the people who would be most directly effected by changes in US immigration policy: the undocumented workers themselves.

In contrast to corporate media's performance, *Democracy Now!* covered the immigration policy debate in a far more comprehensive fashion. Most notably, *Democracy Now!* routinely featured the voices, perspectives and experiences of undocumented workers and immigrant rights advocates in the days and weeks leading up to the Congressional debate over George W. Bush's proposed immigration reform legislation. For instance, *Democracy Now!* reported on Elvira Arellano's defiance of a deportation order that would separate her from her son, Saul, who was born in this country and is a US citizen. Arellano is president of the immigration rights group, United Latino Families, that works on behalf of undocumented workers in their struggle to keep their families together in the face of stepped up deportation proceedings. In spring 2006, Elvira Arellano took sanctuary in Chicago's Adalberto Methodist Church and *Democracy Now!* followed the story for weeks.

Immigration rights are but one of the public policy arenas that *Democracy Now!* covers with such depth. For instance, *Democracy Now!* routinely updates the activities of groups like September Eleventh Families for Peaceful Tomorrows – a citizens group that challenged the Bush Administration's war policy in the wake of the 9/11 attacks. On the first anniversary of the attacks, *Democracy Now!* spent the hour with victims' families who denounced the Bush Administration's rush to war in the name of the innocents killed on September 11, 2001. In short, *Democracy Now!* provides a forum for the dissemination of perspectives, opinion and analysis that challenge the orthodoxy produced within and through the corporate media.

This approach to news reporting serves as a countervailing force to corporate media's over reliance upon "official sources." Indeed, since its inception in 1996, *Democracy Now!* has been steadfast in going where the silence is. According to *Democracy*

Now! host and executive producer, Amy Goodman, "Our objective is to be accurate and objective and to give voice to those who are marginalised by the mainstream media. We act as a balance to the reality of suppressing dissent" (Goodman qtd. in Benthien). Herein lies the critical distinction between the sourcing common to corporate media and that of *Democracy Now!* Billing itself as a "daily, global, grassroots, unembedded news hour" *Democracy Now!* routinely features views and perspectives that receive scant attention in corporate media outlets. In this way, *Democracy Now!* provides a forum for local community groups, peace and environmental activists, civil rights workers and civil liberties attorneys, progressive academics and others directly involved in counter-hegemonic struggles to enter into public discourse.

For their part, corporate media typically ignore or trivialise dissident opinion, preferring instead to limit public deliberation and debate to "legitimate" news sources – such as politicians, government officials, business leaders, and other so-called experts. This approach to journalism is neither a fair nor accurate representation of the social world. As Goodman notes, journalism of this sort abdicates journalism's historic role as a "watchdog" of the powerful by "trading access for truth." In doing so, the corporate media, unwittingly perhaps, serve as "stenographers of power" rather than journalists in search of the truth. Furthermore, by failing to provide a robust and inclusive forum for popular debate, the news routines and practices of corporate media seriously compromise the capacity of a free press to serve a self-governing people.

Thus, by incorporating the views of what Goodman describes as "the silenced majority" into a daily newscast, *Democracy Now!* reinvigorates the practice of journalism as "the conversation of democracy". Rather than inhibit popular participation in the public sphere, *Democracy Now!* provides a forum for discussion and debate that is far more inclusive and egalitarian than the discursive spaces owned and occupied by corporate elites, government officials and other official sources.

The Past Didn't Go Anywhere

In the era of corporate colonisation, political decision-making is reduced to a spectator sport – complete with opposing sides, play-by-play coverage, and color commentary. While this approach may arouse the emotions, it does little to promote substantive, let alone critical engagement with important issues of the day.

News media too often bombard audiences with stories of conflict, scandal, and celebrity *without offering information (or an appeal to the imagination) that could encourage popular political participation.* The news positions audiences as political spectators who are "done to" by politicians and special interest groups, displacing alternative ways of thinking about ourselves (as workers, and as political beings). (Hackett and Zhao 9, emphasis added)

In this climate, apathy and resignation reach epidemic proportions. The adage "You can't fight city hall" seems as immutable as the laws of physics insofar as corporate news places its audiences outside of the realm of politics *writ large* and denies any sense of individual and collective agency in challenging the status quo. *Democracy Now!* takes a distinctive approach to an increasingly depoliticised public culture by appealing to the popular imagination – often through the lessons of history. Or, to be more precise, through the lessons of what Howard Zinn would call "the people's history."

Zinn's approach to history highlights the long struggle of oppressed peoples in the United States and elsewhere to realise the unfulfilled promise of liberal democracy (Zinn). Indeed, when history is viewed in this fashion, the problems of the present come into sharp relief. Rather than promote indifference and helplessness, this perspective encourages active, engaged, and *hopeful* participation in public life. A comparison between corporate media's use (or more properly, abuse) of history with that of *Democracy Now!* reveals the political significance of historical memory to contemporary struggles.

For instance, corporate media applied a familiar frame – the heroic individual who makes a difference – to news of the death of civil rights champion, Rosa Parks. Press reports prominently featured the iconic image of Parks defying racially segregated seating on a bus in Montgomery, Alabama and dutifully noted Ms. Parks' courageous stand for equal treatment under the law. On the whole, however, corporate media's coverage emphasised this seemingly spontaneous individual act of defiance with little or no reference to Park's long-time association with civil rights issues and organisations. In contrast to this sympathetic, but decidedly limited appreciation of Rosa Park's achievement, *Democracy Now!* reviewed the life and times of Rosa Parks with special attention to her role as an organiser and activist. To that end, *Democracy Now!* aired a revealing 1956 interview with Ms. Parks from the Pacifica radio archives. In doing so, *Democracy Now!* placed Rosa Parks' historic act of nonviolent resistance within a larger context that highlighted the collective efforts and strategic planning behind the Montgomery bus boycott.

Like the corporate media, *Democracy Now!* affirmed the historical significance of Rosa Parks' act of civil disobedience. However, by placing that act in the broader context of oppositional politics and community organising *Democracy Now!* celebrated the past while affirming the possibility for progressive political change today. All of which is to suggest that while corporate media's use of history tends to uphold and reinforce the status quo (oftentimes in a congratulatory and self-serving manner) *Democracy Now!* draws on historical memory to challenge received assumptions, to highlight the contingent character of human history, and to appeal to the popular imagination.

For example, while commemorating the terrorist attacks of September 11, 2001, *Democracy Now!* also exposes corporate media's penchant for historical amnesia. As it has done for the past six years, *Democracy Now!* reminded listeners of the historical significance of that date in other parts of the world: the September 11, 1973 US-backed coup of Salvador Allende, the democratically-elected president of Chile; the September 11, 1977 arrest, detention and fatal beating of Steven Biko, founder of the black consciousness movement in South Africa; and the September 11, 1990 murder of American anthropologist Myrna Mack by Guateleman security forces trained and supported by the United States.

In this way, *Democracy Now!* challenges the notion of "American exceptionalism" cultivated by the corporate media in the aftermath of 9/11 – and exploited with unnerving success by the Bush Administration to legitimate its assault on civil liberties at home and to justify its imperial ambitions abroad. Further, by placing the terrorist attacks on the United States in historical context, *Democracy Now!* acknowledges the cultural significance of public memory in forging national identities and shaping collective destinies: for good or ill.

With this in mind, the Bush Administration's recent provocations toward Iran are all the more ominous. Four years and a half years on from the invasion of Iraq, corporate media grudgingly acknowledge they were "asleep at the switch" on the question of WMD. Likewise, news workers haltingly accept responsibility for parroting the administration's specious claims of Iraqi complicity in the 9/11 attacks. And yet, remarkably similar claims surrounding Iranian weapons and Tehran's hostile intentions toward the United States and Israel circulate in the corporate news media with nary a hint of skepticism. The lessons of history, it seems, are lost on a colonised press corps.

DECOLONISING US NEWS MEDIA

In a speech before the 2007 National Media Reform Conference veteran journalist Bill Moyers urged attendees to petition their local public broadcasters to start airing *Democracy Now!* A fierce critic of corporate news in his own right, Moyers has witnessed first-hand the right wing attack on US public broadcasting, the attendant corporate colonisation of public radio and television, and the subsequent dilution of journalistic independence in US public media. In no uncertain terms, Moyers described the significant role *Democracy Now!* is playing in the revitalisation of American journalism.

I can't think of a single act more likely to remind people of what public broadcasting should be, or that this media reform conference really means business. We've got to get alternative content out there to people, or this country is going to die of too many lies. And the opening rundown of news on Amy's daily show is like nothing else on any television, corporate or public. It's as if you opened the window in the morning and a fresh breeze rolls over you from the ocean. (Moyers)

At first blush, the headlines Moyers celebrates are an unremarkable feature of the broadcast; after all a rundown of the day's top stories is a staple of corporate and public news outlets alike. However, in addition to relaying news items from the wire services – the Associated Press, Reuters and Agence France Press – or news stories appearing in "papers of record" such as the *New York Times* or the *Washington Post*, *Democracy Now!* inserts headlines or related stories that don't make the front page, or the evening news for that matter.

For instance, *Democracy Now!* reported extensively on General David Petraeus' assessment on the so-called "troop surge" before Congressional oversight committees in September 2007 – as did corporate and public media. However, few news outlets mentioned the civil disobedience that took place during the high-profile proceedings, despite the fact that television cameras captured the arrest of several activists, including Code Pink founder Medea Benjamin and anti-war activist Cindy Sheehan. *Democracy Now!* gave listeners an account of the incident and ran the accompanying footage as part of its telecast.

Similarly, when Reverend Lennox Yearwood Jr. of the Hip Hop Caucus attempted to enter the hearing room, he was injured during an unprovoked altercation with Capitol Hill police: another incident that went largely unnoticed in the corporate press. Apparently, such blatant and, perhaps, racially motivated violations of constitutional rights are not sufficiently newsworthy for a colonised press corps. For *Democracy Now!* it was another story altogether.

Incorporating these events into the daily headlines, *Democracy Now!* reveals the degree to which corporate media marginalise dissent. Moreover, placing news items detailing the activities of anti-war activists alongside stories featuring political and military elites affirms the news value of counter-hegemonic struggles against American military, economic and political power. Thus, *Democracy Now!* offsets corporate media's strategy of either ignoring or trivialising dissent through frequent and ongoing coverage of direct action campaigns, protests and other forms of civil disobedience. In doing so, *Democracy Now!* acknowledges and helps to legitimise collective resistance to repressive regimes of state or corporate power.

Democracy Now!'s daily headlines are certainly a refreshing alternative to similar formats in other media outlets. However, it is the long-form interviews with activists, analysts, and most especially, independent journalists that make *Democracy Now!* a distinctive and increasingly indispensable resource in the struggle to decolonise US news media.

Independent's Day

Today's media landscape is a mixed blessing for independent journalists. On one hand, corporate consolidation of the media industries represents a formidable obstacle to journalistic autonomy. As we have seen, corporate media exert considerable pressure on working journalists to yield to economic imperatives and adhere to a set of norms, routines and assumptions that all too often preclude reporters from fulfilling the basic functions of a free press: to act as a watchdog of the powerful, to discern truth from lies, and to provide a forum for diverse, competing and informed opinion on matters of common concern (McChesney, *Problem of the Media*).

On the other hand, the era of digital communication affords independent journalists unprecedented opportunities to produce and distribute their work with relative ease. Moreover, as audiences turn away from "traditional" news sources and embrace grassroots and alternative news content and delivery systems – podcasts, blogs, social networking sites, etc. – independent journalists can disseminate their work to audiences that have grown dissatisfied with corporate media behaviors and performance.

Over the course of the past ten years, *Democracy Now!* has acted as a clearinghouse for independent journalism from across the country and around the world. For established and well respected independent journalists like Robert Fiske, Naomi Klein, and John Pilger, to name but a few, *Democracy Now!* amplifies and extends the reach of their work considerably. Equally important *Democracy Now!* provides a nurturing and supportive atmosphere for up and coming investigative reporters whose subject matter is incompatible with corporate interests and the commercial imperatives of the news business.

Democracy Now! correspondent Jeremy Scahill's work is a case in point. Scahill has been filing first-rate investigative reports on Blackwater USA – the North Carolina-based private defence contractor – with *Democracy Now!* for years. A secretive and politically well-connected private militia, Blackwater's activities have, until recently, flown under the corporate media radar. Amidst allegations that Blackwater indiscriminately killed 17 innocent Iraqi civilians, the corporate media has slowly turned its attention to Blackwater.

These charges confirm much of what Scahill has been reporting about all along: that Blackwater's mercenary armies are conducting illegal, paramilitary operations, at the behest of the United States, in Iraq, Afghanistan and, as Scahill notes with chilling detail in his book, in post-Katrina New Orleans (Scahill). In the finest traditions of investigative journalism, *Democracy Now!* enable reporters, like Jeremy Scahill, to practice their craft in an environment that grants journalists remarkable freedom and autonomy.

REMAKING PUBLIC MEDIA

Democracy Now! distinguishes itself from corporate and public service broadcasting in one more crucial arena: what might best be described as "communication politics." As Robert McChesney has documented with great precision and insight, the corporate media are loath to cover debates over US communication policy (*Problem of the Media*). The favoured tactic of corporate media on this score is the media blackout: virtual silence on closed-door meetings between Big Media and the federal and state regulatory agencies charged with promoting and defending the public interest.

In contrast, *Democracy Now!* "breaks the sound barrier" by providing timely reports and thoughtful analysis that supports and encourages public knowledge, awareness, and participation in communication policy debates. Similarly, *Democracy Now!* monitors grassroots and national media reform efforts on a substantive and on-going basis. For example, *Democracy Now!* provided extensive coverage of the aforementioned National Media Reform Conference. In doing so, *Democracy Now!* illuminates what media scholar Clemencia Rodriquez describes as "fissures in the mediascape" (Rodriguez).

That is to say, *Democracy Now!* highlights the way ordinary Americans are taking up the struggle for democratic communication by getting involved in policy debates, demanding greater accountability from the media industries and regulatory bodies, and making use of communication technologies – radio, public access television, community newspapers, and the internet – to reinvigorate the public sphere at a time when corporate colonisation of the communication commons has degraded public discourse and all but eviscerated public culture.

The phenomenal growth of *Democracy Now!* demonstrates how a more inclusive and expansive public media might be realised within and through collaborative approaches to independent journalism. Indeed, forging links between independent journalists and news outlets has been critical to *Democracy Now!*'s success. When it first began, as a special report during the 1996 electoral season, *Democracy Now!* was available over the Pacifica radio network and some affiliate stations. Today, *Democracy Now!* is the leading public media collaborative in the country (McConnell). Airing on over 600 community, low power FM, and NPR affiliate stations, *Democracy Now!* is also available on local public access and on Free Speech TV, via national satellite television services, Dish TV and Direct TV, and on Link TV.

Democracy Now! also makes its content available online, through podcasts, as well as streaming audio and video. In addition, *Democracy Now!* transcripts are available online, and in Spanish, for news outlets to use free of charge. Finally, *Democracy Now!* is available internationally, broadcasting on public service and community radio in Australia and Canada. In short, by tapping into emerging networks of citizens media and building upon existing networks of independent journalists and alternative media outlets *Democracy Now!* is remaking public media in the era of digital communication.

The corporate colonisation of the press has not proceeded unchecked. Across the country, and indeed around the world, efforts are underway to secure and defend a free and independent press. *Democracy Now!* is but one noteworthy example of this process of decolonisation. Significantly, *Democracy Now!* remakes public media by drawing on the talents and resources of people across the United States and elsewhere involved in counter-hegemonic struggles.

In doing so, *Democracy Now!* provides a model for grassroots journalism in the twenty-first century by challenging the conservatising effects of journalistic objectivity and articulating the relationship between local and global struggles for peace and justice. Equally important, because the producers, reporters and independent journalists featured on *Democracy Now!* excel at their craft, journalists working for corporate media are growing more accustomed to picking up stories first aired on *Democracy Now!*: a practice Amy Goodman refers to as "trickle-up journalism."

The unprecedented success of *Democracy Now!* indicates that the American people, dissatisfied with a press corps beholden to corporate and political elites, value independent journalism that challenges the status quo. Moreover, by providing a forum for opinion and perspectives that lie outside the narrow range of debate available through the corporate media, *Democracy Now!* reasserts the importance of public life and promotes deliberative democracy in an otherwise fragmented, isolating and depoliticised culture. All of which is to suggest that the crisis of journalism precipitated by the corporate colonisation of the US news media is neither irresistible nor irreversible.

MEDIA DEMOCRACY

Media democracy is a set of ideas advocating reforming the mass media, strengthening public service broadcasting, and developing and participating in alternative media and citizen journalism. The stated purpose for doing so is to create a mass media system that informs and empowers all members of society, and enhances democratic values. The concept, and a social movement promoting it, have grown as a response to the increased corporate domination of mass media and the perceived shrinking of the marketplace of ideas.

The term also refers to a modern social movement evident in countries all over the world which attempts to make mainstream media more accountable to the publics they serve and to create more democratic alternatives

Key principles

Media democracy advocates argue that corporate ownership and commercial pressures influence media content, sharply limiting the range of news, opinions, and entertainment citizens receive. Consequently, they call for a more equal distribution of economic, social, cultural, and information capital, which would lead to a more informed citizenry, as well as a more enlightened, representative political discourse.

Despite the difficulties in defining the term, the concept broadly encompasses the following notions:

1. that the health of the democratic political system depends on the efficient, accurate, and complete transmission of social, political, and cultural information in society
2. that the media are the conduits of this information and should act in the public interest
3. that the mass media have increasingly been unable and uninterested in fulfilling this role due to increased concentration of ownership and commercial pressures
4. that this undermines democracy as voters and citizens are unable to participate knowledgeably in public policy debates.
5. Without an informed and engaged citizenry, policy issues become defined by political and corporate elites.

More radical thinkers argue that media democracy remains an under-defined concept because of deliberate structural pressures that prevent individuals from questioning the connection between media and democracy. A leading proponent of this view is Noam Chomsky, who argues that

The concept of "democratizing the media" has no real meaning within the terms of political discourse in the United States. In fact, the phrase has a paradoxical or even vaguely subversive ring to it. Citizen participation would be considered an infringement on freedom of the press, a blow struck against the independence of the media that would distort the mission they have undertaken to inform the public without fear or favor... this is because the general public must be reduced to its traditional apathy and obedience, and driven from the arena of political debate and action, if democracy is to survive.

Media Ownership Concentration

A key idea of media democracy is that the concentration of media ownership in recent decades in the hands of a few corporations and conglomerates has led to a narrowing of the range of voices and opinions being expressed in the mass media; to an increase in the commercialization of news and information; to a hollowing out of the news media's ability to conduct investigative reporting and act as the public watchdog; and to an increase of emphasis on the bottom line, which prioritizes infotainment and celebrity news over informative discourse.

This concentration has been encouraged by government deregulation and neo-liberal trade policies. For example, the U.S. Telecommunications Act of 1996 discarded most media ownership rules that were previously in place, leading to massive consolidation in the telecommunications industry. Over 4,000 radio stations were bought out, and minority ownership of TV stations dropped to its lowest point since the federal government began tracking such data in 1990. In its review of the Telecommunication Act in 2003, the Federal Communications Commission (FCC) further reduced restrictions and allowed media corporations to grow and expand into other areas of media.

The past decade has also seen a number of media corporate mergers and takeovers in Canada. For example, in 1990, 17.3% of daily newspapers were independently owned; in 2005, 1% were. These changes, among others, caused the Senate Standing Committee on Transport and Communications to launch a study of Canadian news media in March 2003. (This topic had been examined twice in the past, by the Davey Commission (1970) and the Kent Commission (1981), both of which produced recommendations that were never implemented in any meaningful way.)

The Senate Committee's final report, released in June 2006, expressed concern about the effects of the current levels of news media ownership in Canada. Specifically, the Committee discussed their concerns regarding the following trends: the potential of media ownership concentration to limit news diversity and reduce news quality; the Canadian Radio-television and Telecommunications Commission]] (CRTC) and Competition Bureau's ineffectiveness at stopping media ownership concentration; the lack of federal funding for the CBC and the broadcaster's uncertain mandate and role; diminishing employment standards for journalists (including less job security, less journalistic freedom, and new contractual threats to intellectual property); a lack of Canadian training and research institutes; and difficulties with the federal government's support for print media and the absence of funding for the internet-based news media.

The report provided 40 recommendations and 10 suggestions (for areas outside of federal government jurisdiction), including legislation amendments that would trigger automatic reviews of a proposed media merger if certain thresholds are reached, and CRTC regulation revisions to ensure that access to the broadcasting system is encouraged and that a diversity of news and information programming is available through these services.

Media democracy advocates argue in favour of such legislative policies that encourage a stronger commitment to serving the public interest and a commercial framework that facilitates independent media ownership.

The 2004 documentary film *Outfoxed: Rupert Murdoch's War on Journalism* treats criticism about corporate media concentration.

Alternative and Citizen Media in the World

As a response to the shortcomings of the mainstream media, proponents of media democracy often advocate supporting and engaging in independent and alternative media, in both print and electronic forms as well as video documentary. Through citizen journalism and citizen media, individuals can produce and disseminate information and opinions that are marginalized by the mainstream media. In the book *We the Media: Grassroots Journalism by the People, for the People*, Dan Gillmor urges individuals who are concerned about media ownership concentration and the decreasing amount of public-interest broadcasting to use technology like the internet to create and distribute information they believe is not properly reported in the mainstream news media. This book details strategies that individuals and groups can use to democratize the media.

4

Human Rights and Journalistic Ethics

The foregoing critique of state-run and public-funded electronic media institutions is also valid for newspapers that function under state auspices. Some such criticism is also valid for newspapers that are privately owned and deny editorial autonomy to journalists. Nor do such newspapers foster the observance of journalistic ethics in day-to-day functioning by providing for professional training and observance of ethical norms. Although the newspaper enterprise in most South Asian countries is over 150 years old (except explicitly in Bangladesh and Pakistan for reasons of their recent creation as separate nations) there has been no formal code until recently. However, there are laws pertaining to newspapers and printing presses and the general law, several provisions of which are incorporated in the Penal Code.

It was noted earlier in this essay that private newspapers that were supportive of the ruling power in the respective countries experienced a sense of political, social and economic power. Consequently, they could hire and fire journalists at will and felt that their newspapers had no moral obligation to serve the public interest or to accommodate news and views favourable to those with whom they disagreed or whom they disliked. It was the intensely partial, divisive and restrictive stance of some newspapers, albeit influential with the ruling elites, which led to public clamour for press commissions in some countries of South Asia. Partly, they were inspired by the initiatives taken in Britain (Royal Commission on the Press,

1947-1949) and in the United States with the publication in 1947 of "A Free and Responsible Press." An independent Commission on the Freedom of the Press issued it. Its report deals with the responsibilities of the owners and managers of the press to their consciences and the common good for the formation of public opinion. The Commission comprised persons of standing drawn from civil society.

The special significance of the US commission is that it predates the Universal Declaration of Human Rights of 1948 and the International Covenant on Civil and Political Rights in 1976, in particular Articles 14, 17 and 19. The Commission focused on the moral aspect of freedom of expression, the right being based on the duty of a person to the common good and to his own thought. "In the absence of moral duties, there are no moral rights," the report states. The jurisprudence derived from the recognition of human rights and duties, the inspirational religious and cultural values of the South Asian civilisations and a shared public repugnance at the abuse of power by some newspapers and journalists supportive of regimes that were authoritarian led to the appointment of press commissions.

In India the first press commission was set up in 1952 and reported on the status of the press. Its unique feature is that it is multi-lingual, publishing in as many as 90 languages. The ownership pattern of some 25,000 newspapers and journals is varied, the largest number (nearly two thirds) being published by individuals. Their combined share of circulation is about equal to that of newspapers published by joint stock companies. The number of company newspapers is only about one eighteenth of the number published by private individuals. Societies and associations, firms and partnerships, trusts, cooperative societies and educational institutions are among the other publishers of newspapers. This varied pattern of ownership, the multi-lingual character of the press, the diversity of the readership and the absence of an ethic shared by journalists and the public compound the issue of a common code of communication ethics.

The Press Council of India, set up by an Act of Parliament in 1965, was empowered to draft a code of conduct for newspapers, news agencies and journalists in accordance with high professional standards. But it refrained from doing so, hoping that a code would evolve from its own deliberations.

In 1984 the Press Council published an 11-point set of guidelines, which could serve as norms in the event of editors and journalists themselves deciding to draft a code. They were as follows.

- Accuracy and fairness
- Verification before publication
- Respect for privacy
- Recognition of the right of reply
- Restraint in the coverage of communal disputes/clashes
- Avoidance of plagiarism
- Principles regarding recording interviews and phone conversations
- Avoidance of vulgarity and obscenity
- Caution in criticising judicial actions
- Restraint in the use of photographs of bodies of victims of crime/accidents
- Avoidance of crass commercialism.

It has been observed that there is a low degree of voluntary compliance with the code. Nevertheless, public faith in the Press Council as a forum for redressing complaints against newspapers is borne out by the number of complaints it receives and investigates. The Council has on occasion deplored conflict between owners and editors that tends to affect editorial freedom as well as the proper functional relationship between the proprietors and the staff engaged in the production of the paper. A cause of conflict between owners and editors is the interlocking of the press with industry. Consequently, owners warn editors not to be too critical of the government, fearing reprisals that may affect their business interests.

Another ethical issue arises from the attitude to the newspaper as a saleable commodity, expressed by the Managing Director of Benett Coleman and Company, publishers of "The Times of India." Such an attitude negates the human rights basis of media ethics. It is refreshing therefore to find a Code of Ethics of the All-India Newspapers Editors Conference. In several respects it is similar to the Guidelines of the Indian

Press Council. Significant departures from the Council principles are that journalists are enjoined to promote the unity of the country and to be circumspect in dealing with movements and ideas which promote regionalism at the cost of national unity; the integrity of the country is to be regarded as sacrosanct; confidentiality and professional secrecy; obligations of propriety to fellow journalists, and personal integrity of conduct.

The Code of Conduct 1993 for Newspapers, News Agencies and Journalists of Bangladesh framed under the Press Council Act of 1974 introduces the expression "moral duty" in several of its provisions. Among such moral duties is that the editor must accept full and sole responsibility for all that is published in his newspaper; that journalists should highlight degeneration of moral values in Bangladesh society; and exercise caution in publishing news of man-woman relationships or any report relating to women. In Nepal the preamble to the Code of Conduct for Journalists (1992) states that the country's new Constitution (1990) has established democratic principles and values, and by enhancing the dignity of the press has placed a greater responsibility on its practitioners to fulfil the professional duty entrusted to them by making it responsible to society.

The Code, issued by the Press Council (initially set up in 1970 and reconstituted in 1992) requires journalists to "always remain dedicated to human values, democratic behaviour, national interest and public welfare." Another article of the Code states that "news and views leading to communal fighting, terrorism and differences between different races, religious groups and communities should not be entertained."

Another provision states that resort to blackmail through journalism for economic or other benefit "is a serious moral crime." In other respects the Code is comparable with codes elsewhere.

In 1993 the Nepal Journalists Association adopted a Code of Conduct for Journalists, also called the Birgunj Declaration 1993 after the venue of the meeting. While it is similar to other codes for journalists, it is significant in that it requires journalists to be dedicated to ensuring that the people's right to be informed is secured. They are also required to "remain dedicated to human values, democratic culture, the country's well-being and for the public well-being."

The relaxation of restrictions on the Nepalese press owes a great deal to a 1981 Royal Commission on the Press that led to the enactment of the Press and Publications Act of 1982, a measure of reform. The Constitution of 1990 reinforced the liberalisation. Of special interest is Article 16, which states, "Every person shall have the right to demand and receive information on any matter of public importance." The Press and Publications Act of February 1992 further consolidated the earlier gains.

Pakistan's articulation of media ethics is unique in that it illustrates how Islam tends to reshape the values and ethics of Pakistan's society. The authoritarian regime of Field Marshal Ayub Khan had in 1963 promulgated the restrictive Press and Publications Ordinance. It was replaced by a mild regulatory law, the Registration of Press and Publications Ordinance of 1988, as a result of the Federal Shariat Court judgement on a petition which entailed examination of the 1963 Ordinance.

In its judgment the Shariat Court relied heavily on the Islamic Declaration for the mass media prepared and published by the Islamic Press Union. According to the Islamic Declaration, Islam lays great emphasis on freedom of expression and human dignity. It not only gives people the right of dissent but also makes it obligatory on them to protest against tyranny, injustice and oppression.

The Declaration adds, "Islam aims at creating a disciplined society where the rights and obligations of the individuals are in harmony with the broader interests of the community. "These rights and obligations must not be curtailed, abrogated, suspended or transgressed by individuals, governments, parliaments or other institutions."

The Declaration articulates in some detail the rights of freedom of expression, or protest against injustice and evil and the individual's right to privacy. It goes on to spell out the concept of authenticity, which the media are required to uphold in practice.

Article 19 of the Constitution of the Islamic Republic of Pakistan, besides guaranteeing to citizens freedom of speech and expression, also guarantees freedom of the press, subject, however, to reasonable restrictions imposed by law "in the interest of the glory of Islam, of the integrity, security or defence of Pakistan or any part thereof, friendly relations with foreign states, public order, decency or morality, or in relation to contempt of court, defamation or incitement to any offence." The Sri Lanka Press Council Code of Ethics for journalists was drawn up in consultation with a group of editors and approved by parliament in October 1981. The Press Council was established in 1973 by an act of parliament. Its institution was recommended by the Press Commission of 1963, which recommended the broadbasing of the ownership of the press besides other matters.

The Code of Ethics is comparable with codes in most Western countries, but many journalists are not aware of its existence nor does it form part of whatever training is provided in newspaper establishments. Even some legislators are unaware that the Code has been there since 1981. The principles enshrined in the Code derive from the human rights jurisprudence, which draws attention to both rights and duties.

OBSERVANCE OF MEDIA ETHICS

The South Asian experience points to a gulf between the values and norms enshrined in the respective codes and the actual practice of journalism. It derives partly from a mistaken notion that the press is in a privileged position and that journalists are entitled to greater freedom of expression than ordinary citizens. Further, breach of the code of ethics is not punishable by courts except where the infringement is also an offence against some statutory provision. While freedom of expression is exercised, at times to the point of license, there is insufficient evidence of the duty of care and respect for the rights of others. That the right of expression and publication has to be exercised with responsibility for accuracy, objectivity, fairness and balance appears not to be part of a professional code.

It requires an activist Press Council and a self-regulatory professional body of journalists to ensure high standards of journalism and promotion of the ethical values that the codes seek to uphold. Nevertheless, the interventionist role of the

Press Council is minimal. It often acts only on complaints by aggrieved readers. It does not in addition perform a monitoring role. In any case, after inquiry all that the Press Council can do is to order the newspaper to publish a correction; an apology where it is required; and it could reprimand the offending newspaper. It has no penal power. So it tends to be regarded as toothless.

The situation is further compounded by the absence of a public ethic based on a concept of morality and respect for human rights. At times readers tend to consider public curiosity about the private lives of politicians and celebrities a matter of public interest although the private conduct of such persons does not always impinge on the performance of their public duty.

The fact that newspapers are in a competitive industry is another functional constraint on the observance of media ethics. Papers not only strive to be first with the news, but also tend to sensationalise it to get the edge on competitors.

The link between newspaper circulation and advertising also tends to blur the ethical dimension. Dramatisation of news promotes sales and circulation and helps increase advertising revenue. Note the cynical attitude of the proprietors of The Times of India who regard the newspaper primarily as a saleable commodity.

Journalism schools endeavour to instil an awareness of the ethics of principle. But only a very small proportion of South Asian journalists have had pre-entry training in such schools of journalism. In-plant training is mainly craft-oriented. Even if media ethics is part of the curriculum of such training, the practice of journalism leaves much to be desired. The absence of professional bodies of journalists comparable with bodies for such professions as law, medicine, engineering and accountancy is a drawback to the self-regulation of the profession.

While there are many associations of journalists in the respective countries they function more like trade unions and are concerned mainly with working conditions, salaries, pensions, ancillary facilities and security of service.

The need for codes of media ethics is unquestionable. But codes alone have not been effective in raising ethical standards in the media. This was the consensus of a three-day seminar on "Communication Ethics from a South Asian Perspective," held in Colombo, Sri Lanka, in November 1993. The participants included 20 senior journalists and communication scholars from the South Asian region. The seminar was organised by the Asian Media Information and Communication Centre (AMIC) Singapore, the World Association of Christian Communication, UK, and the International Centre for Ethnic Studies, Colombo, with support from the Friedrich Ebert Foundation, Colombo.

The seminar recommended replacement of press councils by media councils, which, unlike the former, should not be perceived as an extension of the state but as genuinely independent bodies. They should comprise respected media practitioners and eminent persons from public life chosen through a mechanism ensured by appropriate legislation.

The seminar also commented on the paucity of professional bodies of media practitioners in the region and called for the status of such bodies to be recognised by both the state and the social community. It would be the responsibility of such bodies to promote observance of ethical standards among media practitioners and a greater sense of social responsibility among media institutions. While there is a growing degree of awareness among senior media practitioners of the need for adherence to media ethics there is little evidence of discussion of media ethics at the level of media owners. However, there is discussion by media owners on what they perceive as the intrusive role of the state in introducing new regulatory measures especially in relation to electronic media.

Perhaps the weakest aspect of media ethics in South Asia is the absence of an articulate public ethic that could act as a countervailing force to both the state and media institutions. The restraint on such a cohesive public ethic emerging is media audiences being heterogeneous in composition and values, levels of appreciation of media content, diverse in taste and apparently shunning an activist role in safeguarding cultural values and promoting high standards of media performance.

GLOBAL MEDIA: IN 21ST CENTURY

The last decade of the 20th century saw a wave of uncertainty in the media business. The key question was who would own the two main stages of digital entertainment: production and distribution. As a result of that turmoil, a number of different companies have converged on the media industry. Broadcast and content providers such as Sky and onDigital began competing for digital TV subscribers.

Telecommunication companies such as BT and Cable & Wireless promised to deliver video on demand. Services such as pay per view and online shopping added a new dimension to digital broadcasting. But those services also created new complexities for media companies. The bar is quickly being raised for companies that want to succeed in the world of media commerce. Consumers have been shown a glimpse of a more flexible future and their expectations in terms of choice, convenience and quality are higher today than ever before.

For all of those reasons, it's clear that there are plenty of organisational and technological challenges ahead. The first hurdle is the very real imperative to create digital content and to ensure that existing material is digitised for broadcasting over the Internet and by digital service broadcasters across the world. Whatever delivery mechanism is involved, the broadcast media are increasingly content hungry.

REDUCING THE COST

Companies also need to consider the fact that the digitisation of media reduces the cost of entry to media production. A piece of film that took days of work and hundreds of dollars to produce ten years ago can now be shot digitally, stored and broadcast for a fraction of the cost – and within much shorter time-scales. The net effect is that smaller players are able to move much more quickly into the digital media production space just as the desktop publishing (DTP) revolution of the 1980s moved the production of camera ready text and pictures out of the sole preserve of typesetters and designers.

The pressures that these trends create are not trivial. Organisations need to move quickly to meet new competitors head on and to ensure that the assets that they own in the form of film and TV programmes are available in a digital format. They need to reduce the complexity of managing that material so that they can provide a cost-effective, reliable service to customers and partners. Technology clearly plays a vital role.

Once content is in a digital format, it can be stored, managed and distributed as just another information resource. The challenge is that it is a resource that places massive demands on technology platforms.

To meet the expectations of consumers, broadcasters need to provide services of the highest possible quality and availability. They also need platforms that can be re-sized and extended to meet future requirements as well as current needs. A third imperative is that systems can be installed and used quickly by new start-ups moving into the digital broadcasting industry: they must not take organisations into a technological backwater.

FUTURE OF GLOBAL MEDIA INDUSTRY

Media companies will survive or fail in 2010 based not just on content but also on creative intelligence they are able to gather about their customers, the markets which they serve and the value of their digital assets. In the near future the global media majors will have to move towards a more open environment as the media landscape becomes increasingly digital. Computer major IBM has released a report *Media & Entertainment 2010.*

By 2010 to continue remaining healthy media companies will have to form systems by which consumers are allowed 24x7 access to protected media content for variable fees. IBM has stated that it foresees a continuing onslaught of new kinds of content, media forms and devices. Successful media companies will vie for attention by allowing business partners, customers and consumers more freedom to manage their own media and entertainment experiences.

To survive media companies must also be able to negotiate rapid shifts in markets, economic climates and technology innovations. As they go along companies will also need to create new product windows and business models. The report has noted that between now and 2010 digital technologies will become more powerful and affordable at every user level, in digital networks and in product offerings. More and more consumers will be able to compile, programme, edit, create and share content. As a result, they will gain more control and become more immersed in media experiences.

The report states, “We foresee growing participation in media experiences well beyond traditional media, in three additional sectors. We have labelled them multi-media, big media and pervasive media. Successful companies, in transforming their business models to serve these four distinct channels and behaviours, will continue to reposition and restructure. “They will focus on the core components that create value for their customers and consumers, divest unneeded properties, improve the monetisation of assets and importantly, join with other players to achieve scale, lower costs and offer value-added products and services. We call this business model the open media company of the future.”

IBM had ten recommendations for players evolving toward becoming the open media company of the future. The first is creating or converting content to digital formats. The report noted that digital management capabilities would become a core competency and differentiator. Consumers would become more knowledgeable. This means more pressure on the competing content providers to know more about the media habits of individuals as well as the larger segments.

Among other things the media business in the future will leverage advances in technology to provide customers and consumers a more involved experience with the media firm. Changing business model for music, movies: As far as the music industry is concerned the forecast for 2010 is that with the onset of the digital environment some independent artists and producers will offer all their music, short videos and movies for free. They will make money instead from tie-ins, product placements, Webcast concerts and events with pop stars and fan merchandise.

Successful companies will allow customers to purchase and download the rights to a book and have it configured for one or more types of media devices, or delivered in the traditional hard or soft cover within 24 hours. They will also be able to order the film of the book, the soundtrack or only one song from an album, the liner notes or a single quotation which they could then use in a variety of formats. The format could be a term paper, a wall poster etc.

Changes in financial systems: In 2010 the online accounting systems of the surviving media companies will automatically invoice the huge data feeds of digital content ordered by network and cable broadcasters from distributors and streamline payments, as well. Those millions of micropayments aggregate to a sizeable revenue stream from the sale of new or archived digital content, much of which never has to travel to a theater, retail store or TV station. It is delivered online. In an era of pervasive media users from around the globe will be confidentially tracked for their opinions, preferences and tastes in media and entertainment. Actively or passively they will help shape the content they experience as well as how and when they want it.

GLOBAL JOURNALISM ETHICS

Global journalism ethics aims at developing a comprehensive set of principles and standards for the practice of journalism in an age of global news media. New forms of communication are reshaping the practice of a once parochial craft serving a local, regional or national public. Today, news media use communication technology to gather text, video and images from around the world, with unprecedented speed and varying degrees of editorial control. The same technology allows news media to disseminate this information to audiences scattered around the globe.

Despite these global trends, most codes of ethics contain standards for news organizations or associations in specific countries. International associations of journalists exist, and some have constructed declarations of principle. But no global code has been adopted by all major journalism associations and news organizations.

In addition to statements of principle, more work needs to be done on the equally important area of specific, practice guidelines for covering international events. An adequate global journalism ethics has yet to be constructed.

THE GLOBAL MEDIA DEBATE

Since at least the 1970s, a global media ethics has been part of controversial attempts to establish a "new world information order". These international movements have included broad "media" issues that, albeit important, are not a primary focus of journalism ethics per se, e.g., the equal distribution of computer technology in the world. Developing nations and/or UN agencies such as UNESCO have led such movements. None to date has been successful. In the late 1900s, the movement was opposed by governments and news organizations in the United States and Britain. They feared that non-democratic powers might use a global ethic to justify limits to freedom of expression and of the press. The dream of a set of principles for equitable and responsible dissemination of information worldwide has not died. The United Nations is currently holding "World Summits on the Information Society." At a summit in Geneva in December 2003, 175 countries adopted a plan of action and a declaration of principles. A second summit will be held in Tunisia in November 2005.

Why a global ethics?

There are at least two reasons:

(1) Practical: a non-global ethic is no longer able to adequately address the new problems that face a global journalism, and
(2) Ethical: new global responsibilities come with global impact and reach.

Both reasons are grounded in the fact that news media now inhabit a radically pluralistic, global community where the impact of their reports can have far-reaching effects — good or bad. News reports, via satellite or the Internet, reach people around the world and influence the actions of governments, militaries, humanitarian agencies and warring ethnic groups. A responsible global ethic is needed in a world where news media bring together a plurality of different religions, traditions and ethnic groups.

One responsibility is to report issues and events in a way that reflects this global plurality of views; to practice a journalism that helps different groups understand each other better. Reports should be accurate, balanced and diverse, as judged from an international perspective. A biased and parochial journalism can wreak havoc in a tightly linked global world.

Unless reported properly, North American readers may fail to understand the causes of violence in Middle East, or a famine in Africa. Biased reports may incite ethnic groups in a region to attack each other. A narrow-minded, patriotic news media can stampede populations into war. Moreover, journalism with a global perspective is needed to help citizens understand the daunting global problems of poverty, environmental degradation, technological inequalities and political instability.

New Stage in Journalism Ethics

Since the birth of modern journalism in the 17th century, journalism has gradually broaden the scope of the people that it claims to serve — from factions to specific social classes to the public of nations. The journalistic principle of "serving the public interest" has been understood, tacitly or explicitly, as serving one's own public, social class or nation. The other principles of objectivity, impartiality and editorial independence were limited by this parochial understanding of who journalism serves. For example, "impartiality" meant being impartial in one's coverage of rival groups within one's society, but not necessarily being impartial to groups outside one's national boundaries.

Global journalism ethics, then, can be seen as an extension of journalism ethics — to regard journalism's "public" as the citizens of the world, and to interpret the ethical principles of objectivity, balance and independence in an international manner.

Journalism ethics becomes more "cosmopolitan" in tone and perspective.

COMPONENTS OF GLOBAL JOURNALISM ETHICS

The development of global journalism ethics has the following tasks.

Conceptual Tasks

New philosophical foundations for a global ethics, which include:

- global re-interpretation of the ethical role and aims of journalism
- global re-interpretation of existing journalism principles and standards, such as objectivity, balance and independence
- construction of new norms and "best practices" as guides for the practice of global journalism.

Research Tasks

More research into the state of journalism, amid globalization:

- studies of news media in various regions of world
- studies on the evolution and impact of globalization in news media, with a focus on ownership, technology and practice
- studies on the ethical standards of new media in different countries
- studies on news coverage of international problems and issues.

Practical Tasks

Actions to implement and support global standards:

- application of this global perspective to re-define the coverage of international events and issues
- coalition-building among journalists and interested parties with the aim of writing a global code of ethics that has wide-spread acceptance
- initiatives to defend and enhance free and responsible news media, especially in areas where problems are the greatest.

How would a global ethics be different?

Philosophically, the distinct conceptual element of a global ethics can be summarized by three imperatives:

Act as Global Agents

Journalists should see themselves as agents of a global public sphere. The goal of their collective actions is a well-informed, diverse and tolerant global "info-sphere" that challenges the distortions of tyrants, the abuse of human rights and the manipulation of information by special interests.

Serve the Citizens of the World

The global journalist's primary loyalty is to the information needs of world citizens. Journalists should refuse to define themselves as attached primarily to factions, regions or even countries. Serving the public means serving more than one's local readership or audience, or even the public of one's country.

Promote Non-Parochial Understandings

The global journalist frames issues broadly and uses a diversity of sources and perspectives to promote a nuanced understanding of issues from an international perspective. Journalism should work against a narrow ethnocentrism or patriotism. What do these three imperatives imply for specific standards of journalism, such as objectivity? Under global journalism ethics, objectivity becomes the ideal of informing impartially from an international stance. Objectivity in journalism has usually been understood as the duty to avoid bias toward groups within one's own country. Global objectivity takes on the additional responsibility of allowing bias towards one's country or culture as a whole to distort reports, especially reports on international issues.

Objective reports, to be accurate and balanced, must contain all relevant international sources and cross-cultural perspectives. In addition, global journalism asks journalists to be more conscious of how they frame the global public's perspective on major stories, and how they set the international news agenda. The aim of global journalism should be more than helping the public sphere "go well" at home, as civic journalists say. The aim should be to facilitate rational deliberation in a global public sphere.

Global journalism ethics implies a firm journalistic response to inward-looking attitudes, such as extreme patriotism. It was disturbing to see how some news organizations during the Iraq War of 2003 so quickly shucked their peacetime commitments to independent, impartial reporting as soon as the drums of war started beating. Cosmopolitanism means that the primary ethical duty of a global journalism in times of conflict and uncertainty is not a patriotism of blind allegiance, or muted criticism. Public duty calls for independent, hard-edged news, along with investigations and analysis.

PROBLEMS AND OBSTACLES

Universal Values?

Among advocates of global ethics, there is disagreement over whether ethicists need to identify "universal values" among all journalists, or humans. Do such universal values exist?

What might they be? Recently, a growing group of ethicists have attempted to identify a common core of values in various places: in codes of journalism ethics, in international treaties on human rights, in anthropological studies of culture.

One view is that neither universal values nor universal consent is required for a plausible, global code. This view sometimes stems from a contractual or 'constructionist" view of ethics. The constructionist does not believe that ethics depends on "finding" or "discovering", through empirical means, a set of universal values that all rational people acknowledge. Rather, the correct method of global ethics is to see whether all or most interested parties are able to "construct" and agree upon a set of principles through a fair process of deliberation. On this view, it is also not clear that a set of values must gain universal consensus — a demand that seems unduly strong, given the variety of new media in the world. A weaker requirement would aim at the construction of a set of principles agreed to by most major journalism associations and news organizations.

Getting Specific

Global journalism ethics will have to amount to more than a dreamy spiritualism about the brotherhood of man and universal benevolence. Conceptually, there is work to be done. Global journalism ethics must show, in detail, how its ideas imply changes to norms and practices. What exactly do journalists "owe" citizens in a distant land? How can global journalists integrate their partial and impartial perspectives? How can journalists support global values while remaining impartial communicators?

Reforming Media Practices

The slow, complex, practical task of developing better media practices is no less imposing. Exhorting individual journalists to be ethical will be futile unless supported by an institutional climate that encourages global values in the newsroom. Aware of such difficulties, some journalists may accuse global journalism ethicists of being unrealistic in thinking that news organizations will provide the education, expertise and extra resources needed to achieve a high-quality cosmopolitan journalism.

2004 ANNUAL REPORT-NEWSPAPER PUBLIC ATTITUDES

There is an enormous amount of data that has been collected over the years about public attitudes toward the newspaper industry, more perhaps than for any other medium. Taken together, the survey data reveal four key trends.

- People tend to trust newspapers less than other mediums.
- That trust is declining, as it is for other kinds of news mediums.
- People think newspaper journalists are out of touch and motivated by commercial imperatives.
- But people still turn to newspapers, particularly during certain kinds of news events and particularly for local news and for an opinion forum.

Trust: Believability and Credibility

The history and enduring nature of newspapers do not, in the end, give the medium an edge when it comes to public perception. Asked a number of different ways, citizens continuously give newspapers worse marks than other mediums, despite the sense by most print journalists to the contrary.

In general, Americans give newspapers lower marks for believability and credibility than they do for local television news, or any of the three network newscasts and CNN. And this has been the case for decades. NBC's "Dateline," a prime-time television newsmagazine that tends to focus on softer and sometimes more tabloid-oriented subjects, rates nearly as high as newspapers.

While there are various surveys tracking this, one of the latest, a study by the Pew Research Center for the People and the Press, found that a majority of Americans tend to believe their daily newspaper-59% gave it the highest two ratings on a scale of 1 to 4 in May of 2002. Nevertheless, this is lower than the roughly two-thirds of respondents who rated the various television news categories this way. A full 66 percent gave believability ratings to NBC and CNN, 68 percent to ABC and local news, and 64 percent for CBS ("Dateline" received top ratings from 58 percent).

(National Public Radio and the NewsHour with Jim Lehrer appear lower on the believability scale, but that is only because larger percentages of Americans haven't heard of or say they can't rate them, 29% for NPR, and 49% for the NewsHour).

The only news medium that newspapers seemed to surpass when it comes to believability is print magazines. Just more than half deem Time (53 percent), Newsweek (51 percent) and US News and World Report (51 percent) believable. They also still hold and edge over Fox (53 percent) and MSNBC (55 percent).

The picture looks even worse for national newspapers included in the Pew data, as it has in past surveys. According to Pew, the slimmest of majorities (51 percent) believe USA Today, while 25 percent indicated a lack of believability and 23 percent said they could not rate it). The same 51 percent believed The Wall Street Journal, with 15 percent not believing in it and 34 percent not being able to rate it. The New York Times was not included in the survey.

Some of this may have to do with the way people react to news they can see versus what they read, and their attitudes towards local media they know versus national media they are not as familiar with. If so, there may be little newspapers can do about their relative believability versus other media. Perhaps more worrisome for newspapers, however, is the trend line. The percentage of people who rate their daily newspaper as believable has dropped from 80% in 1985 to 59% in 2002. Other media, including network and local TV, have seen similar declines. Here, the NewsHour, NPR, and 60 Minutes stand out for not declining in believability.

Newspapers also have some reason for concern when pollsters turn from asking about believability to asking about quality. When Pew asked, in January 2002, who has been doing the best job of covering the news lately, only 10 percent of respondents named newspapers, compared with 38 percent for cable television, 16 percent for network television news and 13 percent for local television news.

This could be chalked up to a number of factors-the appeal of visual media generally and the increasing availability and convenience of television and online news versus print among them. Yet this finding may also reflect something else. Perhaps since September 11th cable television news, whatever its weaknesses, was the best source of international news generally available in most U.S. communities. Local newspapers, with their focus on local news, were not satisfying reader demand for more news about the war on terror. Though newspapers have not ranked especially well on this question, this still represented a noticeable decline. In January 1999, 13 percent named newspapers as doing the best job, and 14 percent said so in January 1996.

The Readership Institute at Northwestern University has found somewhat more promising results. In a 2000 survey, 11 percent of newspaper readers said their local newspaper was excellent and 39 percent said it was very good, with 35 percent rating it as good. Just 15 percent said it was fair or poor. Also, nearly three-quarters of readers (73 percent) indicated that they would recommend the local paper to a friend. Only 7 percent said they would not recommend it.

The research on public attitudes also suggests the nature of newspapers' appeal and perhaps enduring qualities. People do not tend to turn to newspapers when news is breaking, but they go there later on for a sense of what to make of things.

The percentage of people who name newspapers as their primary news source tends to drop during major breaking news events, such as September 11th or the Iraq war. Only 11 percent cited newspapers as their primary source for news during the terrorist attacks. Just 24 percent saw newspapers as their primary source for the Iraq war in March 2003.

However, as the initial shock of these events subsides, newspapers regain importance. More people began citing newspapers as a main source after the end of combat in Iraq. By October 2003, the latest numbers available, 50 percent said that newspapers were their primary source of news. That is the highest percentage of people citing newspapers as their main source since 1996, making it second only behind television.

This upsurge is probably impossible to explain right now. One reason could be that changes in the nature of the content of cable are pulling people back to print. Another possibility is that the nature of the news in the latter months of 2003 was suited to newspapers. Understanding why the United States had getting into the war, trying to piece together the situation in Iraq and the soundness of Bush administration policies-perhaps these are questions that newspapers may help people sort out more efficiently than turning to fast-breaking cable television or abbreviated local news. It will be helpful to see if this upsurge continues or changes with events.

Another study on public response to coverage of the war, this one by the Readership Institute, offers further clues as to what people like about newspaper versus other media. The study found that during the war in Iraq in March and April 2003, people said they liked the editorial and opinion pages of newspapers, and they also liked papers for giving them a local perspective on the war. The depth and balance that newspapers might provide did not register as strong assets for print in the study, nor did the suggestion that newspapers had more expert sources or dug more aggressively for the news than television might.

5

Freedom of Press and Responsible Journalism

The strength and importance of media in a democracy is well recognized. Article 19(1)(a) of the Indian Constitution, which gives freedom of speech and expression includes within its ambit, freedom of press. The existence of a free, independent and powerful media is the cornerstone of a democracy, especially of a highly mixed society like India. Media is not only a medium to express once feelings, opinions and views, but it is also responsible and instrumental for building opinions and views on various topics of regional, national and international agenda.

The pivotal role of the media is its ability to mobilize the thinking process of millions. The increased role of the media in today's globalized and tech-savvy world was aptly put in the words of Justice Hand of the United States Supreme Court when he said, "The hand that rules the press, the radio, the screen and the far spread magazine, rules the country".

Democracy is the rule of the people. A system which has three strong pillars. But as Indian society today has become somewhat unstable on its 3 legs-the executive, the legislature and the judiciary, the guarantee of Article 19 (1)(a) has given rise to a fourth pillar-media. It plays the role of a conscious keeper, a watchdog of the functionaries of society and attempts to attend to the wrongs in our system, by bringing them to the knowledge of all, hoping for correction. It is indisputable that in many dimensions the unprecedented media revolution has resulted in great gains for the general public. Even the judicial wing of the state has benefited from the ethical and fearless journalism and taken suo motu cognizance of the matters in various cases after relying on their reports and news highlighting grave violations of human rights. The criminal justice system in this country has many lacunae which are used by the rich and powerful to go scot-free. Figures speak for themselves in this case as does the conviction rate in our country which is abysmally low at 4 percent. In such circumstances the media plays a crucial role in not only mobilizing public opinion but bringing to light injustices which most likely would have gone unnoticed otherwise.

However, there are always two sides to a coin. With this increased role and importance attached to the media, the need for its accountability and professionalism in reportage can not be emphasized enough. In a civil society no right to freedom, howsoever invaluable it might be, can be considered absolute, unlimited, or unqualified in all circumstances. The freedom f the media, like any other freedom recognized under the constitution has to be exercised within reasonable boundaries. With great power comes great responsibility. Similarly, the freedom under Article 19(1) (a) is correlative with the duty not to violate any law.

Every institution is liable to be abused, and every liberty, if left unbridled, has the tendency to become a license which would lead to disorder and anarchy. This is the threshold on which we are standing today. Television channels in a bid to increase their TRP ratings are resorting to sensationalized journalism with a view to earn a competitive edge over the others.

Sting operations have now become the order of the day. They are a part of the hectic pace at which the media is evolving, carrying with every sting as much promise as risk. However, though technology cannot be thwarted but it has its limits. It can not be denied that it is of practical importance that a precarious balance between the fundamental right to expression and the right to ones privacy be maintained. The second practice which has become more of a daily occurrence now is that of Media trials. Something which was started to show to the public at large the truth about cases has now become a practice interfering dangerously with the justice delivery system. Both are tools frequented by the media. And both highlight the enormous need of what is called 'responsible journalism'.

STING OPERATIONS VS. RIGHT TO PRIVACY

Television channels have started a series of investigative attempts with hidden cameras and other espionage devices. The advent of miniaturized audio and video technology, specially the pinhole camera technology, enables one to clandestinely make a video/audio recording of a conversation and actions of individuals. Such equipment generally has four components—the miniaturized camera, often of a size of a 25 paisa coin or even smaller, a miniature video recording device, a cord to transmit the signals and a battery cell. The use of the cord can be avoided through wireless transmissions.

In law enforcement, a sting operation is an operation designed to catch a person committing a crime by means of deception. A typical sting will have a law-enforcement officer or cooperative member of the public play a role as criminal partner or potential victim and go along with a suspect's actions to gather evidence of the suspect's wrongdoing. Now the moot question that arises is whether it is for the media to act as the 'law enforcement agency'!

The carrying out of a sting operation may be an expression of the right to free press but it caries with it an indomitable duty to respect the privacy of others. The individual who is the subject of a press or television 'item' has his or her personality, reputation or career dashed to the ground after the media exposure. He too has a fundamental right to live with dignity and respect and a right to privacy guaranteed to him under Article 21 of the Constitution.

The movement towards the recognition of right to privacy in India started with Kharak Singh v. State of Uttar Pradesh and Others, wherein the apex court observed that it is true that our constitution does not expressly declare a right to privacy as fundamental right, but the said right is an essential ingredient of personal liberty. After an elaborate appraisal of this right in Gobind v. State of Madhya Pradesh and Another, it has been fully incorporated under the umbrella of right to life and personal liberty by the humanistic expansion of the Article 21 of the Constitution.

Today, it is being witnessed that the over-inquisitive media, which is a product of over-commercialization, is severely encroaching the individual's right to privacy by crossing the boundaries of its freedom. Yet another observation of the court which touched this aspect of violation of right to privacy of the individuals, is found in the judgment of the Andhra Pradesh High Court in Labour Liberation Front v. State of Andhra Pradesh. The Court observed as follows:

Once an incident involving prominent person or institution takes place, the media is swinging into action and virtually leaving very little for the prosecution or the Courts to examine the matter. Recently, it has assumed dangerous proportions, to the extent of intruding into the very privacy of individuals. Gross misuse of technological advancements and the unhealthy competition in the field of journalism resulted in obliteration of norms or commitment to the noble profession. The freedom of speech and expression, which is the bedrock of journalism, is subjected to gross misuse. It must not be forgotten that only those who maintain restraint can exercise rights and freedoms effectively.

In Mr. X v. Hospital Z the Supreme Court held that the right to privacy may, apart from contract, also arise out of a particular specific relationship, which may be commercial, matrimonial or even political. Public disclosure of even true private facts may amount to an invasion of the right to privacy. The following observations of the Supreme Court in R. Rajagopal and Another v. State of Tamil Nadu and Others are true reminiscence of the limits of freedom of press with respect to the right to privacy:

A citizen has a right to safeguard the privacy of his own, his family, marriage, procreation, motherhood, child bearing and education among other matters. Noone can publish anything concerning the above matters without his consent-whether truthful or otherwise and whether laudatory or critical. If he does so, he would be violating the right to privacy of the person concerned and would be liable in an action for damages. Position may, however, be different, if a person voluntarily thrusts himself into controversy or voluntarily invites or raises a controversy. U.S. law enforcement agencies use sting operations to target any entry point, which is being knowingly used to introduce proceeds of crime into the financial system. Sting operations have therefore been used against such entry points as car dealerships, restaurants, bookmakers, cheque-cashing services, pawnshops, and even churches. The justification for undercover operations generally has been expressed as follows:

Covert investigative techniques are often the most efficient, effective and, in the case of the most virulent strains of criminality, such as organized and major drug related crime, the only practical way of obtaining evidence for the purposes of prosecuting and convicting those responsible However, former U.S. Chief Justice Earl Warren in Sherman v United States, made an important observation stating that 'a line must be drawn between a trap for the unwary innocent and a trap for the unwary criminal.'

On the other hand, the authorities of the United Kingdom have set down a defined and set code for the commission of undercover operations. The ability to do great good rarely comes without some power to do harm, and the free press is no exception to this general rule. The press should do what it can to minimize the abuse of power (self-scrutiny can help and so can competition), but we should also try to understand with clarity why and how press freedom can enrich human lives, enhance public justice, and even help to promote economic and social development. Technology is being used by the media to throw light upon 'truths' which may never have been known to the public at large. However, the use of technology in a rightful manner is what needs to be adequately emphasized upon and proper guidelines be framed for the same.

MEDIA TRIAL VS. RIGHT TO FREE AND FAIR TRIAL

Trial by media has created a 'problem' because it involves a tug of war between two conflicting principles – free press and free trial, in both of which the public are vitally interested. The freedom of the press stems from the right of the public in a democracy to be involved on the issues of the day, which affect them. This is the justification for investigative and campaign journalism. At the same time, the right to fair trial, i.e., a trial uninfluenced by extraneous pressures is recognized as a basic tenet of justice in India. Provisions aimed at safeguarding this right are contained under the Contempt of Courts Act, 1971 and under Articles 129 and 215 of the Constitution of India. Of particular concern to the media are restrictions which are imposed on the discussion or publication of matters relating to the merits of a case pending before a Court. A journalist may thus be liable for contempt of Court if he publishes anything which might prejudice a 'fair trial' or anything which impairs the impartiality of the Court to decide a cause on its merits, whether the proceedings before the Court be a criminal or civil proceeding.

A number of decisions of the U.S Supreme Court confirm the potential dangerous impact the media could have upon trials. In the case of Billie Sol Estes, the U.S. Supreme Court set aside the conviction of a Texas financier for denial of his constitutional rights of due process of law as during the pre-trial hearing extensive and obtrusive television coverage took place. The Court laid down a rule that televising of notorious criminal trials is indeed prohibited by the "due process of law" clause of Amendment Fourteen. In another case of Dr.Samuel H.Sheppard, the Court held that prejudicial publicity had denied him a fair trial. Referring to the televised trials of Michael Jackson and O.J.Simpson, Justice Michael Kirby stated: The judiciary which becomes caught up in such entertainment, by the public televising of its process, will struggle (sometimes successfully, sometimes not) to maintain the dignity and justice that is the accused's due. But these are not the media's concerns. Jurists should be in no doubt that the media's concerns are entertainment, money-making and, ultimately, the assertion of the media's power.

In England too, the House of Lords in the celebrated case of Attorney General v. British Broadcasting Corporation has agreed that media trials affect the judges despite the claim of judicial superiority over human frailty and it was observed that a man may not be able to put that which he has seen, heard or read entirely out of his mind and that he may be subconsciously affected by it. The Courts and Tribunals have been specially set up to deal with the cases and they have expertise to decide the matters according to the procedure established by the law. Media's trial is just like awarding sentence before giving the verdict at the first instance. The court held that it is important to understand that any other authority cannot usurp the functions of the courts in a civilized society.

Similarly there have been a plethora of cases in India on the point. The observations of the Delhi High Court in Bofors Case or Kartongen Kemi Och Forvaltning AB and Ors. v. State through CBI are very much relevant, as the Court weighed in favour of the accused's right of fair trial while calculating the role of media in streamlining the criminal justice system:

It is said and to great extent correctly that through media publicity those who know about the incident may come forward with information, it prevents perjury by placing witnesses under public gaze and it reduces crime through the public expression of disapproval for crime and last but not the least it promotes the public discussion of important issues. All this is done in the interest of freedom of communication and right of information little realizing that right to a fair trial is equally valuable. Such a right has been emphatically recognized by the European Court of Human Rights:

Again it cannot be excluded that the public becoming accustomed to the regular spectacle of pseudo trials in the news media might in the long run have nefarious consequences for the acceptance of the courts as the proper forum for the settlement of legal disputes. The ever-increasing tendency to use media while the matter is sub-judice has been frowned down by the courts including the Supreme Court of India on the several occasions. In State of Maharashtra v. Rajendra Jawanmal Gandhi, the Supreme Court observed:

There is procedure established by law governing the conduct of trial of a person accused of an offence. A trial by press, electronic media or public agitation is very antithesis of rule of law. It can well lead to miscarriage of justice. A judge has to guard himself against any such pressure and is to be guided strictly by rules of law. If he finds the person guilty of an offence he is then to address himself to the question of sentence to be awarded to him in accordance with the provisions of law.

The position was most aptly summed up in the words of Justice H.R.Khanna,:-Certain aspects of a case are so much highlighted by the press that the publicity gives rise to strong public emotions. The inevitable effect of that is to prejudice the case of one party or the other for a fair trial. We must consider the question as to what extent are restraints necessary and have to be exercised by the press with a view to preserving the purity of judicial process. At the same time, we have to guard against another danger. A person cannot, as I said speaking for a Full Bench of the Delhi High Court in 1969, by starting some kind of judicial proceedings in respect of matter of vital public importance stifle all public discussions of that matter on pain of contempt of court. A line to balance the whole thing has to be drawn at some point. It also seems necessary in exercising the power of contempt of court or legislature vis-à-vis the press that no hyper-sensitivity is shown and due account is taken of the proper functioning of a free press in a democratic society. This is vital for ensuring the health of democracy. At the same time the press must also keep in view its responsibility and see that nothing is done as may bring the courts or the legislature into disrepute and make the people lose faith in these institutions.

The Hon'ble Supreme Court in the case of Rajendra Sail v. Madhya Pradesh High Court Bar Association and Others, observed that for rule of law and orderly society, a free responsible press and an independent judiciary are both indispensable and both have to be, therefore, protected. The aim and duty of both is to bring out the truth. And it is well known that the truth is often found in shades of grey. Therefore the role of both can not be but emphasized enough, especially in a 'new India', where the public is becoming more aware and sensitive to its surroundings then ever before. The only way of functioning orderly is to maintain the delicate balance between the two. The country can not function without two of the pillars its people trust the most.

STING OPERATION AND RIGHT TO PRIVACY

Look if One can Violate Your Privacy

A question mark is raised on Human Rights Commissions by the reputed News Channel Star News in a Sting Operation where Police Officials in a police station of Haryana and Agra are ready to torture anyone if money is given to them. For then Human Rights Commission is a non-existent body. It can be said that the state bodies meant for the purpose are nonfunctional or it do not want to take cognisance Human Rights. So, the role is taken by media of exposing such felonious act in the society through Sting Operations. But, at the same time this is called violation of a major Human Right by media, i.e., Right to Privacy, as in some way they intrude the privacy of a person. Privacy is what is demanded by and for each and every person in his or her life. And this privacy literary means nothing but being aloof from society on some issues of personal life. But, the question is, can Sting Operation, known as '*Dansh Patrakarita*' in Hindi, can take away this privacy and make it public. This is the most burning issue in the entire world today. Article 12 of Universal Declaration of Human Rights (1948) defines Right to Privacy as—*No one shall be subjected to arbitrary interference with his privacy, family, home or correspondence not to attack upon his honour and reputation. Everyone has the right to protection of law against such interference or attack.*

Sting Operation Vis-à-vis Right to Privacy

Article 19(2) of the Constitution of India provides for nothing in sub-clause (a) shall affect the operation of any existing law in so far as it relates to, or prevent the state from making any law relating to libel, slander, defamation, contempt of court or nay matter which offends decency or morality or which determines the security of, or tends to overthrow the state.

In *Romesh Thapar Case* the Supreme Court laid down an important principle and giving restrictive interference to clause 2 of Article 19 having allowed the imposition of restrictions on the freedom of speech and expression for specified purposes, any law imposing restriction which are capable of being applied in causes beyond the express purposes cannot be held to be constitutional or valid to any extent.

On the other hand, '*Freedom of Press*' has been held to be a part of the Fundamental Right of '*Freedom of Speech and expression*' guaranteed by article 19(1)(a) to the citizens of India. Is had been held that '*Freedom of Press*' is necessary for exercise of fundamental freedom of citizens of 'speech and expression'.

And so '*Freedom of Press*' cannot be termed as unconstitutional and void. And as the Constitution says this can only be exercised till it does not harm the decency/morality of a person. The Constitution of India gives full liberty to press but with stings attached. On 18th June, 1951 Amended Article 19(2) by adding "*reasonable*" to restrictions. The restriction must be reasonable. In other words, it must not be excessive or misappropriate. The procedure and the manner of imposition of the restriction also must be just, fair and reasonable.

In a landmark judgement in the case of *Sakal papers*, the Supreme Court held that Article 19(2) of the Constitution permits imposition of reasonable restrictions on the heads specified in Article 19(2) and on no other grounds. It is, therefore, not open for the state to curtail the *Freedom of Speech and Expression* for promoting the general welfare of a section or a group of people unless its action can be justified by the law falling under clause 2 of Article 19. And moreover it is valid point that at a certain point all Sting Operations do violate *Right to Privacy* in some degree because during a Sting Operation, in nearly all its cases, the person being filmed is not aware of the presence of a hidden camera. This means that he does not consent to be filmed, without which, in ordinary course, no one has the right to film anyone. However, it may be argued that a illegal act being committed by a public servant during his office hours and in abuse of spirit of his office are not worthy of protection under Right to Privacy law. Besides, what a public servant does while discharging his duty is in public domain. In such cases, public interest does seem to weigh heavier compared to *Right to Privacy*. If a person has no duty towards general public, his morality questionable conduct is not open to public scrutiny unless he violates the law by such conduct. Right to Privacy is implicit to Article 21. According to Subba Rao J '*liberty*' in Article 21 is comprehensive enough to include privacy. His Lordship said that although it is true that he does not explicitly declare the *Right to Privacy* as a Fundamental Right but the right is an essential ingredient of personal liberty. It is regarded as a Fundamental Right but cannot be called absolute. It can be restricted on the basis of compelling public interest.

The court, however, has limited to personal intimacies of the family, marriage, motherhood, procreation and child bearing. On the other side, in the Sting Operations done by the media in India, only the working of the public servants in their offices is covered. The official work of the public servant should be transparent and open to all as it is in the public interest. But the court's decision the *Right to Privacy* does not cover this official work into the purview of its definition. Sting Operation began with a laudable objective of exposing corruption in high places and degenerated into cheap entertainment.

Sting Operations are generally carried out to trap the corrupt, the underworld dons and spies. They are also undertaken to establish adultery. Sting Operation can also be useful in the arrest of terrorists and anti-national elements. The spy camera of media caught 11 M.L.A.s accepting bribe for asking question in the parliament. When the media gets all the evidence against the corrupt and the wrongdoer and their aim is public interest, why do media not file a case in court and submit these as proof? This will lead to punishing of these wrongdoers, which is in public interest. Or, even after getting such evidences, why no report is given to public authorities and make them take some actions? By interviewing Mr. Prakash Tiwari, Bureau chief, Sahara Samaya, Bhopal, and Mr. Brajesh, a correspondent of Star News, Bhopal and Mr. Rajendra, a correspondent of Zee News, Bhopal it was found that Sting Operations are a good way to get evidences for exposing things and submitting these in court. It is a way of helping law, as media is the fourth estate of governance.

But, on the other hand, such cases cannot be filed in courts with these tapes, or audio or video recording as evidence or proof because courts do not consider theses as credible evidence and proof. Moreover, as the Government Machinery is not functioning properly, that is why such instances are increasing and so what is the point taking it to public authorities. Apart from this, when all this is exposed by media, the general crowd gets aware of the illegal business going on in the so called " Government Machinery". The news Broadcasters Association (NBA) justified Sting Operation as "illegitimate journalistic tool". In a discussion with Mr. Kumar Shakti Shekhar, a correspondent of N.D.T.V., Bhopal, he said that Sting Operation take place in public interest where public money is involved. Sting Operations are carried out in hospitals which bring out the problems of paucity of doctors in hospitals, absence of medicines and medication. But, it can easily be made out from all these interviews that one of the basic reasons to carry out Sting Operation is to increase TRP ratings or to '*interest the public*' rather than '*public interest*'. Hence the 17th Law Commission in its 200 th report has made recommendations to the centre to enact a law to prevent the media from interfering with the privacy rights of the individuals.

Which Fundamental Right is more Important?

Freedom of Press is derived from the *Freedom of Right to Speech and Expression* guaranteed in article 19(1)(a) of the Constitution of India. Moreover, *Right to Privacy* flows from *Right to Life and Personal Liberty* guaranteed in article 21 of the Constitution of India. Both theses come under Part III of the Constitution, i.e., the Fundamental Rights. So there is a clash in two major Fundamental Rights guaranteed by the Constitution of India. Although, these Fundamental Rights are not absolute and can only be taken away under Article 19(2), under reasonable restrictions. 6 This leads to burning debate between the two major Fundamental Rights which the makers of Constitution would never have thought of.

THE GOOD AND BAD OF STING OPERATIONS

Banning Sting Operations is not the Answer

In a proposed draft code for television broadcasters, the government has suggested that sting operations be banned. While the idea of formulating a codebook for broadcasters with clearly spelt out dos and don'ts is a good one, banning sting operations is not desirable. As shown by the BMW case, they are an integral part of investigative journalism. The clause in the code is against the "violation of the privacy of individuals", which lends credence to the theory that the government is attempting to use protection of privacy as an excuse to block journalistic investigations.

Sting operations have been criticised for being nothing more than entrapment. The detractors may be correct in their view of stings as a base form of journalism, but in banning a particular method of investigation, the government only creates the impression that it has something to hide. Newspapers are allowed to conduct their investigations and break stories —

news channels should have the same option. Ratings might go up in the process, good. Even better, these operations might shed light on insider information and corruption prevailing in the country.

To hide their misdoings, politicians try to pass legislations to curb freedom of the media. Whilst sting operations might blur the lines between what is ethical and what is not, the results often justify the methods. Investigative journalism is a distinctive aspect of the work undertaken by the media. Essentially an information-gathering exercise, it looks for facts that are not easy to obtain by simple requests and searches, or those that are actively being concealed, suppressed or distorted. Some subterfuge may be necessary in order to obtain the information required to bring unlawful activities to light. The growth of electronic media over the past decade has drastically altered the rules of the game for journalists. The media should decide what form of investigative journalism is acceptable and what is not. The I&B ministry has no place interceding and peremptorily deciding to simply ban an entire method of reporting.

Counter View: Exposes Undermine Public Interest

Following an expose by a TV news channel, the infamous BMW hit-and-run case is back in the news. It has triggered off another round of middle-class activism, complete with SMS polls, much like the public outcry over the Jessica Lal and Priyadarshini Mattoo murder cases. While there is no denying that justice must prevail, especially in high-profile cases where the powerful often go scot-free, it is not the media's job to conduct a sting operation to ensure this.

However honourable the inten-tion, a sting operation is unethical. It is simply another name for entrapment. The person who is 'caught on camera' is often coerced into making statements that are then plucked out of context and presented as a confession of wrongdoing. With technology making it possible to doctor footage at the editing table, the veracity of the evidence is often under a cloud.

A sting operation is a classic case of lazy journalism. The profusion of 24-hour television news channels mandates that journalists constantly confect sensation. The pressure to outdo competition is so immense that most reporters have little interest in, or respect for, the facts of the matter. Half-baked stories are passed off as gospel truth; often they fall apart under close scrutiny. Unfortunately, the issues raised and cases in question actually suffer as a result of patchy sting operations that hide more than they reveal.

Media's oft-repeated defence of sting operations is that the exposes serve public interest. But, increasingly, the fine line between responsible journalism and sheer voyeurism is getting blurred. For instance, how does it affect the well-being of the nation if the casting couch in Bollywood were exposed on prime time TV? The media has not distinguished itself in the selection of stories it chooses to 'expose' and draw public attention to. Very often, it is a gimmick aimed at boosting viewership and little else. It is precisely in public interest, and for the sake of due judicial process, that sting operations be banned.

THE STING HAS LOST ITS THING

There's a bee in my bonnet, and I am afraid it's got a sting that can kill. The killing machine is out at large, in search of victims who thrive on the no-nos of the society. Yes, the bee has a mission. Only sometimes, the sting misfires like an unguided missile – losing track of why it was fired in the first place. My poor bee needs a lesson. But I am not sure how to train the supercilious sting.

All right, metaphors apart, what we are talking about are the sting operations carried out by news media. In what seems to be the call of the day, sting operations have become a source for higher TRPs more than the principle on which they are conducted in the first place. The channels may defend their stand under the guise of investigative journalism, but who can explain the loose ends nearly all the sting operations seem to leave behind.

Sex, Sex, and More Sex

Sting operations first became popular with Tehelka.com in 2000, when they carried out an exposé on former several prominent politicians accepting bribes from a decoy. It's been seven years since, the case has been going back and forth, and the Tehelka case became a mere flash in the pan. This was followed by the sting on actors Shakti Kapoor and Aman Verma. The nation went in a tizzy when the sting was aired on news channels, depicting the two (among others), leeringly suggesting a casting couch in front of the hidden camera. However, the two stings raised some ethical questions. Would a sting qualify as investigative journalism when firstly, there was no obvious relevance of the sting to the public? Secondly, how fair is a sting when there is clear ensnarement? The journalists in both the cases trapped the two actors into propositioning them. While one is not defending the two "victims" of the sting, the issue remains that the two stings in question were motivated by attempts to sensationalize news and raise TRPs rather than highlight legitimate public interest issues.

It is not just India, the recent covert mission to nab Senator Larry Craig has brought forth a debate on the hypocrisy of sting operations. The debate questions the moral grounds on which sting operations are carried out, and the thin line between consent and criminal intent. The case of Larry Craig is reminiscent of the ouster of singer George Michael from his closet, in a similar operation carried out by the police.

While Larry Craig has been vocally homophobic in his views, this operation apparently fans homophobia. The focus is not so much on Craig's double standards, but on the fact that he engaged in homosexual acts – but is that reason enough to incriminate him because what he engaged in was purportedly consensual?

Seducation

Among the numerous sting operations carried out since the revelation of the casting couch, the latest involving Uma Khurana stands out as one of the most disturbing. The sting alleged that Uma Khurana, a mathematics teacher at Sarvodaya Kanya Vidyalaya in Delhi, was pushing her students into prostitution. The sting, aired on the TV channel Live India, led to a large-scale riot on Asaf Ali Road. Uma Khurana was almost lynched by a violent mob.

In a latest development, the police said that they have no evidence against Uma Khurana. The sting was a frame-up and was allegedly motivated by a petty dispute between Virendra Arora, a businessman, and Uma Khurana. Arora's friend

Prakash Singh, the journalist with LiveIndia channel who masterminded the sting, asked a friend, Rashmi Singh, to pose as a student who was pushed into prostitution by Khurana. A study of the unedited tapes showed that Uma Khurana refused to admit to any prostitution ring or provide any students for prostitution. The police has now arrested Rashmi Singh for cheating.

The whole sting was motivated by petty revenge on the part of the businessman who gave the journalist a tip-off and a desire for cheap publicity on the part of the channel. The operation focused chiefly on the sexual angle in the whole story, which is a whole deal more glamorous than say corruption in the education system. Corruption has been the country's bane and it starts early—right in our schools. If the schools are a breeding ground for illicit liaisons and undue favors, is it surprising then that we have not been able to do away with corruption? But, somehow, the channels do not seem to highlight such instances.

Growing up in small towns in the country, I know for a fact that teachers coerce students to join their private tuitions, lest the student fail in exams. Some teachers resort to bribes to leak examination papers, while others look for favors in kind. Students oblige, parents give in. Who wants to take on a hassle for a few rupees more?

There are sting operations that bring out corruption in the bureaucracy, but as the bureaucracy functions in India, these operations lead nowhere. Taking action on those found guilty is a long-winded process, and no one seems to have the patience, nor the inclination to wait for the outcomes. It's just convenient to bring out stories that do not deserve more than a day's worth of attention.

Close on the heels of the Uma Khurana sting operation in Delhi, comes another one from down south. Professor Suryanarayan of Osmania University met almost the same fate as the math teacher from Delhi – minus the public thrashing. The charge here is the professor sought sexual favors from students in lieu of a doctorate degree. Again, the focus of the story seemed sex, and not the moral responsibility education entails.

Superfluity of the Sting

So, while the channels are sting-happy, hopping from one operation to another, the issues they set out to address seem lost as soon as the buzz dies down. Follow ups mean a small story covered a few months down the line. If sting operations are part of investigative journalism, since when has leaving issues in lurch become acceptable to the journo community? Justifications apart, where has the idea of a proper closure to a story gone? Is the media itself a victim of attention deficit disorder, like its viewers who flip channels every two seconds?

Rhetorical questions these, but getting underneath the skin of today's journalist is not easy. It is a matter of who can cast the first stone. Sex sells – the kinkier the better. Does this take away the significance of issues that question basic ethics of a society? We seem to be too afraid to dig out the larger monsters that work at a deeper level than purely sexual, lest we all fall down.

6

An Analysis of Parliamentary Privileges in India

The term parliamentary privileges is used in Constitutional writings to denote both these types of rights and immunities. Sir Thomas Erskine May has defined the expression ?Parliamentary privileges? as follows: The sum of the peculiar rights enjoyed by each house collectively is a constituent part of the High Court of Parliament, and by members of each house of parliament individually, without which they cannot discharge their functions, and which exceed those possessed by other bodies or individuals.

Parliamentary Privileges

A.105.Powers, privileges, etc., of the Houses of Parliament and of the members and committees thereof

1. Subject to the provisions of this Constitution and the rules and standing orders regulating the procedure of Parliament, there shall be freedom of speech in Parliament.
2. No member of Parliament shall be liable to any proceeding in any court in respect of anything said or any vote given by him in Parliament or any committee thereof, and no person shall be so liable in respect of the publication by or under the authority of either House of Parliament of any report, paper, votes or proceedings.
3. In other respects, the powers, privileges and immunities of each House of Parliament, and the members and the committee of each House, shall be such as may from

time to time be defined by Parliament by law, and until so defined, [shall be those of that House and of its members and committees immediately before the coming into force of Section 15 of the Constitution (44th Amendment) Act, 1978].

4. The provision of clauses (1), (2), and (3) shall apply in relation to persons who by virtue of this Constitution have the right to speak in, and otherwise to take part in the proceedings of, a House of Parliament or any committee thereof as they apply in relation to the members of Parliament.

Parliamentary privileges-this article defines parliamentary privileges of both Houses of Parliament and of their members and committees. Article 194, which is an exact reproduction of Article 105, deals with the State Legislatures and their members and committees. To enable Parliament to discharge functions properly the Constitution confers on each member of the Houses certain rights and immunities and also certain rights and immunities and powers on each house collectively. Parliamentary privilege is an essential incident to the high and multifarious functions which the legislature is called upon to perform. According to May, the distinctive mark of a privilege is its ancillary character a necessary means to fulfilment of functions. Individual members enjoy privileges because the House cannot perform its function without unimpeded use of the services of its members and by each House for the protection of its members and the vindication of its own authority and dignity. In defining parliamentary privilege this article adopts certain method. Two privileges, namely, freedom of speech and freedom of publication of proceedings, are specifically mentioned in clauses (1) and (2). With respect to other privileges of each House, clause (3) before its amendment in 1978 laid down that the powers, privileges and immunities shall be those of the House of Commons of the United Kingdom at the commencement of the Constitution until they are defined by an Act of Parliament. Though since 1978 position has changed in so far as the privileges of parliament, its members and committees have to be determined on the basis of what they were immediately before the commencement of 1978 amendment i.e., before 20th June 1979.

Freedom of Speech

Article 105, clause (1), expressly safeguards freedom of speech in parliament. It says: there shall be freedom of speech in parliament. Clause (2) further provides that no member of Parliament shall be liable to any proceedings in any court in respect of anything said or any vote given by him in parliament or any committee thereof. No action, civil or criminal, will therefore lie against a member for defamation or the like in respect of things said in parliament or its committees. The immunity is not limited to mere spoken words; it extends to votes, as clause (2) specifically declares, viz. any vote given by him in parliament or any committee thereof. Though not expressly stated, the freedom of speech would extend to other acts also done in connection with the proceedings of each House, such as, for notices of motions, questions, reports of the committee, or the resolutions.

It may be noted that clause (1) of Article 105 is made Subject to the provisions of this constitution and to the rules and standing orders regulating the procedures of Parliament. The words regulating the procedures of Parliament occurring in clause (1) should be read as covering both the provisions of the Constitution and the rules and standing orders. So read, freedom of speech in Parliament becomes subject to the provisions of Constitution relating to the procedures of Parliament, i.e., subject to the articles relating to procedures in Part V including Articles 107 and 121. Thus for example, freedom of speech in Parliament would not permit a member to discuss the conduct of any judge of the Supreme Court or of a High Court. Likewise, the freedom of speech is subject to the rules of procedures of a House, such as use of unparliamentary language or unparliamentary conduct.

The freedom of speech guaranteed under clause (1) is different from that which a citizen enjoys as a fundamental right under Article 19 (1) (a). the freedom of speech as a fundamental right does not protect an individual absolutely for what he says. The right is subject to reasonable restrictions under clause (2) of Article 19. The term ?freedom of speech? as used in this article means that no member of Parliament shall be liable to any proceedings, civil and criminal, in any court for the statements made in debates in the Parliament or any committee thereof. The freedom of speech conferred under this article cannot therefore be restricted under Article 19 (2). Clauses (1) and (2) of Article 105 protect what is said within the house and not what a member of Parliament may say outside. Accordingly, if a member publishes his speech outside Parliament, he will be held liable if the speech is defamatory. Besides, the freedom of speech. To which Article 105 (1) and (2) refer, would be available to a member of Parliament when he attends the session of Parliament, no occasion arises for the exercise of the right of freedom of speech, and no complaint can be made that the said right has been invalidly invaded.

Article 105 (2) confers immunity, inter alia, in respect of anything said in Parliament the word anything is of the widest import and is equivalent to everything. The only limitation arises from the words in Parliament, which means during the sitting of Parliament and in the course of business of Parliament. Once it was proved that Parliament was sitting and its business was transacted, anything said during the course of that business was immune from proceedings in any court.

This immunity is not only complete but it is as it should be. It is one of the essence of parliamentary system of government that people's representative should be free to express themselves without fear of legal expenses. What they say is only subject to the discipline of the rules of Parliament, the good sense of the members and the control of proceedings by the speaker. The courts have no say in the matter and should really have none.

In a much publicized matter involving former Prime Minister, several ministers, Members of Parliament and others a divided Court, in P.V.Narsimha Rao v. State has held that the privilege of immunity from courts proceedings in Article 105 (2) extends even to bribes taken by the Members of Parliament for the purpose of voting in a particular manner in Parliament. The majority (3 judges) did not agree with the minority (2 judges) that the words in respect of in Article 105 (2) mean, arising out of and therefore would not cover conduct antecedent to speech or voting in Parliament. The court was however unanimous that the members of Parliament who gave bribes, or who took bribes but did not participate in the voting could not claim immunity from court proceeding's under Article

105 (2). The decision has invoked so much controversy and dissatisfaction that a review petition is pending in the court.

RIGHT OF PUBLICATION OF PROCEEDINGS

Clause (2) of Article 105 expressly declares that no person shall be liable in respect of the publication by order under the authority of a house of Parliament, of any report, paper, votes or proceedings. Common law accords the defence of qualified privilege to fair and accurate unofficial reports of parliamentary proceedings, published in a newspaper or elsewhere. In Wason v. Walter, Cockburn, C.J. observed that it was of paramount public and national importance that parliamentary proceedings should be communicated to public, which has the deepest interest in knowing what passes in Parliament. But a partial report or a report of detached part of proceedings published with intent to injure individuals will be disentitled to protection. The same is the law in India. The Parliamentary Proceedings (Protection of Publication) Act, 1956 enacts that no person shall be liable to any proceedings, civil or criminal, in a court in respect of the publication of a substantially true report of the proceedings in either House of the Parliament, unless it is proved that the publication is made with malice.

Other Privileges

Clause (3) of Article 105, as amended declares that the privileges of each House of Parliament, its members and committees shall be such as determined by Parliament from time to time and until Parliament does so, which it has not yet done, shall be such as on 20th June 1979 i.e., on the date of commencement of Section 15 of the 44th Amendment. Before the amendment this clause has provided that until Parliament legislates the privileges of each House and its members shall be such as those of the House of Commons in England at the time of commencement of the Constitution. As the position till 20th June 1979 was determined on the basis of original provision, it is still relevant to refer to the law as it has been in the context of English law. In that perspective it may be emphasized that there are certain privileges that cannot be claimed by Parliament in India. For example, the privileges of access to the sovereign, which is exercised by the House of Commons through its Speaker to have at all times the right of access to the sovereign through their chosen representative can have no application in India. Similarly, a general warrant of arrest issued by Parliament in India cannot claim to be regarded as a court of record in any sense. Also the privilege of the two Houses of Parliament, unlike the privileges of the House of Commons and House of Lords in England are identical. To each House of Parliament, accordingly, belong the privileges, which are possessed by the House of Commons in the United Kingdom.

In India freedom from arrest has been limited to civil causes and has not been applied to arrest on criminal charges or to detention under the Preventive Detention Act. Also there is no privilege if arrest is made under s.151 Criminal Procedure Code. It has been held in K. Anandan Kumar v. Chief Secretary, Government of Madras, that matters of Parliament do not enjoy any special status as compared to an ordinary citizen in respect of valid orders of detention. In India, the rules of procedure in the House of People give the chair the power, whenever it thinks fit, of ordering the withdrawal of strangers from any part of the House and when the House sits in a secret session no stranger is permitted to be present in the chamber, lobby or galleries. The only exceptions are the members of the Council of States and the persons authorized by the Speaker.

In Pandit M.S.M Sharma v. Shri Krishna Sinha, proceedings for the breach of privilege had been started against an editor of a newspaper for publishing those parts of the speech of a member delivered in Bihar legislative assembly which the speaker had ordered to be expunged from the proceedings of the Assembly. The editor in a writ petition under A. 32 contended that the House of Commons had no privilege to prohibit either the publication of the publicly seen and heard proceedings that took place in the House or of that part of the proceedings which had been directed to be expunged. The Supreme Court by a majority of four to one rejected the contention of the petitioner. Das C.J., who delivered the majority judgment, observed that the House of Commons had at the commencement of our Constitution the power or privilege of prohibiting the publication of even a true and faithful report of the debates or proceedings that took place within the House. A fortiori the House had at the relevant time the power or privilege of prohibiting the publication of an inaccurate version of such debates or proceedings. Now Article 361-A inserted by the 44th Amendment with effect from June 20, 1979 provides that no person shall be liable to any proceedings civil or criminal for reporting the proceedings of either House of Parliament or a State Legislature unless the reporting is proved to have been made with malice. This provision does not apply to the reporting of proceedings of secret sittings of the Houses.

In India there also vest a right of the House to regulate its own constitution. When a seat of a member elected to the house becomes vacant, the Election Commission, by a notification in the Gazette of India calls upon the Parliamentary constituency concerned to elect a person for the purpose of filling the vacancy. In India, Article 103 expressly provides that if any question arises as to whether a member of either House of Parliament has become subject to any of the disqualifications, the question shall be referred to the President whose decision shall be final. The President is however required to act in this behalf according to the opinion of Election Commission.

As far as right to regulate internal proceedings are concerned Article 122 expressly provides that the validity of any proceedings shall not be called in question on the ground of any alleged irregularity of procedure, and no officer or member of Parliament in whom powers are vested by or under the Constitution for regulating the procedure or the conduct of business or for maintaining order in Parliament shall be subject to the jurisdiction of any court in respect of the exercise by him of those powers.

LAW COURTS AND PRIVILEGES

Article 105, so also Article 194 subjects the powers, privileges and immunities of each House as well as all its members and all its committees not only to the laws made by the appropriate legislature but also to all other provisions of the Constitution. Both these articles far from dealing with the legislative powers of the Houses of Parliament or of State Legislature respectively are confined in scope to such powers of each House as it may exercise separately functioning as a House.

A House of Parliament or Legislature cannot try anyone or any case directly as a court of justice can, but it can proceed quasi judicially in cases of contempt of its authority or take up motions concerning its privileges and immunities in order to seek removal of obstructions to the due performance of its legislative functions. If any question of jurisdiction arises as to a certain matter, it has to be decided by a court of law in appropriate proceedings. For example, the jurisdiction to try a criminal offence such as murder, committed even within a House vests in ordinary courts and not in a of Parliament or in a State Legislature. Also, a House of Parliament or State Legislature cannot in exercise of any supposed powers under Articles 105 and 194 decide election disputes for which special authorities have been constituted under the Representation of People Act, 1951 enacted in compliance with Article 329.

Parliamentary Privileges and Fundamental Rights

In Pandit M.S.M. Sharma's case it was also contended by the petitioner that the privileges of the House under A.194 (3) are subject to the provision of Part III of the Constitution. In supposrt of his contention the petitioner relied the Supreme Court's decision in Gunupati Keshavram Reddi V. Nafisul Hasan. In this latter case Homi Mistry was arrested at his B'bay residence under a warrant issued by the Speaker of U.P. Assembly for contempt of the House and was flown to Lucknow & kept in a hotel in Speaker's custody. On his applying for a writ of habeas corpus, the Supreme Court directed his release as he had not been produced before a magistrate within 24 hours of his arrest as provided in Article 22 (2). This decision therefore indicated that Article 194 (or Article 105) was subject to the Articles of Part III of the Constitution.

In Sharma's case the Court held that in case of conflict between fundamental right under Article 19 (1) (a) and a privilege under Article 194 (3) the latter would prevail. As regards Article 21, on facts the Court did not find any violation of it. In Powers, Privileges and Immunities of the State Legislature, Re, the proposition laid down in Sharma's case was explained not to mean that in all cases the privileges shall override the fundamental rights.

The rules of each House provide for a committee of privileges. The matter of breach of privilege or contempt is referred to the committee of privileges. The committee has power to summon members or strangers before it. Refusal to appear or to answer or to knowingly to give false answer is itself a contempt. The committee's recommendations are reported to the House which discusses them and gives its own decision.

Article 194

Powers, privileges, etc., of the Houses of Legislature and of the members and committees thereof.

1. Subject to the provisions of this Constitution and to the rules and standing orders regulating the procedure of the Legislature, there shall be freedom of speech in the Legislature of every State.
2. No member of the Legislature of a State shall be liable to any proceeding in any court in respect of anything said or any vote given by him in the Legislature or any committee thereof, and no person shall be so liable in respect of the publication by or under the authority of a House of such a Legislature of any report, paper, votes or proceedings.
3. In other respects, the powers, privileges and immunities of a House of the Legislature of a State, and of the members and the committees of a House of such Legislature, shall be such as may be defined from time to time be defined by the Legislature by law, and until so defined, shall be those of that House and of its members and committees immediately before the coming into force of Section 26 of the Constitution (Forty Fourth Amendment) Act, 1978.
4. The provisions of clauses (1), (2) and (3) shall apply in relation to persons who by virtue of this Constitution have the right to speak in, and otherwise to take part in the proceedings of, a House of the Legislature of a State or any committee thereof as they apply in relation to members of that Legislature.

This article that applies to the State Legislatures and members and committees thereof is an exact reproduction of Article 105, which applies to both Houses of Parliament and committees thereof.

Clause (1)-of this article declares that there shall be freedom of speech in the legislature of every State. This freedom is subject to the provisions of Articles 208 and 211. A member cannot accordingly raise discussions as to the conduct of a Supreme Court or High Court judge as A. 211 prohibits it. The provisions of the Constitution subject to which freedom of speech has been conferred on the legislators are not the general provisions of the Constitution but only such of them as relate to the regulation of the procedure of the Legislature. The freedom of speech guaranteed to citizens under A. 19 (1) (a) is therefore separate and independent of Article 194 (1) and does not control the first part of clause 1 of A.194.

Clause (2)-emphasizes the fact that the freedom of speech conferred on the Legislatures under clause (1) is intended to be absolute and unfettered. Similar freedom is guaranteed to the legislators in respect of the votes they may give in the Legislature or committees thereof. Thus, if a legislator exercises aright of freedom of speech in violation of A. 211 he would not be liable for any action in any court. Likewise, if the legislator by his speech or vote is alleged to have violated any of the fundamental rights guaranteed by Part III of the Constitution in the Legislative Assembly, he would not be answerable for the said contravention in any court. If the speech amounts to libel or becomes actionable or indictable under any other provision of the law immunity has been conferred on him from any action in any court by clause (2). He may be answerable to the House for such a speech and the Supreme Court may take appropriate action against him in respect of it. Thus clause (1) confers freedom of speech to the legislators within the legislative chambers and clause (2) makes it plain that the freedom is literally absolute.

Clause (3)-the first art of this clause empowers the State Legislature to make laws Prescribing its powers, privileges and immunities. If the Legislature of a State under the first part of clause (3) makes a law which prescribes its powers, privileges and immunities, such law would be subject to Article 13 and clause (2) of that article would render it void if it contravenes or abridges any of the fundamental rights guaranteed by Part III. The right of State Legislatures to punish for contempt can be discussed with the case law of Powers, Privileges and Immunities of State Legislature, Re. The reference was a sequel to the passing of an order by an unprecedented Full Bench of

28 judges staying, under Article 226, the implementation of the U.P. Assembly resolution ordering two judges of Allahabad High Court to be brought in custody before the Bar of the House to explain why they should not be punished for the contempt of the House. The two judges had admitted the habeas corpus petition of and granted bail to one Keshav Singh who was undergoing imprisonment in pursuance of the Assembly Resolution declaring him guilty of the breach of privilege. The resolution of the Assembly and the stay order issued by the Full Bench resulted in a constitutional stalemate. Consequently, the president referred the matter under Article 143 to the Supreme Court for its opinion. The Supreme Court by a majority of 6:1, through an elaborate and learned opinion delivered by Gajendragadkar, C.J., held that in India notwithstanding a general warrant issued by the Assembly, the Courts could examine the legality of the committal in proper proceedings.

Other propositions were also laid down in the majority judgment. It said that Article 194 (3) cannot be read in isolation. The impact of Articles 226, 32 and 211 had to be ascertained in order to determine the scope of Article 194. Article 226 empowers the High Court to issue a writ of habeas corpus against any authority. This would include the legislature since no exception is made in favour of a detention order by the House for the breach of its privileges. Article 211 on the other hand unambiguously indicates that the conduct of a judge in the discharge of his duties can never become the subject matter of any action taken by the House in exercise of its powers or privileges conferred by the latter part of Article 194 (3). The fact that the first part of Article 194 (3) refers to future laws defining the privileges as being subject to fundamental rights is a significant factor in construing the latter part of Article 194. Such a state legislation would be law within the meaning of article 13 and the courts will be competent to examine its validity vis-à-vis the fundamental right. Although no opinion was tendered as regards fundamental rights in general, it was made clear that so far as Articles 21 and 22 are concerned, any privileges etc., which are claimed, must be consistent with these articles in the context of Article 208.

There is a clear demarcation as to what all rights and privileges are absolute and what are not. For example, in India

Legislative Assemblies and Parliament never discharge any judicial function and their historical and constitutional background does not support their claim to be regarded as courts of record in any sense. No immunity from scrutiny by courts of general warrants issued by House in India can therefore be claimed.

Both the Parliament and State Legislatures have a duty to look carefully before making any law, so that it doesn't harm other rights. It is also a duty of the members to properly use these privileges and not misuse them for alternate purposes that is not in the favour of general interest of nation and public at large. Thus what we must keep in mind is the fact that ?power corrupts and absolute power corrupts absolutely. For this not to happen under the privileges granted, the public and the other governing body should always be on vigil.

TELECASTING AND BROADCASTING OF PARLIAMENTARY PROCEEDINGS

Parliaments throughout the world have wrestled with the question of whether or not to allow the television cameras into the Chamber. Many have done so, but many more continue to hesitate or might not have even considered it. Radio broadcasting of parliamentary proceedings has proved less controversial, and the New Zealand Parliament was a pioneer in this field, having introduced it in its House of Representatives as long ago as in 1936. In the following year, it instituted continuous broadcasting of proceedings. In 1946, Australia introduced sound broadcasting of the debates in both Houses of Parliament, the broadcasts being governed by statute and controlled by a Joint Committee of both Houses. Regular sound broadcasting of the proceedings of both Houses of the British Parliament was introduced in 1978. The Parliament of the Solomon Islands is one of the smaller Parliaments whose proceedings are broadcast live by radio.

Television, being a visual medium, reveals a great deal more than sound alone. The arguments for and against televising Parliament have been exhaustive both in parliamentary debate, in Committee studies and in published articles. Television undoubtedly brings to the fore, the actual face of Parliament, but at least it is seen by the viewer as it really is and not simpl as it is represented by others. The television camera in the chamber is an extension of the public gallery, bringing Parliament into the homes of all who care to tune in. It is always likely to transform parliamentary behaviour whether for better or worse, being in the hands of parliamentarians themselves. Television is a factor to be reckoned with in Parliament's public relations. Whatever Parliaments do, it is here to stay and cannot be ignored. Of those Parliaments which have admitted the television cameras, only a few provide continuous live coverage of all the proceedings. They are Bulgaria, Canada, Denmark, Hungary, Iran, Scotland, UK and USA. The latest to join the select group is India. Most of the other countries permit live telecast of special events only and Highlights of the proceedings in the News Inserts.

Continuous live television coverage of a Parliament's proceedings does not by itself guarantee that the public will have a balanced view of Parliament. Since its advent in the Canadian House of Commons, for example, public attention has largely focused on the daily question period, a period of confrontation between the Government and the Opposition Parties when parliamentary behaviour is seldom seen at its best. The House must, therefore, expect to be judged to a great extent by what goes on during this part of the parliamentary day.

Position in India

In order to make the citizens aware of the deliberations in Parliament, the Lok Sabha Secretariat has taken several steps to record and telecast/broadcast the proceedings of its House with the help of the official Media, *viz.* Doordarshan/All India Radio. A beginning was made in this direction when, for the first time, the President's Address to members of both the Houses of Parliament was telecast on 20 December 1989.

As a prelude to complete live telecast of parliamentary proceedings throughout the nation, a Low Power Transmitter (LPT) was set up in Parliament House on 25 August 1994 to provide for live telecast of Lok Sabha proceedings, within a range of 10 to 15 kms. from Parliament House. With the installation of another Low Power Transmitter, the Rajya Sabha proceedings are also being telecast live since 7 December 1994.

The proceedings of the Question Hour of both the Houses are being telecast live on alternate weeks throughout the country on the National Channel of Doordarshan from 1100 hrs. to 1200 hrs. since 7 December 1994. With the launch of a new DD-News Channel, Doordarshan has been telecasting live the Question Hours of both Lok Sabha and Rajya Sabha simultaneously on National Channel and DD-News Channel of Doordarshan on alternate weeks from the Winter Session of 2003. While telecasting the Question Hour of one House on the National Channel, Doordarshan is telecasting live the Question Hour of the other House on DD-News Channel.

All India Radio has been broadcasting the recording of the Question Hour of both the Houses on alternate weeks on their National Channel the same night. It has been arranged in such a manner that during the week, Doordarshan covers live the Question Hour of one House (*e.g.* Rajya Sabha) on their National Channel, All India Radio covers the recorded broadcast of the Question Hour of Lok Sabha that night. In the following week, it is *vice versa*. Other important events like President's Address to members of both the Houses, presentation of General and Railway Budgets and debates on Motions of Confidence/No-confidence in the Council of Ministers. Elections of Speaker and Deputy Speaker, oath taking by Members and certain other debates of national importance have also been telecast/ broadcast live on the Primary Channel of Doordarshan/All India Radio.

Dedicated Satellite Channels for Live Telecast: In a significant landmark in the history of telecasting of our parliamentary proceedings, on 14 December 2004; two separate dedicated satellite channels for telecasting live the entire proceedings of Rajya Sabha and Lok Sabha nationwide were launched. The entire proceedings of the two Houses of Parliament are since being telecast live through separate dedicated satellite channels by Doordarshan. The Audio-Video Unit which was set up in 1992 provides facilities for viewing/ listening to the video records of Lok Sabha and Rajya Sabha debates, proceedings of national and international Parliamentary Conferences/Seminars/Symposia/Workshops, media persons and other visiting dignitaries. This Unit of the Library preserves the Video (U-matic, Betacam and VHS) cassettes, Video Compact Discs (VCDs) of all Lok Sabha Debates, proceedings of national and international parliamentary Conferences/Seminars/Symposia/Workshops and other parliamentary functions, which have immense archival value for the parliamentarians, Media persons, scholars, academicians and even common people. It also looks after the work of selection and collection of audio-visual materials; accession, classification and preservation of cassettes of important parliamentary functions and events like Conferences, Seminars, Symposia and Workshops and telefilms on different aspects of parliamentary practices and procedures. Arrangements have also been made for dubbing of speeches of members into VHS cassettes/CDs on nominal payment.

The Audio-Visual Unit has acquired Linguaphone Courses in various Indian and foreign languages and has also added to its holdings audio-cassettes pertaining to classical/instrumental music and patriotic songs for use at various parliamentary functions. The various Linguaphone Courses (audio and video cassettes) are available for listening/viewing in the Viewing Room.

The Audio-Visual Unit has VHS cameras, editing equipment and a Viewing Room in the Parliament Library Building. With the help of the VHS cameras, the video crew of the Unit records all important parliamentary functions/events, including National and International Parliamentary Conferences/ Seminars/Symposia/Workshops and various other events and activities. As a part of the modernization of A.V. facilities, a state-of-the-art studio and production control room (in digital format) equipped with post-production editing facilities are being set up in the Parliament Library Building. Video viewing arrangements would also be modernized by providing multi-media facilities.

A number of domestic and foreign broadcasting and news agencies have been showing increasing interest in telecasting and broadcasting of parliamentary proceedings, events, functions, etc. because of their news value. Guidelines for recording, telecasting and broadcasting of the proceedings of Lok Sabha and supply of video cassettes or compact discs thereof to the members, Media and other interested persons, have been issued from time to time. Incidentally, many roadblocks for live telecast of the entire proceedings and/or providing footage to various agencies have since been cleared by the present Speaker of Lok Sabha.

Robotic Camera System in Parliament House / Parliament Library Building: In order to telefilm and telecast live the complete proceedings of Parliament in a better manner, a sophisticated modern robotic camera system and a studio have been set up in Parliament House. The system became operational with effect from the Winter Session of Parliament in 1997. Under the new robotic camera system, there are eight robotic cameras which are operated by remote control from the studio set-up in Parliament House.

A robotically-controlled TV set up has also been introduced for the purpose of coverage of the functions/events held in the G.M.C. Balayogi Auditorium and the Committee Rooms in the Parliament Library Building. Robotically-controlled Multi-Camera System and their Production Control Rooms have been set up for the Auditorium and the BPST Main Committee Room. A Mobile Unit has also been developed for on-line production of the events/functions in other Committee Rooms of the Parliament Library Building. The latest digital broadcasting quality equipment have also been installed in the Production Control Room.

Parliamentary Films: As an extension of telefilming and televising of parliamentary proceedings, video films are prepared on different aspects of parliamentary practices and procedures and related parliamentary topics, especially for the use of new members of Parliament and State Legislatures.

These films also help in educating students, Media persons and others about various facets of the functioning of Parliament. Six parliamentary films which have been prepared so far are:

(i) Private Members' Bills;

(ii) Parliamentary Questions;

(iii) Parliamentary Etiquette and Manners;

(iv) Financial Committees;

(v) Enriching the Debates in Legislatures; and

(vi) How to be an Effective Parliamentarian?

Two films *viz.* 'Parliamentary Etiquette and Manners' and

'How to be an Effective Parliamentarian?' were also dubbed in Russian language and shown at the State *Duma*, Moscow, during an Exhibition on "Parliamentary History and Activities" set up as part of the Golden Jubilee Celebrations of India's Independence in November 1998. This Service is in the process of preparing some more informative and educative films on the functioning of Parliament.

Parliamentary Museum and Archives

The museums and archives are today designed to function as treasure-houses and research centres. The concept of the functions and activities that appropriately belong to a museum and/or archives today, however, is very different from what it used to be 25 or 30 years ago. Modern museums and archives are expected to be places of learning, research and communication. They seek to preserve, interpret, educate, inspire and stimulate. In the best of the modern museums and archives, the collections have not only to be stored, cared for and meticulously preserved, but also to be intensively studied, displayed and explained.

In the evolution and operation of the constitutional system and parliamentary institutions, museums and archives have particular relevance. What the schools and colleges offer by way of instruction is inadequate and needs to be supplemented and enriched by the first-hand exposure which museums and archives and their trained staff alone can provide. While all over the world there are national or state level museums and archives devoted to a wide range of subjects and all the fields of fine art, science, history, government, etc., preserving a varied selection of paintings, art works, manuscripts of old scriptures and a large number of other antiquities, in the very nature of things they cannot afford to provide the necessary breadth and depth in a specific specialized area like that of Parliament.

Although not much effort seems to have been made to create institutional frameworks for parliamentary museums and archives, in some countries, such as Australia, New Zealand and Uganda, setting up such an institution has already received attention. In the United Kingdom, there is no parliamentary museum or archives as such, but the Clerk of the Journals exercises overall responsibility for the preservation of all records. In Canada, the institution of the Public Archives has assumed responsibility for collecting historically valuable parliamentary papers accumulated by Prime Ministers, Cabinet Ministers, Members of Parliament and Senators.

Japan has set up a Parliamentary Museum (*The Kensei Kinenkan*). It was opened to the public on 21 March 1972. The Museum, which is a subordinate body of the House of Representatives, has as its main purpose the collection and preservation of reference materials relating to Japan's parliamentary politics. In Poland also, a decision has been taken to establish an organized Museum Exhibition within the Parliament buildings with a view to presenting the rich Polish parliamentary history. The institution, it is expected, would become a significant link in the activities aiming to document and popularize the history of the Polish Parliament.

Position in India

Origin: The origin of the Parliamentary Museum and Archives can be traced to 1976, when as a part of the Parliament Library and Reference, Research, Documentation and Information Service (LARRDIS) of the Lok Sabha Secretariat, it was set up as the Parliamentary Archives of Photographs and Films to preserve an authentic and up-to-date pictorial record of the history of the institution of Parliament, its activities and on eminent personalities. In the years ahead, efforts were made to collect papers, objects and other materials connected with the Parliament and previous legislative bodies. It was done with a view to preserving the past and the present for the future by protecting from the ravages of time and neglect all the precious records, historic documents and articles connected with the Constitution and the Parliament and through them to make the history and growth of parliamentary institutions and the political system better understood. The outcome of these efforts led to the inauguration of the Parliamentary Museum and Archives (PMA) on 29 December 1989. After the inauguration of the *Sansadiya Gyanpeeth, i.e.* the Parliament Library Building on 7 May 2002, a permanent museum is in the process of being set up in a spacious Hall here.

Aims & Objectives: The basic aim of the PMA is to function as a treasure house and research and communication centre. In fulfilment of this aim, it has set its objectives to acquire, collect and preserve the following objects/materials connected with the Parliament and parliamentary institutions in India abroad: rare objects, relics, models, art works, paintings, photographs, audio-video tapes/cassettes/discs, computer floppies/CDs; gifts/other parliamentary antiques like old/historical furniture, pens, writing pads, wigs/dresses of parliamentary officers; official records, manuscripts, private papers of eminent parliamentarians; unpublished dissertations, etc. connected with the origin, growth, structure and functioning of the parliamentary institutions in India and their predecessor bodies.

The Parliamentary Museum and Archives at present has three distinct wings, *viz.*

(i) Parliamentary Museum;

(ii) Parliamentary Archives; and

(iii) Parliamentary Photographs and Films.

(i) *Parliamentary Museum*: In the current phase of its growth, gift items presented to the Indian Parliamentary Delegations visiting abroad on goodwill missions and portraits of national leaders unveiled in the Central Hall of Parliament House, from time to time, are being added to the Museum collection. The collection of the Museum is so planned and exhibited as to give an integrated look and to provide a ready record of the developments, achievements, experiences, ideas, persons and events.

The Museum is further divided into three sectors, *viz.*

(a) History of Parliament;

(b) Parliaments of the World; and

(c) State Legislatures.

In due course, it will undertake other tasks directed towards the dissemination of information about Parliamentary Institutions and the projection of a proper image of and the encouragement of healthy respect for Parliament by stimulating interest in its growth, activities and achievements. At present, the collection of Parliamentary Museum has models of 15 State Legislature buildings of India and 8 foreign Parliament buildings. Besides, blown-up colour photographs of 80 foreign Parliament buildings are available in the Museum. The other interesting objects added to the collections of the Museum include the Gown and Wig worn by the erstwhile President of the Central Legislative Assembly and personal articles of G.V. Mavalankar, the first Speaker of Lok Sabha. The Museum also has 1,079 stamps and 100 First Day Covers issued by the Department of Posts from time to time and stamps of various other countries of the world, ashes of Mahatma Gandhi in a silver-bronze container and 63 gift items presented by various Parliamentary Delegations, including a fragment of moon presented by a Parliamentary Delegation from the United States.

(ii) *Parliamentary Archives*: The Parliamentary Archives is mainly concerned with the acquisition, storage, systematic cataloguing and preservation of precious records, private papers of parliamentarians irrespective of their political affiliations, historical documents and other documentary materials for promotion and dissemination of research and other literary activities in the field of nation-building. It also acquires books on constitutional developments, parliamentary activities and books on and by former and present Speakers, members of Parliament and Secretaries-General for furtherance of academic pursuits. The Parliamentary Archives presently has a collection of 36,474 documents/private papers/correspondence of 61 eminent parliamentarians and freedom fighters on the working of Parliament and related matters. It also has a collection of 492 books on Constitution, parliamentarians and parliamentary activities.

(iii) *Parliamentary Photographs and Films*: This Section acquires, preserves, catalogues and displays photographs concerning parliamentary activities, including those relating to Parliamentary Delegations visiting India and foreign countries. It also caters to the needs of photographs and organises temporary exhibitions on different occasions. The Parliamentary Photographs and Films Section has acquired up-to-date pictorial record of the activities of Parliament and of eminent parliamentarians. The present collection of this Section has 10,104 photographs, 37 films, 106 video cassettes, 38 audio cassettes and 1,539 spool tapes.

***Exhibitions*:** The PMA endeavours to organize exhibitions on various themes, depicting the ancient democratic heritage of India and its growth and development into a modern democratic institution, with the help of photographs, charts, diagrams, write-ups and quotations. Exhibitions are organized by the PMA after the constitution of each new Lok Sabha, on the occasion of Presiding Officers' Conference every year and whenever the statue of a national leader is unveiled and installed in the Parliament Complex.

Setting up a Permanent Museum in PLB : The proposal for developing and setting up a permanent state-of-the-art museum on an area of 11,500 sq. ft. in the Parliament Library Building is under active consideration. The proposal envisages a world class high-tech museum, with the most impressive communication techniques and a dynamic display with flexibility of incorporating future additions in exhibit structures.

The plan being visualized by internationally renowned Museologists would take about 15 months after the work starts on the project.

MEDIA AND LEGISLATIVE PRIVILEGES

An oddly-phrased cricketing metaphor used by the editor of The Hindu – which prides itself on its 'proper' English – to describe the crisis occasioned by the decision of the Tamil Nadu Assembly to imprison the editor and senior staff of The Hindu and the Murasoli for breach of legislative privilege. This decision of the House Privilege Committee of the Legislative Assembly was adopted as a resolution by the majority in the House. The immediate provocation for this resolution was the publication of an editorial piece titled "Rising Intolerance", which criticized the alleged attempts of the Chief Minister and the speaker of the Legislative Assembly to muzzle the media. A Tamil translation of this editorial was published in Murasoli, a newspaper sponsored by the Dravida Munnetra Kazhagam (DMK), a leading regional political party. Predictably, the editors of The Hindu proceeded to the Supreme Court to obtain a stay on the Assembly's orders and thereby authored another legal episode in the continuing struggle between legislative assemblies and the press. On previous occasions, these battles have raised some significant constitutional issues regarding the scope and nature of the un-codified powers of legislative privilege in the Constitution, and its claims of superiority over the fundamental rights guaranteed in the Constitution. This essay explores why the exercise of legislative privilege provokes the constitutional outrage that it does and attempts to clear some of the theoretical confusion that plagues such cases. This essay does not aim to comprehensively work through the dense legal argument that a full response to these issues would require. Instead, it illuminates some crucial themes that such cases raise.

Source of Legislative Privileges

Unlike the conventional basis of privilege in the British Constitution, the source of legislative privilege may be traced to Articles in the text of the Indian Constitution. The Constitution sets out in Articles 105 and 194 the powers and privileges that Parliament and the State Legislatures are entitled to. These articles are identical in structure and content. Clauses 1 and 2 grant members of the House the privilege of freedom of speech and immunity from civil liability for anything said or published under the authority of the House. Clause 4 extends both these privileges to apply to any person who is not a member of the House but who participates in proceedings of the House or its committees. These clauses ensure that participants in House proceedings are not impeded from performing their functions in the House in any manner.

Clause 3 allows the legislatures to define other powers, privileges and immunities by passing laws in this respect. Till such time as they pass these laws, the privileges they are entitled to in 1947 continue to accrue to them. The constitutional framers intended the legislatures to enjoy the privileges enjoyed by the British Parliament in 1947 till such time as they enacted new laws that spelt out these privileges. Unsurprisingly, the

Indian legislatures have not passed any legislation on the subject and have cashed this blank cheque whenever they have seen fit! It is under the blanket authority of this clause that the Tamil Nadu legislature seeks to proceed against newspersons for a breach of privilege.

We must note at this stage that the privileges of the legislature have both an external and internal effect. Clauses 1 and 2 in these articles protect the internal practices and conduct of members and non-members in the House in order to allow it to conduct its affairs as well as prevent members of the House from abusing their privileges in the House. Clause 3 empowers the House to deal with the conduct and expressions of outsiders who, for good reason, are found to have violated the privileges and immunities of the House. This essay is concerned primarily with the latter external effects of legislative privileges. Interestingly the South African Constitution of 1996 anticipates the Indian scenario and provides for privilege rather differently. Section 58 sets out the privileges of Parliament.

This section adopts a structure very similar to that in Article 105 and 194. Apart from the rights to free speech and immunity from civil proceeding spelled out in sub-sections 1 and 2, Parliament is empowered to make national legislation to provide for other privileges and immunities. The crucial difference lies in the approach to un-codified privileges. Till Parliament passes such a law, it is not entitled to any such privilege. By extinguishing any extant privileges and providing only for codified privileges, the South African Constitution avoids the possibility of any claims of unqualified privilege by Parliament.

Taking a cue from the South African Constitution, the Indian Supreme Court should deny the Indian Legislatures' claim to conventional privileges and compel them to legislate on this crucial subject. Significantly, such a law would need to pass the test of compliance with the fundamental rights under Article 13, thereby ensuring that such a law would imbibe due process norms and respect the guarantees to life, liberty and speech. This step alone will guarantee against any future possibility of flagrant abuse. Till such time we would do well to engage with the problems of the debate as it presently stands.

A Definition of Privilege

One key element that plagues the debate in India is the absence of an acceptable definition of the idea of "privilege". Presently, the debate proceeds on the assumption that privileges are what the legislature defines them to be. So it would be useful to begin with a recent definition of legislative privilege developed by the Report of the Joint Committee on Parliamentary Privilege in the United Kingdom: "Parliamentary privilege consists of the rights and immunities which the two Houses of Parliament and their members possess to enable them to carry out their parliamentary functions effectively. Without this protection members would be handicapped in performing their parliamentary duties, and the authority of Parliament itself in confronting the executive and as a forum for expressing the anxieties of citizens would be correspondingly diminished".

This definition does not work by setting out an exhaustive listing of privileges that the legislature may claim. Instead, it speaks to the functions that the doctrine of legislative privilege seeks to achieve. The definition marks out two essential functions: first, that legislative privilege allows the house to maintain independence and autonomy from the executive, and secondly, that legislative privilege maintains the representative capacity of the house.

A noteworthy omission from this list of functions is the reputation and dignity of the house and its members, which are not sought to be protected by the exercise of legislative privilege. In the Indian experience, the reputation and dignity of the House has sought to be invoked as the fundamental purpose of the powers of legislative privilege. By omitting these concerns, the Report does not suggest that these are unimportant, but only that these interests are best protected by the ordinary civil law of defamation and libel and not through the constitutional powers of privilege. In the present case, there has been a tendency to conflate the interests of the executive wing of government with that of the legislature, so that legislative privilege may be invoked to protect the reputational interests of the executive wing of government, particularly that of the Chief Minister. Any attempt by the Supreme Court to circumscribe the scope of these privileges by naming the functions that they are to achieve would prevent the excessive range of interests that Indian legislatures have tended to protect using these powers.

Language of 'Privileges'

It is odd to come across a republican constitution that speaks in the language of privileges of the legislature. Despite the proud proclamation of the republican character of our Constitution in the Preamble, the inability of the courts to develop legal principles that reflect the republican aspects of the independence struggle has diminished our constitutional and political tradition.

Madison in the Federalist Papers Number 39 opposes "republicanism" to a state founded on aristocratic, monarchical or feudal power. At the very least, a republican constitution embodies the principles of legal authority that derives from the people at large and admits of no royal privileges, prerogatives or immunities. The United States Constitution does not grant Congress or the House of Representative the "privilege" to punish those who offend its sensibilities. It leaves it to the ordinary courts to mould remedies that protect the functioning of the Houses.

Given that our Constitution does use the word "privilege" in Articles 105 and 194, the courts are obliged to provide a reasonable construction of the term.

The use of the word privilege to describe the powers of legislature no doubt has its origins in the English common law and political tradition. As its inclusion in a republican constitution is anachronistic and hinders clarity of thought, the court should clarify the precise nature and scope of the "privilege" enjoyed by the legislatures in tune with the principles of public authority in a republican constitution.

The ideas about the interpretation of the Constitution set out above must not be seen as a disgruntled academic semantic complaint about the use of inappropriate words. As Adam Tomkins argues, the metaphorical use of the word "Crown" in English public law has prevented public lawyers from asking difficult questions that would have allowed them to develop "a modern and sophisticated understanding of the State" and ensured that they did not "under-estimate the continuing and extraordinary powers of the Crown". The use of the word "privilege" in Articles 103 and 163 of the Constitution has a similar effect.

The language of privilege suggests a mystical source of power that lies beyond and above the Constitution, when the written Constitution sets out to be the exclusive and supreme source of secular and temporal power in the State. While no constitutional arrangement of power can be completely written in a single document, or even in several documents, we must remember that conventions and other sources of constitutional authority are subject to the express arrangements and language of the Constitution. The granting of unnamed and unregulated privileges to the Houses of Legislature invites them to take an anachronistic view of such a power and thereby violate other constitutional guarantees.

Legislative Privilege and the Courts

The history of legislative privilege may be usefully divided into three stages. The early origins of the privilege clauses are closely tied to the history of conflict between the House of Commons and the Tudor and Stuart monarchs, during which successive monarchs utilized criminal and civil law to suppress and intimidate critical legislators. Subsequently, the courts and Parliament locked horns to delineate their respective boundaries of power.

The more recent history of the privilege clause is tied to its use by legislatures against citizens. In this last stage, citizens look to the courts to protect their rights of liberty and speech, thereby pitting these two types of powers against each other.

Though it is this last stage that we are concerned about in this essay, it is rewarding to pay attention to the previous conflicts between the courts and the legislatures on the exercise of privilege, as they provide us with insight into the historical context and attitudes that ground these conflicts. Two historical precedents will enhance our ability to see through the patterns arising out of such a conflict. The first of these relates to the state of the law in England.

In 1839 Hansard had, by order of the House of Commons, printed and sold to the public a report by the inspectors of prisons which noted that an indecent book published by

Stockdale was circulating in Newgate prison. When Stockdale brought an action for defamation, Hansard was ordered by the House to plead that he had acted under an order of the House of Commons and that the House had declared that the case was a care of privilege.

The court rejected this defence and held that no resolution of the House could place anyone beyond the control of the law, and when dealing with persons outside the House, the courts would determine the nature and existence of privileges of the Commons. Though courts are willing to grant the House a wider brief to deal with matters of privilege internal to the House, they concede far less latitude to the House when dealing with outsiders.

But like all good stories, this one has a sequel! The sheriffs executing the order of the court had proceeded to recover damages of the princely sum of 600 pounds from Hansard.

The House committed Hansard and the two sheriffs who had intended to implement the orders of the court. Sensing the resolve of the House, the court backed down and refused to entertain a writ of habeas corpus to release the sheriffs from the custody of the House.

This particular sort of dispute was sought to be resolved by the Parliamentary Papers Act of 1840, which overturned the decision of the court in the Stockdale case and established that a non-member who published material on the orders of the House was immune from prosecution for libel. However, the broader question of whether it would be the courts or the House who would determine the scope of privilege is an open question that is yet to be settled conclusively.

The bright sides to this story are, first, that it reflected the position in English law 163 years ago, and secondly, that this is not the position in Indian law. Moreover, the Nicholls Committee which reviewed the English law on this point went so far as to suggest that the power to punish non-members of the House for contempt should be taken away from the Legislature and passed on to the High Court which would have the limited power to impose a fine. The Committee pointed out that with the passing of the Human Rights Act, 1998, the privileges which accrue to the Houses were thereafter subject to the right to free expression and fair trial guaranteed by Article 12 and Article 6 of the European Convention on Human Rights.

Though the ideal solution would be the establishment of an independent and autonomous tribunal to try such cases, the least that should be followed is a procedure that affords a person accused of breach of privilege the procedural protections of the notice and hearing before any action can be taken.

The second incident which we will investigate was closer to home and relates to the Indian Supreme Court's ruling in the Keshav Singh case. Keshav Singh had published a pamphlet maligning a member of the State Legislative Assembly. The House found him guilty of contempt and sentenced him to prison for seven days. He challenged this order before the High Court, which granted him interim bail. The House responded by finding that the judges who issued interim orders were themselves guilty of contempt of the House and liable to be punished. The judges moved petitions before the High Court, which sat in a full bench and stayed the orders of the House. As this confrontation seemed to be spiraling out of control, the Union government requested the President to refer the matter to the Supreme Court.

The key argument before the Supreme Court was about the scope and nature of the power of legislative privileges. While the State Legislative Assembly contended that this power was sui generis, supreme and independent of the other provisions, the petitioners argued that the power, like all others in the constitution, was subject to the fundamental rights of citizens. The historical parallels between the circumstances in the Stockdale v Hansard and Keshav Singh cases end with the decision of Supreme Court. The court rightly concluded that it had the power to review unspeaking warrants issued by the Legislature for compliance with the due process requirements under Article 21, among others, thereby asserting the supremacy of the Constitution in general, and some fundamental rights in particular, over the exercise of the privileges powers.

On 'Rising Intolerance'

Notwithstanding this assertion of constitutional supremacy in the Keshav Singh case, state legislative assemblies continue to exercise their powers of legislative privilege in an indiscriminate and uncontrolled fashion. A motivation for such an exercise might lie with an earlier ruling of the court which found that legislative privilege may be exercised even if it were to violate the rights of citizens to free speech under Article 19(1)(a).

The present case of The Hindu provides the Supreme Court with an opportunity to overrule this decision and spell out the limited scope and nature of legislative privilege in a republican constitution which guarantees fundamental rights. Legislative privilege, rightly conceived, would extend only to the protection of the autonomy of the House from the executive, and to maintaining its ability to represent the people.

7

Media Culture in Globalization

CULTURE, MEDIA AND HEGEMONY

Among the new areas and horizons of knowledge and research in the closing decades of the 20th century, nothing else is more abiding and widespread than the new discipline on "Cultural Studies". It is interesting and instructive that Marxists tools of investigation, terminology and insights play a crucial role in this expanding area of new knowledge.

It does not follow from this assertion that all what is discussed and debated in this field is just a paraphrase or linear expansion of what Marx, Engles or Lenin said or wrote. Though the basic springs of these new ideas may be traced to their classic works, the new findings have gone much further ahead from them, with Antonio Gramsci and number of neo-Marxists and the so-called Western Marxists contributing substantially to its corpus.

These new findings were made possible and necessary because of the great technological and scientific transformations in the late 20th Century like information revolution, genetic engineering, particle physics and quantum mechanics. These new scientific 2 ideas and technological practices have accelerated the process of global integration via multi-national corporate spread and phenomenal communication revolution.

That the humans are communicating animals is a rider of assessment that humans are social animals. And society is a communication network. What they communicate is culture. Communication is the vehicle of culture. Culture is the cement, which keeps the bricks of society in their places intact. To change the position and order of the pattern the bricks are placed, the cement has to be broken, and re-mixed, i.e., the culture has to be recast.

What does the communication of culture do in society – it keeps the power structure, where some dominate and others are dominated. Here comes another concept germane to our theme, Hegemony. Though person-to-person communication is common practice in social science in general and cultural studies in particular, communication through various forms of media is the most significant and decisive factor.

After Culture, Media and Hegemony the fourth term, which envelop all these and tie them in a knot, as it were, is ideology. Like Culture Ideology too is an elusive term with several meanings both descriptive and pejorative, sometimes mutually contradictory. Terry Eagelton lists sixteen meanings for ideology in his book of the same name (Verso, 1991).

What is Culture?

"Culture," Raymond Williams said three decades ago, " is one of the two or three most complicated words in the English language. This is so partly because of its intricate historical-development, in several European languages, but mainly because it has now come to be used for important concepts in several distinct intellectual disciplines and several distinct and incompatible systems of thought." (Key Words 1976) Though the evolution and the chequered career of this evocative word could be traced back to the Latin roots and old English usages, most of its present connotation began to gain momentum only in the last quarter of the 19th century. The equivalents of culture in Indian languages have even a shorter history.

Then comes the differentiation between civilization and culture, which too is nebulous and evasive. At present it is almost taken for granted that 'Culture' represents mental, artistic and intellectual aspects and achievements, civilization represents the political, economic and such other aspects of social life. Soc what we to do with the concept of "material culture," handed down to us from Anthropology, from Edward Tylor's Primitive Culture of 1870 onwards. It is interesting in this instance to remember that Baron Von Humboldt used the word civilization for intellectual and artistic attainments and culture for material and physical attainments — almost a reversal of our current practice.

Then the question arises: may we legitimately divorce the material from the mental achievements? The classical Marxist concept of basis and superstructure consider the economic and production structure as primary and the mental accomplishments as derivative, as superstructure. Basing on Engels' clarification of Marx's architectural metaphor, and Gramsci's ideas on civil society, ideology and hegemony, the modern Marxists have rejected the mechanical one-to-one relation between basis and superstructure as an over-simplification and even distortion. Without rejecting the idea of the primacy of the economic basis, the modern trend among Marxists is to accept a certain measure of autonomy for the cultural superstructure, with its own laws of functioning, and its impact on the movements on the basis – instead of the superstructure being a lifeless derivative of the basis and simply as a mirror reflection.

Though the anthropological sense of culture, which includes material culture like how we clear our forest and till our lands, how we design our houses and build them, and how the power structure is ordered etc. is certainly interesting and important. But for the purpose of the present discourse, we may confine to the sociological and current forms and practices of culture. That culture as Raymond Williams defined is the total mode of life of a people, or group shared by values, traditions, beliefs, material objects and territory. There may be a valid sense in which we talk of an entire people or country – but caste, class and ethnicity do make inroads into the monolith of nations and people. Also forms and means of domination and resistance mark out and differentiate the cultural patterns.

These important functions and expressions of culture need not always be obtrusive and shrill. The grand total is made up by seemingly trivial details of human actions and reactions, interactions and inter-relations. As James Lull says: "Culture is a complex and dynamic ecology of people, things and world views, activities and settings that fundamentally endures, but is also changed in routine communication and inter-actions. Culture is context. It is how we talk and dress, the food we eat and how we prepare and consume it, the gods we invent and how we worship them, how we divide up time and space, how we dance, the values to which we socialize our children, and all the other details that make up everyday life. This perspective on culture implies that no culture is inherently superior to any other and that cultural richness by no means derives from economic standing Culture as every day life is a steadfastly democratic idea"

Certainly this democratic idea comes into conflict with those who privilege certain types of culture as "high brow" and denigrate others as either "low brow" or even "vulgar". These questions are related to the real division in society on the basis of caste and class, elite and common, metropolitan and colonial.

IDEOLOGY AND HEGEMONY

Like culture, Ideology too is now common coin in every day parlance. But like culture this common but pregnant term too eludes attempts to tie it dawn to a definition. As stated earlier Terry Eagleton has listed 16 meanings of ideology in current use as follows:

(a) The process of production of meanings, signs and values in social life;
(b) A body of ideas characteristic of particular social group or class;
(c) Ideas which help to legitimate a dominant political power;
(d) False ideas which help to legitimate a dominant political power;
(e) Systematically distorted communication;
(f) That which offers a position for a subject;
(g) Forms of thought motivated by social interests;
(h) Identity thinking;
(i) Socially necessary illusion;
(j) The conjuncture of discourse and power;
(k) The medium in which conscious social actors make sense of their world;
(l) The confusion of linguistic and phenomenal reality;
(m) Semiotic closure;

(n) The indispensable medium in which individuals live out their relations to a social structure;

(o) *The process whereby social life is converted to a natural* reality;

As is clear from this list, some of these meanings run parallel to each other, some even intersect and contradict. We need not get lost in this jungle of interpretations and misinterpretations, academic-hair splitting and journalistic loose talk. But we must certainly be aware of the pitfalls and blind spots in grasping this extremely useful through thoroughly confusing term. In order to keep our tracts simple and straight, let us turn to Marx himself who set the ball rolling, though the term was first coined during the French Revolution by one of its philosophers, Destutt de Tracy and propagated by no less a person than Napoleon himself – though he used it in a pejorative sense.

Marx's seminal ideas on this appear in many places and it occurs as a running theme in many of his works and analyses. In German Ideology, one of his early works in collaboration with Engles he says: "....men, developing their material production and their material intercourse, alter, along with this their actual world, also their thinking and the products of their thinking, it is not consciousness that determines life, but life that determines consciousness."

Here he traces the orgin of the ideas and the modes of production relations which give rise to them. But as was noted earlier both Marx and Engles have warned against falling into a mechanistic trap and allotting ideas and consciousness only as a secondary or derivative role. For example Marx explains: "Men make their history themselves, only they do so in a given environment, which conditions it, and on the basis of actual relations already existing, among which the economic relations, however much they may be influenced by the other – the political and ideological relations – are still ultimately the decisive one, forming the keynote which runs through *them and alone leads to understanding.*" (K.Marx & F.Engles Selected Correspondence, Moscow, 1962)

Marx has also tried to emphasis the role of ideas by stating that, though the ideas are immaterial at first sight they become a material force when they are appropriated by the masses. How do we account for the variety and clashes of ideas in society?

We have already seen that if ideas are born and developed from the forms of social existence of humans. Or as Mao put it more precisely and simply: Ideas do not fall from skies, they spring from practice. They vary according to differing living experience of humans and human groups. They also articulate and produce ideas which specifically suit their station in life and interests they wish to promote. Therefore, ideas exist not in variety alone but also in opposition to one another. Marx and Engles explained the hierarchy of ideas and ideologies. They said in German Ideology:

"The ideas of the ruling class are in every epoch the ruling ideas: i.e., the class which is the ruling material force of society is at the same time its ruling intellectual force. The class which has the means of material production at its disposal, consequently also controls the means of mental production, so that the ideas of those who lack the means of mental production are on the whole subject to it...The individuals composing the ruling class...rule also as thinkers, as producers of ideas and regular the production and distribution of the ideas of their age: thus their ideas are the ruling ideas of the epoch."

From these discussions, we should not limit the concept of ideology purely into a set of abstract ideas and theories. Ideology from the very beginning with de Tracy onwards to modern theorists include ideas, feelings, orientations traditions and conscious and unconscious interests. Ideas and theories operate mainly in conscious mind, on a plane of reason and debate. But when we speak of ideology it seeps down into the realm of the unconscious and influence human ideas that operate on a plane of reason and even distort the reasoning process, buttress prejudices, and priorities by ideological pre-dilections. Because of this tendency of ideological action and interaction, many writers have considered ideology as "false consciousness". Marx and Engles have also occasionally resorted to this critical characterization of ideologies. The variety of meanings attached to the term ideology springs form this dual aspect of the term.

It is here that the idea of hegemony becomes relevant in our discussion. There is no doubt that the state is an organ of violence exercised by one class over another or others. The sanction of the state structure is the violence and instruments of violence wielded by the ruling class. All other arms of the state are only contributory factors to this decisive character of the state. Granting this premise we have to admit that violence of the ruling class alone in a limited sense cannot hold the society together or the ruling class in power.

Antonio Gramsci has dealt with this problem in detail by the concepts for civil and political society. Political society is a power structure held together by the sanction of violence by the ruling class. But civil society is a corpus of ideas, ideologies and culture. Unless a class is able to hold a dominant position in civil society, its grip on political society will slip from its hands. Though this concept of ideological hegemony was developed in detail by Antonio Gramsci in his famous "Prison Note Books" the seeds of the idea we present in the classical writings on scientific socialism.

Its perpetrators include what Marx calls 'vulgar economists' who go around 'proclaiming for everlasting truths, the banal and complacent notions held by the bourgeois agents of production about their own world, which is to them the best possible one.' This ideological slavery of the classes and masses derives not only form the articulated propaganda of the ruling class apologists, but also from the inherited traditions, religious prejudices and superstitions. The struggle for power or the hegemony in political society has to be fought decisively in civil society, for hegemony of the ideology of the rising classes. Therefore the cultural struggle is an unavoidable pre requisite for not only the capture of political power but also its sustainance and strengthening. There are many commentators who adopt the Gramscian concepts and ascribe the collapse of the European Socialist system to the decline of working class ideological hegemony in civil society. All the other factors which went into the collapse of European Socialist system are related to this decline in the arena of civil society though we may not ignore the decay which was corroding its economic system.

COMMUNICATION AND MEDIA

As we have seen, when we say humans are social animals, it is inevitable that they are communicating animals. Without communication the idea of collectivity and society is meaningless. Nonhuman animals also have communication systems and practices but their communication are by instinct, derived through tens of thousands or millions of years in organic evolutionary process. Therefore their systems of communication never change or if at all they change it may take unimaginably long ages or stages of evolution. But systems of human communication along with human production and reproduction of the means of livelihood change in comparatively short durations, sometimes changes take place with in a few hundred years, like printing, telegraph, wireless and the latest gadgets like internet of the information etc. Humans communicate mainly through various forms of media, though person-to-person communication is still prevalent and may continue forever. Media are made of material equipment and as technical advances take media to higher and more efficient levels, they need capital and machinery. In class society, capital and machinery are owned and operated by, and therefore, to promote the interests of the propertied classes.

Parallel to and as a part of the development of monopoly capitalism the media industry also has come under monopolist control and manipulation. The sponsorships and advertisements by large producers and sellers of consumer products directly exert their power in media to promote their interests. The drive towards globalization, privatization and liberalization has condemned all moral and altruistic aims of human endeavour, and placed on the supreme pedestal the selfish pursuit for pelf and profit as the measure of all things. The media not only part take this objective but has become itself the most potent instrument for promoting their amoral endeavour. As Edward S Herman and Robert W McChesney inform us: "Since the early 1980s there has been a dramatic restructuring of national media industries, along with the emergence of a genuinely global commercial media market. The new developing global media system is dominated by three or four dozen large transnational corporation (TNCs), with fewer than ten mostly U.S.-based media conglomerates towering over the global market. In addition to the centralization of media power, the major feature of the global media order is its thorough going commercialism, and an associated market decline in the relative importance of public broadcasting and the applicability of public service standards. Such a concentration of media power in organizations dependent on advertiser support and responsible primarily to shareholders is a clear and potent danger to citizens' participation in public affairs, understanding of public issues, and thus to the effective working of democracy."

We have said that the questions of culture is inextricably bound up with media and mode of communication. It is because communication is the vehicle through which culture is passed on from generation to generation, people to people and person to person. If that communication and its media is controlled and guided by vested interests in a highly inequitous and class-ridden society, communication looses its community and common aspect and becomes an instrument of hidden persuasion, hegemony and oppression. As Antonio Gramsci taught us, hegemony in civil society buttresses dominance and oppression in political society.

MEDIA AND CULTURE

Having explained the monopolistic character of media and its total dependence in Capital let us examine how media influence and interact on culture. For this I may be permitted to quote in extenso Doughlas Keller, who seems to me a very perceptive theorist: "A media culture has emerged in which images, sounds, and spectacles help produce the fabric of everyday life, dominating, leisure time, shaping political views and social behaviour, and providing the materials out of which people forge their very identities. Radio, television, film and the other products of culture industries provide the models of what it means to be male or female, successful or a failure, powerful or powerless. Media culture also produces the materials out of which many people construct their sense of class. of ethnicity and race, of nationality, of sexuality, of "us" and "them". Media culture helps shape the prevalent view of the world and deepest values; it defines what is considered good or bad, positive or negative, moral or evil. Media stories and images provide the symbols, myths and resources which help constitute a common culture for the majority of individuals insert themselves into contemporary techno-capitalist societies and which is producing a new form of global culture".

"Media culture consists of systems of radio and the reproduction of sound (albums, cassettes, CDs and their instruments of dissemination such as radios, cassette recorders and so on); of film and its modes of distributions (theatrical playing, video-cassette rental, TV showing); of print media ranging from newspapers to magazines; and to the system of television which stands at the center of media culture. Media culture is a culture of image and often deploy sight and sound. The various media-radio, film, television, music and print media such as magazines, newspapers, and comic books – privilege either sight or sound or mix the two senses. Playing as well on broad range of emotions, feelings and ideas. Media culture is industrial culture, organized on the model of mass production and is produced for a mass audience according to types (genres), following conventional formulas, codes, and rules. It is thus a form of commercial culture and its products are commodities that attempt to attract private profit produced by giant corporations interested in the accumulation of capital. Media culture aims at a large audience, thus it must resonate to current themes and concerns, and is highly topical, providing hieroglyphics of contemporary social life."

"But media culture is also high-tech culture, deploying the most advanced technologies. It is vibrant sector of the economy, one of the most profitable sectors and one that is attaining global prominence. Media culture is thus a form of techno-culture that merges culture and technology in new forms and configurations, producing new types of societies in which media and technology become organizing principles." "Media culture spectacles demonstrate who has power and who is powerless, who is allowed to exercise force and violence, and who is not. They dramatize and legitimate the power of the forces that be and demonstrate to the powerless that if they fail to conform, they risk incarceration of death. For those immersed in from cradle to grave in media and consumer society it is therefore important to learn how to understand, interpret, and criticize its meanings and messages. In a contemporary media culture, the dominant media of information and entertainment are a profound and often misperceived source of cultural pedagogy they contribute to educating us how to behave and what to think, feel, believe, fear and desire – and what not to.

Consequently, the gaining of critical media literacy is an important resource for individuals and citizens in learning how to cope with this seductive cultural environment. Learning how to read, criticize, and resist media manipulation can help individuals empower themselves in relation to dominant media and culture It can enhance individual sovereignty vis-à-vis media culture and give individuals more power over their cultural environment and the necessary literacy to produce new forms of culture." (Media Culture, Cultural Studies, Identity and Politics between the Modern and Postmodern, Doughlas Kellner, Routledge, London, 1995)

STRATEGIES OF RESISTANCE AND PROMOTION OF ALTERNATE CULTURE

The picture presented above is rather gloomy. The prospects in India too is none too rosy. The decline of renaissance and democratic values, especially secularism, in the last decade spanning form Ayodhya 1992 to Gujarat 2002 poses a challenge to the very existence of India as a united nation. It is significant that the new rulers who guide our nation down the slippery path of communal violence, neo-fascism and subservience to neocolonialist globalization have taken up culture as their weapon for nefarious objectives and the cultural and research organizations like ICHR, ICSSR, UGC, NCERT is assuming alarming proportions. Not only the official media but also the nations private TV channels with very few exceptions are feeling the line with the saffronisation drive. The film industry and various state and central academies are reorganized and manned to suit the aims of the new ruling elite.

All these reversals of Indian traditional policies are carried out with the tacit and as was proved in Gujarat, vociferous support of a substantial sections of people. They could do so with impunity because they have established the hegemony of Hindutva Ideology over significant sections of civil society. The Gujarat Chief Minister Narendra Modi succeeded albeit temporarily, in galvanizing his vote bank by unleashing waves of communal hysteria. That was why he was making ugly haste in conducting the elections before the receding of the communal wave. Therefore, it is highly urgent that forces of secularism and culture open up a second front of onslaught against this malignant growth, before it spreads to the rest of India. The first front of course is the political and class struggle. Both these fronts are complementary to each other.

This struggle has two aspects, resistance to ruling ideology and Hindutva culture is one, the other is the creation and propagation of alternate forms of culture, imbued the humanist values of renaissance, the spirit of secularism and the thrust towards democracy and socialism. Along with air time-tested agenda, new emphasis is to be given to dalit liberation, environmental protection and women empowerment. The attempt to highjack these crucial issued by pseudo-radicals and fascists must be resisted in a principled manner both in the field of action and ideas.

In our struggle for the reassertion of secular and renaissance culture, we must consciously avoid two deviations – which in the absence of better terms we may call "techno-phobia" and "techno-mania". As we explained in detail, the current technological advance, communication revolution and media transformations are posing formidable challenges to peoples culture and democratic advance in a class society it is inevitable. We need not be apologetic about the opposition to computerization when it began to be applied in Banks, offices and factories as measure of rationalization to increase the profit of the managements and others at the expense of employees and workers. We were correct in opposing computerization and other mechanical devised to retrench workers and increase the capitalist profit. We still do so. But a totally negative attitude to technology is both futile and counter productive. It is futile because the history has shown that once a technology is invented and applied there is no way of retreat, no escape routes. That is why very well-meaning and powerful thinkers and political leaders like Rousseau, Tolstoy and Gandhi failed in their anti-machinery struggle as did the machine breaking generations primitive trade union movement. Therefore the only reasonable and feasible course is to criticize and oppose the anti people consequences of technology and try to make use of technology to advance peoples interests

Making use of modern technology in the interests of people should not lead us to the opposite deviation for "technological mania" and the tendency to indulge in high-tech hyperboles must be avoided at all cost. This critical attitude d is now al the more important because of the exaggerated claims put forward by bourgeois and peti-bourgeois politicians about the millennium to be ushered in by the panacea of IT, without restructuring the society. Their hyperboles are designed to hide the class oppression and the class meaning of the high-tech mania. They are either ignorant or seek to hide from people the al-pervading crisis that is taking place inn countries of great IT advances like USA, Germany and Japan. They also seek to legitimize the emergence of a narrow high-tech IT elite and a mass of IT wage labourers (some call them coolies) with the gulf between them expanding both between countries and with in countries. This adds a new dimension to the traditional class divisions of the classical capitalist society.

Never slackening our campaign against the in-built anti-people proclivities of the monopolist electronic media, and never nursing any idea competing with them in their court, we have to make use of the immense potential of the new media to the extent possible. In many countries and on a very limited scale in India too, revolutionary and progressive movements are tapping its potential. In Latin America both legal and illegal liberation movements and peoples organisations establish TV channels, sponsor websites, and enter the Internet world to reach the masses at home and abroad. We must make a detailed study of such networks and activities so that we too may learn and apply them in our specific milieu.

I do not claim that Kerala's experience of participating in a leftoriented TV channel was a resounding success. Problems of capital, sponsorships and advertisements do lead occasionally to compromise on quality of the programs. But with all these infautle disorders and draw-backs Kairali Channel has to stay and serve the secular and democratic movements in two ways: one by its own programmes and coverage and two: setting certain standards for others to copy and forcing them to take note of the peoples movements and struggles – which they may not have done in the absence of a left-oriented channel.

Still wider use of cassettes, CD ROMs, slide projections and documentary films and organisation for clubs and community listening and viewing centres are certainly within our means. Our cadre must be given Training to produce such programmes to suit every locality and organisations, centered around panchayats, schools and rural libraries. The beginning of such activities in Kerala and elsewhere are crowned with immense success such centres with discussion, shows, performances, speeches will prove to be effective forums of resistance to monopolist communication aggrandizement.

The Film Society movement is now in decline. Our movement and organisation should take initiative to revive it- and attach it to schools, panchayats, colleges, libraries, trade unions, kisan sabhas etc. Selected films from India and abroad and documentaries should be centrally collected and distributed to these societies.

Computerization in governance and education was begun in Kerala during the LDF rule. In some other states like Madhya Pradesh too such experiments are being tried, I understand. If possible with the Governments assistance and even with out it on the initiative of progressive panchayats and local-self government leaderships this reform is possible. Along with governance and various services to people, it is not difficult to add a cultural and entertainment component to computer set up. It must be tried.

HASHMI'S IDEAL, HASHMI'S STYLE

The new era of communal and neo-fascist resurgence in the last decade of the 20th century also marked a new era of cultural resistance inaugurated by the glorious martyrdom of Safdar Hashmi. His example liberating performing arts from the locked chambers of the elite minority to the open fields and streets where the milling crowd to toil and struggle contains the key new stage of cultural renaissance. Not that the traditional folk style of street and open fields shows and performances in any thing unheard of in the past. But Hashmi following the IPTA example of the forties of fifties of 20th Century took this form to higher levels, upgrading it to the needs of late 20th Century and even 21st Century after him.

Though the TV, films and documentaries have the capacity for immensely larger reach, still they are tricks played by light and shadows, echoes of real sounds and voices. The performance by actual human beings in front of human being in flesh and blood conveys a sense of reality which is unthinkable in electronic and image shows. In drama and other performances the performer and audience forma a common community. The barrier between the performer and viewer is thin and disappear altogether in moments of higher acting and climax. That is why authorities like the former producer with BBC and theorist Martin Essdin said in Drama the audience and performers merge into a community and in the process recreate the social experience as if in church or temple congregation. Such lived experience of art is alien to an electronic show, where the performers are far away in time and space. Therefore in our strategies of resistance performing arts must be accorded the pride of place.

According the pride of place to performing arts in our scheme of resistance and creation of alternate cultural forms is easier said than done. In films and TV shows a group of people can perform and the cultural product may be preserved to cater to virtually tens for thousands of people and repeated again and again. But the live performances in front for an audience of hundreds (even a few dozens in street corners) on streets or factory gates, or village common needs to be repeated physically to reach tens of thousands. For this dozens or hundred of artist troups have to be organized and trained. This pattern is qualitatively different from a highly paid and sophisticated group in some air conditioned studio somewhere faraway, with no contact what ever with the people for whom they perform. So the Hashmi's style breaks down the barrier between the elite performer and common audience, both artistically and physically Hashmi's mode and style, like those of our traditional folk performers, are essentially a popular and democratic exercise, while the other is a mind manipulating exercise of hidden persuaders.

This argument in favour of folk style and a wide-spread network of hundreds of troupes and thousands of performers does not lead us to the conclusion that professionalism and training are not necessary. There must be centres and troupes of excellence in art also, but all that should be to set the pattern and provide examples for the larger and ever growing network for popular artists and performers. These higher units of talented and trained performer and directors and writers should be entrusted with the task of imparting their skills to the popular groups. They also should prepare sufficiently large and versalite repertoire of scripts and themes. This should not be a one-way traffic-there must be a process of give-and take from the top to bottom and vice versa.

Along with lonely touring groups performing in different places and occasions, we must also have grand secular festivals. The People Science Movement in Kerala (KSSP) and DYFI have successfully conducted such festivals and attracted talented village artists and big crowds of audiences. Besides performances of plays, music, dance etc we may also have exhibitions, seminars, lectures etc. National and interstate exchange, cooperation's, and consultations will go a long way to raise the level and variety of cultural perform once and activities. Many comrades in our state long for some are to take initiate to bring about National Forum, to coordinate activities one a national level and facilitate the process of exchange of ideas and examples.

GROWTH MEDIUM

A growth medium or culture medium is a liquid or gel designed to support the growth of microorganisms or cells, or small plants like the moss *Physcomitrella patens*. There are different types of media for growing different types of cells.

There are two major types of growth media: those used for cell culture, which use specific cell types derived from plants or animals, and microbiological culture, which are used for growing microorganisms, such as bacteria or yeast. The most common growth media for microorganisms are *nutrient broths* and agar plates; specialized media are sometimes required for microorganism and cell culture growth. Some organisms, termed *fastidious organisms*, require specialized environments due to complex nutritional requirements. Viruses, for example, are obligate intracellular parasites and require a growth medium containing living cells.

Types of Growth Media

The most common growth media for microorganisms are *nutrient broths* (liquid nutrient medium) or *Luria Bertani medium* (LB medium or *Lysogeny Broth*). Liquid media are often mixed with agar and poured into petri dishes to solidify.

These agar plates provide a solid medium on which microbes may be cultured. They remain solid, as very few bacteria are able to decompose agar. Bacteria grown in liquid cultures often form colloidal suspensions.

The differences between growth media used for cell culture and those used for microbiological culture are because cells derived from whole organisms and grown in culture often cannot grow without the addition of, for instance, hormones or growth factors which usually occur *in vivo*. In the case of animal cells, this difficulty is often addressed by the addition of blood serum to the medium. In the case of microorganisms, there are no such limitations, as they are often unicellular organisms. One other major difference is that animal cells in culture are often grown on a flat surface to which they attach, and the medium is provided in a liquid form, which covers the cells. In contrast, bacteria such as *Escherichia coli* may be grown on solid media or in liquid media.

An important distinction between growth media types is that of *defined* versus *undefined* media. A defined medium will have known quantities of all ingredients. For microorganisms, they consist of providing trace elements and vitamins required by the microbe and especially a defined carbon source and nitrogen source. Glucose or glycerol are often used as carbon sources, and ammonium salts or nitrates as inorganic nitrogen sources. An undefined medium has some complex ingredients, such as yeast extract or casein hydrolysate, which consist of a mixture of many, many chemical species in unknown proportions. Undefined media are sometimes chosen based on price and sometimes by necessity-some microorganisms have never been cultured on defined media.

A good example of a growth medium is the wort used to make beer. The wort contains all the nutrients required for yeast growth, and under anaerobic conditions, alcohol is produced. When the fermentation process is complete, the combination of medium and dormant microbes, now beer, is ready for consumption.

Nutrient Media

This is an undefined medium because the amino acid source contains a variety of compounds with the exact composition being unknown. Nutrient media contain all the elements that most bacteria need for growth and are non-selective, so they are used for the general cultivation and maintenance of bacteria kept in laboratory culture collections.

An *undefined medium* (also known as a *basal* or *complex* medium) is a medium that contains:

- a carbon source such as glucose for bacterial growth
- water
- various salts needed for bacterial growth

Defined media (also known as chemically defined media)

- all the chemicals used are known
- does not contain any yeast, animal or plant tissue.

Differential medium

- some sort of indicator, typically a dye, is added, that allows for the differentiation of particular chemical reactions occurring during growth.

Minimal Media

Minimal media are those that contain the minimum nutrients possible for colony growth, generally without the presence of amino acids, and are often used by microbiologists and geneticists to grow "wild type" microorganisms. Minimal media can also be used to select for or against recombinants or exconjugants.

Minimal medium typically contains:

- a carbon source for bacterial growth, which may be a sugar such as glucose, or a less energy-rich source like succinate
- various salts, which may vary among bacteria species and growing conditions; these generally provide essential elements such as magnesium, nitrogen, phosphorus, and sulfur to allow the bacteria to synthesize protein and nucleic acid
- water

Supplementary minimal media are a type of minimal media that also contains a single selected agent, usually an amino acid or a sugar. This supplementation allows for the culturing of specific lines of auxotrophic recombinants.

Selective Media

Selective media are used for the growth of only select microorganisms.

For example, if a microorganism is resistant to a certain antibiotic, such as ampicillin or tetracycline, then that antibiotic can be added to the medium in order to prevent other cells, which do not possess the resistance, from growing. Media lacking an amino acid such as proline in conjunction with *E. coli* unable to synthesize it were commonly used by geneticists before the emergence of genomics to map bacterial chromosomes.

Selective growth media are also used in cell culture to ensure the survival or proliferation of cells with certain properties, such as antibiotic resistance or the ability to synthesize a certain metabolite. Normally, the presence of a specific gene or an allele of a gene confers upon the cell the ability to grow in the selective medium. In such cases, the gene is termed a marker.

Selective growth media for eukaryotic cells commonly contain neomycin to select cells that have been successfully transfected with a plasmid carrying the neomycin resistance gene as a marker. Gancyclovir is an exception to the rule as it is used to specifically kill cells that carry its respective marker, the Herpes simplex virus thymidine kinase (HSV TK).

Some examples of selective media include:

- eosin-methylene blue agar (EMB) that contains methylene blue – toxic to Gram-positive bacteria, allowing only the growth of Gram negative bacteria
- YM (yeast and mold) which has a low pH, deterring bacterial growth
- blood agar (used in strep tests), which contains bouvine heart blood that becomes transparent in the presence of hemolytic *Streptococcus*
- MacConkey agar for Gram-negative bacteria
- Hektoen enteric agar (HE) which is selective for Gram-negative bacteria
- mannitol salt agar (MSA) which is selective for Gram-positive bacteria and differential for mannitol

- Terrific Broth (TB) is used with glycerol in cultivating recombinant strains of Escherichia coli.
- xylose lysine desoxyscholate (XLD), which is selective for Gram-negative bacteria
- buffered charcoal yeast extract agar, which is selective for certain gram-negative bacteria, especially *Legionella pneumophila*

TRANSPORT MEDIA

Temporary storage of specimens being transported to the laboratory for cultivation.

Maintain the viability of all organisms in the specimen without altering their concentration.

Contain only buffers and salt.

Lack of carbon, nitrogen, and organic growth factors prevents microbial multiplication.

Transport media used in the isolation of anaerobes must be free of molecular oxygen.

Enriched Media

Enriched media contain the nutrients required to support the growth of a wide variety of organisms, including some of the more fastidious ones. They are commonly used to harvest as many different types of microbes as are present in the specimen. *Blood agar* is an enriched medium in which nutritionally rich whole blood supplements the basic nutrients. *Chocolate agar* is enriched with heat-treated blood (40-45°C), which turns brown and gives the medium the color for which it is named.

8

Public Broadcasting and Digital Media

Public broadcasting includes radio, television and other electronic media outlets that receive some or all of their funding from the public. Public broadcasters may receive their funding from individuals through voluntary donations, a specific tax such as a television license fee, or as direct funding by the state. The extent to which public broadcasters can be considered "non-commercial" varies from country to country. In the United States, most public radio and television stations are licensed as non-commercial broadcasters, yet many stations air underwriting spots (resembling advertisements on commercial broadcasting but with some content limitations) in exchange for corporate contributions. In some other countries, public broadcasters are permitted to air commercials.

Public broadcasting may be nationally and/or locally operated, depending on the country and the station. In some countries, public broadcasting is dominated by a single organization (such as the BBC in the UK and the Australian Broadcasting Corporation in Australia) and its radio and television services broadcast throughout the country. However, some countries have multiple public broadcasting organizations operating regionally (such as in Germany) or in different languages. In the United States, public broadcasting stations are always locally licensed, but range from stations that mostly broadcast programming from national networks (such as the Public Broadcasting Service (PBS) and National Public Radio (NPR)) to stations that broadcast only locally produced content.

Historically, in many countries (with the notable exception of the US), public broadcasting was once the only form or the dominant form of broadcasting. However, commercial broadcasting now also exists in most of these countries; the number of countries with only public broadcasting has declined substantially during the latter part of the 20th century. In some countries, commercial broadcasting and the emergence of a wider variety of broadcast media have created competition that makes it more difficult for public broadcasters to retain their audiences and survive.

DEFINING PUBLIC BROADCASTING

There is no standard definition for public broadcasting, although a number of official bodies have attempted to identify key characteristics. Public-service broadcasters generally transmit programming that aims to improve society by informing viewers. In contrast, the aim of commercial outlets is to provide popular content that attracts a large audience, maximizing revenue from advertising and sponsorship. For this reason, the ideals of public broadcasting are often hard to reconcile with commercial goals. The Broadcasting Research Unit lists the following as possible goals or characteristics of a public broadcaster.

Geographic universality — The stations' broadcasts are available nationwide, with no exception. Generally, the "nationwide" criterion is satisfied by either having member stations across the country (as is the case with PBS) or, as is the case with most other public broadcasters around the world, the broadcaster's use of sufficient transmitters to broadcast nationwide.

Catering for all interests and tastes — as exemplified by the BBC's range of minority channels (BBC Two and BBC Radio 3).

Catering for minorities — much as above, but with racial and linguistic minorities. (for example S4C in Wales, BBC Asian Network, Radio-Canada, and Australia's multicultural Special Broadcasting Service (SBS)).

Concern for national identity and community — this essentially means that the stations mostly part commission programmes from within the country, which may be more expensive than importing shows from abroad.

Detachment from vested interests and government in which programming is impartial, and the broadcaster is not be subject to control by advertisers or government.

Even when a broadcast medium is removed from corporate and government interests, critics argue that it may nonetheless have a bias towards the values of certain groups, such as the middle class, the politics of the incumbent government, or in the case of partially or wholly commercially funded networks, the advertisers.

One broadcasting system to be directly funded by the corpus of users — For example, the licence fee in the case of the BBC, or member stations asking for donations in the case of PBS/ NPR.

Competition in good programming rather than numbers — quality is the prime concern with a true public service broadcaster. Of course, in practice, ratings wars are rarely concerned with quality, although that may depend on how "quality" is defined.

Guidelines to liberate programme-makers and not restrict them — in the UK, guidelines, and not laws, govern what a programme-maker can and cannot do, although these guidelines can be backed up by hefty penalties.

Some of these definition points may not be acceptable everywhere. For example in the US, public broadcasting may see part of its mission to bring in foreign content, such as from the CBC/Radio-Canada and the BBC, since such content is not commonly aired by American commercial broadcasters.

An alternative model for implementing public-service media exists, known as Citizen Media. As it relates to broadcasting, this generally means a radio or television outlet which has some sort of public access, that is, most or much of the programming is created by members of the public which receives the programming. This can be in the form of community radio, campus radio, and public access television, although the latter is not a form of over-the-air broadcasting, as it is only available on cable television systems.

Advantages and Disadvantages

Public broadcasters may receive all or a substantial part of their funding from government sources, either from the general tax revenues or from licence fees. Public broadcasters do not rely on advertising as a source of revenue to the same degree as commercial broadcasters; this allows public broadcasters to air programs that are less saleable to the mass market, such as public affairs shows, radio and television documentaries, and educational programs. That public broadcasters do not chase ratings in the same way as commercial broadcasters can lead to the criticism that they are unresponsive to what their viewers want, but also to the positive claim that they can explore issues in greater depth and with more complexity than is possible in commercial media, and that they can present cultural fare that has social value but would not be supported by markets. It may also be pointed out commercial broadcasters program not for audiences but for those audiences which will buy their products.

Additionally, public broadcasting facilitates the implementation of cultural policy (an industrial policy and investment policy for culture). Some examples include:

- The Canadian government is committed to official bilingualism (English and French). As a result, the public broadcaster, the CBC employs translators and journalists who speak both official languages and it encourages production of cross-cultural material. Quebec separatists argue that this is also a policy of cultural imperialism and assimilation.
- In the UK, the BBC supports multiculturalism and diversity, in part by using on-screen commentators and hosts of different ethnic origins.
- In New Zealand, the public broadcasting system provides support to Maori (native New Zealander) broadcasting, as a way to improve the opportunities, maintain the cultural heritage and promote the language of these New Zealanders.

Critics of public broadcasting systems argue that this implementation of cultural policy imposes the values of the public broadcaster on the populace. However, it can also be argued that commercial broadcasting has a bias for certain values or cultural forms, such as pop culture, militarism, culture bias, and consumerism.

Public broadcasting, and also some pirate broadcasting, provides a counterweight to the commercial media. Advocates of deliberative democracy argue that public broadcasting helps to maintain modern democracies, since public broadcasters can engage in journalism for its own sake. In wealthier countries public broadcasters tend to not be beholden to political parties or the government of the day. This is especially true where the broadcaster is funded by licensing fees and so, theoretically, not dependent on the government for any of its funding.

Economics of Public Broadcasting

An economic rationale for public broadcasting is that it exists to provide coverage of interests for which there are missing markets. Public broadcasting can supply those topics which have social benefit that would otherwise not be broadcast due to believed unprofitability. Society is willing to pay for such programming, but markets fail to provide it. Typically, such underprovision exists when the benefits to viewers are relatively high in comparison to the benefits to advertisers from contacting viewers. This frequently is the case in undeveloped countries that normally have low benefits to advertising, which helps explain their tendency to have public broadcasting. However, concern exists that public broadcasting can crowd out potential private broadcasting. One study compared classical and jazz music programming provided by private radio to that provided by public radio. It found that in large markets, public broadcasting appears to displace private entry. Additionally, publicly funded broadcasting does not necessarily mean that the optimal level will be produced. A government failure can arise in which the cost of public funding exceeds its benefits

In the United States, public broadcasting amounts to a coalition effort. On average, professionally staffed stations receive substantial sums, between 26 percent and 16 percent, from four major sources: audience members ("subscribers" or "members"), the federal government, state governments, and businesses ("underwriters"). Individual stations and programs carried on them rely on highly varied proportions of funding.

Program-by-program funding creates the potential for conflict-of-interest situations, which must be weighed program by program under standards such as the guidelines established by PBS. Donations are widely dispersed to stations and producers, giving the system a resilience and broad base of support but diffusing authority and impeding decisive change and priority-setting.

The American structure also diffuses responsibility. A minority of viewers and listeners makes donations, creating a "free-rider" situation for most of the audience, though this is the nature of philanthropy. But with no single supporter, such as a parliament, taking responsibility for adequacy of service, the American public broadcasting system is weak in comparison with those of other countries.

Implementation of Public Broadcasting around the World

The model, established in the 1920s, of the British Broadcasting Corporation – an organization widely trusted, even by citizens of the Axis Powers during World War II – was widely emulated throughout Europe, the British Empire, and later the Commonwealth. The public broadcasters in a number of countries are basically an application of the model used in Britain.

Modern public broadcasting is often a mixed commercial model. For example, the CBC has always relied on a subsidy from general revenues of the government, in addition to advertising revenue, to support its television service. This means they must compete with commercial broadcasting. Some argue that this dilutes their mandate as truly public broadcasters, who have no commercial bias to distort their presentation.

The rest of this section looks at some specific implementations of public broadcasting around the world.

Asia

India

In India, Prasar Bharati is India's public broadcaster. It is an autonomous corporation of the Ministry of Information and Broadcasting, Government of India and comprises the Doordarshan television network and All India Radio. Prasar

Bharati was established on November 23, 1997 following a demand that the government owned broadcasters in India should be given autonomy like those in many other countries. The Parliament of India passed an Act to grant this autonomy in 1990, but it was not enacted until September 15, 1997.

Pakistan

In Pakistan, the public broadcaster is the state owned PBC which is short for "Pakistan Broadcasting Corporation." It consists of PTV (Pakistan Television) and Radio Pakistan. In the past PBC was funded publicly through money obtained from television, radio and VCR licensing. Pakistan entered into Television Broadcasting age with a small pilot TV Station established at Lahore from where transmission was first beamed in Black & White with effect from 26 November 1964. Television centres were established in Dhaka, Karachi and Rawalpindi/ Islamabad in 1967 and in Peshawar and Quetta in 1974. PTV has various channels trasmitting throughout the world including PTV National, PTV World, PTV 2, PTV Global, PTV Bolan etc. Radio Pakistan has stations covering all the major cities, it covers 80% of the country serving 95.5 Million listeners. It has world service in 07 languages daily.

Hong Kong (China)

In Hong Kong, the Radio Television Hong Kong (RTHK) is the sole public service broadcaster. Although a government department under administrative hierarchy, it enjoys editorial independence. It operates seven radio channels, and produces television programmes and broadcast on commercial television channels, as these channels are required by law to provide time slot for RTHK television programmes.

RTHK would be assigned a digital terrestrial television channel within 2013 to 2015, when the new broadcasting building is completed in Tseung Kwan O.

Japan

In Japan, the main public broadcaster is the NHK (Japan Broadcasting Corporation), sometimes informally referred to as Radio Tokyo by English speakers. The broadcaster was set up in 1926 and was modelled on the British Broadcasting Company, the precursor to the British Broadcasting Corporation created in 1927. Much like the BBC, NHK is funded by a "receiving fee" by every Japanese household, with no commercial advertising and the maintenance of a position of strict political impartiality. NHK runs two national terrestrial TV stations (NHK General and NHK Educational) and three satellite only services (NHK BS-1, BS-2 and the hi-definition NHK Hi-Vision services). NHK also runs 3 national radio services and a number of international radio and television services, akin to the BBC World Service. NHK has also been an innovator in television, developing the world's first high definition television technology in 1964 and launching high definition services in Japan in 1981.

Malaysia

In Malaysia, the public broadcaster is the state owned RTM which is short for "Radio Televisyen Malaysia" (Malaysian Radio and Television). RTM was previously funded publicly through money obtained from television licensing, however it is currently state subsidised as television licences have been abolished.

At present, RTM operates 8 national, 16 state and 7 district radio stations as well as 2 national terrestrial television channels called TV1 and TV2. RTM has also done test transmissions on a new digital television channel called RTMi. Tests involving 2000 residential homes in the Klang Valley began in September 2006 and ended in March 2007.

Europe

In most countries in Europe, state broadcasters are funded through a mix of advertising and public money, either through a licence fee or directly from the government.

Croatia

Croatian Radiotelevision (Croatian: *Hrvatska radiotelevizija, HRT*) is a Croatian public broadcasting company. It operates several radio and television channels, over a domestic transmitter network as well as satellite. As of 2002, 70% of HRT's funding comes from broadcast user fees with each house in Croatia required to pay 79 HRK, kuna, per month for a single television), with the remainder being made up from advertising.

Estonia

ERR (Estonian Public Broadcasting) organizes the public radio and television stations of Estonia. ETV (Estonian Television), the public television station, made its first broadcast in 1955, during the Soviet Occupation, and together with its sister channel ETV2 has ca. 20% audience share.

Germany

Following World War II, when regional broadcasters had been merged into one national network by the Nazis to create a powerful means of propaganda, the Allies insisted on a decentralized, independent structure for German public broadcasting and created regional public broadcasting agencies that, by and large, still exist today. In addition to these nine regional radio and TV broadcasters, which cooperate within ARD, a second national television service—actually called Second German Television (German: *Zweites Deutsches Fernsehen*, ZDF)—was later created in 1961 and a national radio service with two networks (Deutschlandradio) emerged from the remains of Cold War propaganda stations in 1994. All services are mainly financed through license fees paid by everybody who keeps a radio, TV set, PC or mobile phone with internet access "ready for use", and are governed by councils of representatives of the "societally relevant groups". Public TV and radio stations spend about 60 % of the ~10 Bil. € spent altogether for broadcasting in Germany per year.

Ireland

In Ireland a system of TV licencing and advertising to fund public services operates. RTÉ the incumbent offers a range of free to air services on TV and Radio. The Sound and Vision Fund is operated by the Broadcasting Commission of Ireland, this fund receives 5% of the licence fee. The fund is used to assist broadcasters to commission public service broadcast programming. It is open to all independent producers provided they get a free to air or community broadcaster's backing, including TV3, Today FM, BBC Northern Ireland, RTÉ, Channel 4, UTV etc. An off-shot of RTÉ, TG4 is an independent Irish language broadcaster that is funded by the government through subsidy, and through advertising revenue.

Italy

Italian national broadcasting company is the RAI-Radiotelevisione Italiana, born as URI in 1924. RAI transmits on analogical television on three channels, named Rai Uno, Rai Due and Rai Tre, but also works via satellite, in radiophonic sector, book and cinema. It is considered the biggest and one of the most authoritative television companies in Europe. With 45% of share, RAI also is the most viewed public television of the continent. Proceeds derive from a periodical standing charge and from advertising. The main competitors of RAI are Mediaset, the biggest national private television, divided in three channels, and La7, owned by Telecom Italia.

Montenegro

RTCG (Radio Television of Montenegro) is the public broadcaster in Montenegro.

Netherlands

In the Netherlands a different system is used to most other countries. Public-broadcasting associations are allocated money and time to broadcast their programmes on the publicly owned television and radio channels. The time and money is allocated in proportion to their membership numbers. The system is intended to reflect the diversity of all the groups composing the nation.

United Kingdom

The United Kingdom has a strong tradition of public service broadcasting. In addition to the BBC, established in 1922, there is also Channel 4, a state-owned commercial public service broadcaster, and S4C, a Welsh language broadcaster in Wales. Furthermore, the two commercial analogue broadcasters ITV and Five also have significant public service obligations imposed as part of their licence to broadcast.

Scandinavia

National public broadcasters in the Scandinavian countries were modelled after the BBC and established a decade later: Radioordningen (now DR) in Denmark, Kringkastingselskapet (now NRK) in Norway, and Radiotjänst (now Sveriges Radio and Sveriges Television) in Sweden (all in 1925), and YLE in

Finland in 1926. All four are funded from television licence fees costing (in 2007) around €230 (US$300) per household per year.

Spain

In Spain, being a highly decentralized country, two public broadcasting systems coexist: a national broadcasting television, Radio y Televisión Española (RTVE), that can be watched all around Spain, and many autonomic TV channels, only broadcasted within their respective Autonomous Community. Televisión Española, founded in 1937 and modelled after the BBC, broadcasts two different TV-channels: TVE1 (a.k.a *La Primera* or *La uno*), that is a wide-range audience general channel; and TVE2, (a.k.a *La dos*), that tends to offer cultural programation, as well as sport competitions. Till 2008, RTVE was founded both with public funding and with private advertising; however, the Spanish government has recently decreed that starting in September 2009, RTVE's channels shall be founded with taxpayer's money and with private founding raised from the rest of Spain's private TV stations, thus removing advertising from the broadcaster. A TV licence fee has been suggested, but with little popular success.

Moreover, each of the autonomous communities of Spain have their own public broadcaster, usually consisting in either one or two public channels that tend to reproduce the model set up by Televisión Española: a general channel and a more cultural related one. In the Autonomous Communities that have their own official language besides Spanish, those channels may broadcast not in Spanish, but in the other co-official language. For example, this occurs in Catalonia, where Televisió de Catalunya broadcasts mainly in catalan. In the Basque Country, Euskal Telebista has three channels, two of which broadcast only in basque (ETB 1 and ETB 3), whereas the other (ETB 2) broadcasts in Spanish. In Galicia, the Television de Galicia and the G2. All the autonomic networks are publicly founded, and also admit private advertising.

North and South America

Argentina

Despite a moderate state presence in television media since

the 1970s, it never had a strong history of European style public service radio or television. The private sector has taken the leading role in the development of television networks. In opposition, state broadcasters tend to be either very weak and under-funded (as the Argentinian Canal 7, formerly known as ATC

Canada

In Canada, the main public broadcaster is the national Canadian Broadcasting Corporation (the CBC), which operates two television networks (CBC Television and Télévision de Radio-Canada), four radio networks (CBC Radio One, CBC Radio Two, Première Chaîne and Espace musique) and two 24-hour news channels (CBC Newsworld and RDI) in both of Canada's official languages. CBC's television operations are funded in part by advertisements, in addition to tax dollars from the federal government (Newsworld and RDI are funded entirely by commercials). CBC's radio operations are commercial-free. In recent years, the CBC was frequently battered by budget cuts and labour disputes.

In addition, several provinces operate public broadcasters; these are not CBC subentities, but distinct networks in their own right. These include the English-language TVOntario and the French-language TFO in Ontario, Télé-Québec in Quebec, SCN in Saskatchewan, public radio station CKUA in Alberta, and Knowledge in British Columbia. Some of the provincial broadcasters operate through conventional transmitters, while others are cable-only channels.

Alberta also has a semi-public television network, Access, which is licensed to provide some public service programming but is owned and operated by a commercial broadcaster. The network, formerly a public broadcaster operated by the provincial government, was sold to CHUM Limited in 1995. CJRT-FM in Toronto also operated as a public government-owned radio station for many years; while no longer funded by the provincial government, it still solicits most of its budget from listener and corporate donations and is permitted to air only a very small amount of commercial advertising. One television station, CFTU in Montreal, operates as an educational station owned by the Université de Montréal. Some other universities have dedicated cable channels to broadcast educational programming, but no other university in Canada operates a conventional broadcast television station.

Some local community stations also operate non-commercially with funding from corporate and individual donors. In addition, cable companies are required to produce a local community channel in each licensed market. Such channels have traditionally aired community talk shows, city council meetings and other locally oriented programming, although it is becoming increasingly common for them to adopt the format and branding of a local news channel.

Canada also has a large number of campus radio and community radio stations.

Chile

The closest model to the British BBC is that of Chile's Televisión Nacional, an open channel which serves the entire country (including Easter Island and Antarctica bases). Televisión Nacional, popularly known as channel 7 because of its Santiago frequency, is governed by a seven-member board appointed by the Chilean Senate. It is meant to be independent of political pressures, although accusations of bias have been made, especially during election campaigns.

United States

Public broadcasting in the United States is as old as broadcasting itself. Most early public stations were operated by state colleges and universities, and were often run as part of the schools' cooperative extension services. Stations in this era were internally funded, and did not rely on listener contributions to operate; some accepted advertising. Networks such as Iowa, South Dakota, and Wisconsin Public Radio began in this way.

The concept of a "non-commercial, educational" station *per se* does not show up in U.S. law until the 1940s, when the FM band was moved to its present location; the part of the band between 88.1 and 91.9 MHz is reserved for such stations, though they are not limited to those frequencies. For example, WBAA-West Lafayette, Ind. has its FM frequency at 101.3 MHz. Houston's KUHT was the nation's first public television station, and signed on the air in 25 May 1953 from the campus of the University of Houston. This phenomenon continued in other big cities in the 1950s; in rural areas, it was not uncommon for colleges to operate commercial stations instead (e.g., the University of Missouri's KOMU-TV, an NBC affiliate).

In the United States, public broadcasting is decentralized and is not government operated, but does receive some government support. The majority of funding comes from community support to hundreds of public radio and public television stations, each of which is an individual entity licensed to one of several different non-profit organizations, municipal or state governments, or universities. Sources of funding also include on-air fund drives and-on public radio stations-the sale of underwriting "spots" (typically 15–30 seconds) to sponsors. Public radio and television organizations often produce their own programs, but purchase or receive most of their programming from national producers and program distributors such as National Public Radio (NPR), Public Broadcasting Service (PBS), Public Radio International (PRI), American Public Television (APT), and American Public Media. U.S. Federal government support for public radio and television is filtered through a separate organization, the Corporation for Public Broadcasting (CPB).

Television

In the United States the Public Broadcasting Service (PBS) (formerly National Educational Television) television network operates on a largely viewer-supported basis, with commercial sponsors of specific programs. Over time, sponsorship announcements ("underwriting") have slowly transformed into something resembling regular (commercial) TV advertisements, though they are usually shorter and have a more muted tone than what normally appears on commercial and cable TV, and many organizations still only receive a short thanks for their contributions. Underwriting may only issue declarative statements (including slogans) and may not include "calls to action". Most communities also have public access services on local cable television stations, which are sometimes supported in part through donations. US public broadcasting for television has, from the late 1960s onward, dealt with severe criticism from conservative politicians and think-tanks, which allege that its programming has a leftist bias.

As European public broadcasting systems tend to dominate their national marketplaces, radio and television broadcasting in the US was incubated (in the first half of the 20th century), and eventually dominated, mainly through the private sector, with a heavy emphasis on program sponsorships being sold to businesses attempting to promote their products and services to a mass audience; in many cases (especially in US broadcasting's earliest decades) these sponsors had near-total control over the content they paid for, resulting in most programs, such as situation comedies, soap operas and popular sporting events, only being geared to the perceived tastes and attitudes of the widest possible audience. Therefore, US public broadcasting is, and has always been, a niche service that provides programming considered less attractive to corporate advertisers, and as a result, not found elsewhere on the system; this includes cultural and educational programs, documentaries, public affairs and political affairs shows.

Radio

A public radio network, National Public Radio (NPR), was created in 1970, following the passage of the Public Broadcasting Act of 1967 which established the Corporation for Public Broadcasting. This network (generally exclusive of Pacifica Radio, described below) is colloquially though inaccurately referred to as *Public Radio*. Independent local public radio stations buy their programming from distributors such as NPR; Public Radio International (PRI); American Public Media (APM); The Public Radio Exchange (PRX); and Pacifica, most often distributed through the Public Radio Satellite System (PRSS). Around these distributed programs, stations fill varying amounts of local programming.

Public radio stations in the U.S. tend to broadcast a mixture of news and talk radio programming along with some music. Some of the larger operations split off these formats into separate stations or networks. Public music stations are probably best known for playing classical music, although other formats have been used, including the time-honored "eclectic" music format that is rather freeform in nature common among college radio stations; jazz is another public radio programming staple, dominating the airwaves in the major markets L.A. and New Jersey, KKJZ 88.1 FM and WBGO 88.3 FM. Also, XM Satellite Radio provides a station of public radio programs licensed from all three content providers.

Local stations derive most of the funding for their operations through regular pledge drives and corporate sponsorship (euphemistically termed "underwriting" on-air). They also derive significant combined public funding from federal, state and local governments and government-funded colleges/universities (in addition to receiving use of the radio spectrum for free). The local stations then contract with program distributors and also provide some programming themselves. NPR produces some of its own programming such as *Morning Edition*; *Weekend Edition*; and *All Things Considered*. PBS, by contrast, does not create its own content. NPR also receives some direct funding from private donors, foundations, and from the Corporation for Public Broadcasting.

Some other public networks, such as Pacifica Radio, are almost entirely member-funded and do not receive significant sponsorship from corporations or governmental sources; Pacifica Radio is known for a general body of programming of (what is considered) a mainly leftist social and political viewpoint, with many programs, especially news and public affairs shows, critical and/or challenging of trends and issues in mainstream government, society and corporations.

Venezuela

Recently, under the initiative of the Venezuelan government of president Hugo Chávez, and with the sponsorship of the governments of Argentina, Bolivia, Cuba, Ecuador and Nicaragua, the news and documentary network teleSUR was created with the intended to be an instrument toward the "concretizing of the Bolivarian idea" through the integration of America, and as a counterweight to what the governments that funds it consider a "distorted view of Latin American reality by privately run networks that broadcast to the region". There is an ongoing debate on whether teleSUR will be able become a neutral and fair news channel able to counter the huge influence of global media outlets, or whether it will end up as a propaganda tool of the Venezuelan government, which owns a 51 percent share of said channel.

Oceania

Australia

In Australia, the Australian Broadcasting Corporation (ABC) is funded entirely through an Australian Government grant-in-aid. The multicultural Special Broadcasting Service (SBS), another public broadcaster, now accepts limited sponsorship and advertising. Imparja is an Aboriginal community broadcaster in Australia that receives funding from the Federal Government. Most of its programs are bought from Australia's commercial broadcasters, and it only airs a small amount of local content.

In addition, there is a large Australian community broadcasting sector, funded in part by Federal grants via the Community Broadcasting Foundation, but largely sustained via subscriptions, donations and business sponsorship. As of June 2005, there were 442 fully-licensed community radio stations (including remote Indigenous services) and a number of community television stations (most operating as Channel 31 despite being unrelated across different states). They are organised similarly to PBS and NPR stations in the US, and take on the role that public access stations have in the US.

New Zealand

In New Zealand, the former public broadcaster BCNZ (formerly NZBC) was broken up into separate state-owned corporations, Television New Zealand (TVNZ) and Radio New Zealand (RNZ). While RNZ remains commercial-free, about 90% of funding for TVNZ comes from selling advertising during programmes on their two stations. TVNZ continues to be a public broadcaster; however like CBC Television in Canada it is essentially a fully commercial network in continuous ratings battles with other stations.

Programmes offered on TVNZ include popular US-produced shows like *Desperate Housewives*, *ER*, *Lost*, *Cold Case*, and *Dancing with the Stars*. TVNZ operates five stations: *TV ONE*, *TV2*, *TVNZ 6*, *TVNZ 7* and *TVNZ Sport Extra* and hold majority ratings in the country. Because of its high ratings some of the most expensive advertising slots in the country are on TV ONE and TV2. TVNZ 6 and 7 are fully-funded and advertisement-free.

The Government owns a network of reserved channels for non-commercial regional access broadcasting, and some of them have been awarded to local community trusts to provide public service and access television. Examples are *Triangle TV* in Auckland and Wellington; and *Channel 7* in Taranaki.

DIGITAL MEDIA

Digital media (as opposed to analog media) are usually electronic media that work on digital codes. Today, computing is primarily based on the binary numeral system. In this case digital refers to the discrete states of "0" and "1" for representing arbitrary data. Computers are machines that (usually) interpret binary digital data as information and thus represent the predominating class of digital information processing machines. Digital media ("Formats for presenting information" according to Wiktionary:media) like digital audio, digital video and other digital content can be created, referred to and distributed via digital information processing machines. Digital media represents a profound change from previous (analog) media.

Digital data is per se independent of its interpretation (hence representation). An arbitrary sequence of digital code like "0100 0001" might be interpreted as the decimal number 65, the hexadecimal number 41 or the glyph "A".

Florida's digital media industry association, Digital Media Alliance Florida, defines digital media as "the creative convergence of digital arts, science, technology and business for human expression, communication, social interaction and education".

There is a rich history of non-binary digital media and computers.

Electronic Business Media

According to Schmid, media can basically be defined as follows: They are enablers of interaction (i.e. they allow for exchange) particularly the communicative exchange between agents. Such interaction enablers can be structured into three main components:

First, a physical component (*C-Component*) allows for the actual interaction of physical agents. This component can also be referred to as carrier medium or channel system. Second, a logical component (*L-Component*) comprises a common "language" (i.e. symbols used for the communication between agents and their semantics). Without such a common understanding, the exchange of data is possible (with the help of the C-Component), but not the exchange of knowledge. Third, an organizational component (*O-Component*) defines a structural organization of agents, their roles, rules which impact the agents' behaviour as well as the process-oriented organization of agents' interactions.

Together, these basic three components have been identified to constitute various kinds of media. Among others, it is appropriate to describe electronic media such as those deployed to support cross-organizational collaboration. Based on these components which already represent a first, scientific approach to modeling, understanding and reorganizing media, a layer/ phase reference model has been introduced as well.

The Media Reference Model (MRM) comprises four different layers (which all represent dedicated views on media) and structures the use of media into four sequential phases. Similar to the emerging field of software engineering in the software context, the MRM aims to provide a comprehensive, coherent and systematic framework for the description and analysis of various media.

The Community View (first layer) thereby accounts for the set of interacting agents, the organization of the given agents' population, i.e. the specific roles of involved stakeholders, the situations in which they act as well as the objects with which they deal. Summing up, it models the structure of the social community sphere in a situation-dependent, but static fashion. The Process View (Implementation Aspects) deals with the modeling of the process-oriented organization of agents and can also be referred to as "Interaction Programming". It is also called implementation view as it connects the needs of the community with the means provided by the carrier medium and thus implements the "community-plot" on the basis of the carrier medium. The Service View (Transaction View) models the services provided by the carrier medium which can be used in the different interaction steps to reach the respective interactions' goals. The Infrastructure View models the production system, which creates the services provided by the service view, i.e. in the case of electronic media the actual underlying information technology.

The above discussed three major components can seamlessly be integrated into the MRM: The upper two views (Community Aspects and Implementation Aspects) represent the organizational component (O-Component) which accounts for the structural as well as process-oriented organization. The lower two layers are mapped to the physical component (C-Component) which focuses on the creation and provision of services. Last, the logical component (L-Component) concerns all four layers as it ensures that interaction of agents is based on a common understanding of exchanged symbols.

Data Conversion

The transformation of an Analog signal to Digital information via an Analog-to-digital converter is called sampling. According to information theory, sampling is a reduction of information. Most digital media are based on translating analog data into digital data and vice-versa.

Data Processing

As opposed to analog data, digital data is in many cases easier to manipulate and the end result can be reproduced indefinitely without any loss of quality. Mathematical operations can be applied to arbitrary digital information regardless of its interpretation (you can add "2" to the data "65" and interpret the result either as the hexadecimal number "43" or the letter "C"). Therefore, it is possible to use the same compression operation onto a text file or an image file or a sound file. The foundations of operation on digital information are described in digital signal processing.

Examples

The following list of digital media is based on a rather technical view of the term media. Other views might lead to different lists.

- Cellphones

- Compact disc
- Digital video
- Digital television
- e-book
- Internet
- Minidisc
- Video game
- e-Commerce
- game systems
- and many interactive media.

Art

Digital art is any art in which computers played a role in production or display of the artwork. Such art can be an image, sound, animation, video, CD-ROM, DVD-ROM, videogame, web site, algorithm, performance or gallery installation. Many traditional disciplines are now integrating digital technologies and, as a result, the lines between traditional works of art and new media works created using computers has been blurred. For instance, an artist may combine traditional painting with algorithm art and other digital techniques. As a result, defining computer art by its end product can thus be difficult. Nevertheless, this type of art is beginning to appear in art museum exhibits.

Comic book artists in the past would generally sketch a drawing in pencil before going over the drawing again with India ink, using pens and brushes. Magazine illustrators often worked with India ink, acrylics or oils. Currently, an increasing number of artists are now creating digital artwork.

Digital artists do, simply, what centuries of artists have always done by exploring and adopting a culture's new technology toward the making of a personal imagery. In doing so the culture is also reflected in the artwork as is the artist's personal vision. As our culture becomes increasingly digitized, digital artists are leading the way in exploring and defining this new culture. Digital Artists use a medium that is nearly immaterial, that being binary information which describes the color and brightness of each individual pixel on a computer screen. Taken as a whole an image consisting of pure light is the feedback devise that tells an artist what is being made and simultaneously stored on the computer's hard drive. Digital Artists employ many types of user interfaces that correspond to the wide variety of brushes, lenses or other tools that traditional artist use to shape their materials. Rather than manipulating digital code directly as math, these electronic brushes and tools allow an artist to translate hand motions, cutting and pasting, and what were formerly chemical dark room techniques into the mathematical changes that effect the arrangement of screen pixels and create a picture.

Digital Art is created and stored in a non-material form on the computer's memory systems and must be made physical, usually in the form of prints on paper or some other form of printmaking substrate. In addition, digital art may be exchanged and appreciated directly on a computer screen in gallery situations or simultaneously in every place on the globe with access to the web. Being immaterial has its advantages and with the advent of high quality digital printing techniques a very traditional long lasting print of this artwork can also be produced and marketed.

The list of digital artists continues to lengthen:

- David Álvarez
- Miguel Álvarez-Fernández
- Winston Blakely
- Craig Boldman
- Brian Bolland
- Thomas Charveriat
- Ernie Colon
- Andrew Dabb
- Matthew Forsythe
- J.D. King
- Roger Langridge
- Liu Dao
- Jim McDermott
- Dave McKean
- Shawn McManus
- Manfred Mohr

- Joseph Nechvatal
- Ariel Olivetti
- Zina Saunders
- Antoine Schmitt
- Barclay Shaw
- Jim Steranko
- Michael Whelan
- Andrew Wildman
- Nam June Paik
- Yoko Ono
- Lev Manovich
- Michael Mandiberg
- Judy Malloy.

Companies

Several design houses are active in this space, prominent names being:

- Publicis
- McCann Erickson.

Companies offering training in Digital Media:

- Digital Media Academy
- Giant Campus
- John Lennon Educational Tour Bus
- Sterling Ledet & Associates.

ELECTRONIC MEDIA

Electronic media are media that use electronics or electromechanical energy for the end user (audience) to access the content. This is in contrast to static media (mainly print media), which are most often created electronically, but don't require electronics to be accessed by the end user in the printed form. The primary electronic media sources familiar to the general public are better known as video recordings, audio recordings, multimedia presentations, slide presentations, CD-ROM and Online Content. Most new media are in the form of digital media. However, electronic media may be in either analog or digital format.

Although the term is usually associated with content recorded on a storage medium, recordings are not required for live broadcasting and online networking.

Any equipment used in the electronic communication process (e.g. television, radio, telephone, desktop computer, game console, handheld device) may also be considered electronic media.

HISTORY OF DEVELOPMENT

- Transmission

Wire

- Telegraph 1795-1832
- Facsimile 1843-1861
- Telephone 1849-1877
- Cable 1962 (Coaxial Standard)
- Fiber Optics 1956-1970

Wireless

- Radio 1897-1920
- Satellite 1958-1972
- Free Space Optics 1960s

Internet

- Download 1969 (file transfer protocols)
- Live Streaming 1996 (RTP Protocol)
- Display and Output
    - o Information Processing 1940's (Term)
    - o Galvanometer 1832
    - o Telegraph Sounder 1844
    - o Telephone Receiver 1849-1877
    - o Light Bulb 1801-1883
    - o Neon 1893-1902
    - o Teletype Receiver 1910
    - o CRT 1922
    - o Radio/Television Tuner 1894-1927
    - o Speaker/Headphones 1876-1928/1930s
    - o LED/LCD 1955-1962/1968

- o Laser Light Show 1970s
- o Computer Monitor 1950s/1976 (for PCs)
- o Large Electronic Display 1985
- o HDTV 1936 (Term) 1990s (Standards)

- HMD 1968-current Signal Processing
  - o Capture 1745 (Capacitor)
  - o Analog Encoding 1830's (morse code)
  - o Electronic Modulating 1832-1927
  - o Electronic Multiplexing 1853 (TDM)
  - o Digitizing 1903 (PCM Telephone)
  - o Electronic Encryption 1935-1945
  - o Online Routing 1969
  - o Electronic Programming 1943-current
- Electronic Information Storage

Recording Medium

- Punch Card and Paper Tape 1725/1846
- Phonograph Cylinder and Disk 1857-1958
- Film 1876-1889
- Magnetic Storage 1898-2003
- RAM 1941-current
- Barcodes 1952/1973 (UPC)
- Laser Disc 1969-1978
- Compact Disc/DVD 1982/1993-current

Content Formats

- Content in general 1877-current
- Audio Recording 1877-current
- Video Recording 1952-current
- Digital File Formats
- Database Content and Formats 1963-current
- Interactivity
  - o Control Panel
  - o Input Device
  - o Game Controller
  - o Handheld

- o Wired Glove
- o Brain computer interface (BCI).

Uses

Electronic media are ubiquitous in most of the developed world. As of 2005, there are reports of satellite receivers being present in some of the most remote and inaccessible regions of China. Electronic media devices have found their way into all parts of modern life. The term is relevant to media ecology for studying its impact compared to printed media and broadening the scope of understanding media beyond a simplistic aspect of media such as one delivery platform (e.g. the World Wide Web) aside from many other options. The term is also relevant to professional career development regarding related skill sets.

INTERACTIVE MEDIA

Interactive media normally refers to products and services on digital computer-based systems which respond to the user's actions by presenting content such as text, graphics, animation, video, audio etc.

Terminology

Though the word *media* is plural, the term *interactive media* is often used as a singular noun. Interactive media is related to the concepts interaction design, new media, interactivity, human computer interaction, cyberculture, digital culture, and includes specific cases such as, for example, interactive television, interactive narrative, interactive advertising, algorithmic art, videogames, social media, ambient intelligence, virtual reality and augmented reality.

An essential feature of interactivity is that it is mutual: user and machine each take a more or less active role. Most interactive computing systems are for some human purpose and interact with humans in human contexts. Manovich complains that 'In relation to computer-based media, the concept of interactivity is a tautology..... Therefore, to call computer media "interactive" is meaningless – it simply means stating the most basic fact about computers.'. Nevertheless the term is useful to denote an identifiable body of practices and technologies.

Any form of interface between the end user/audience and the medium may be considered interactive. Interactive media is not limited to electronic media or digital media. Board games, pop-up books, gamebooks, flip books and constellation wheels are all examples of printed interactive media. Books with a simple table of contents or index may be considered interactive due to the non-linear control mechanism in the medium, but are usually considered non-interactive since the majority of the user experience is non-interactive sequential reading.

MASS MEDIA

Mass media denotes a section of the media specifically designed to reach a large audience. The term was coined in the 1920s with the advent of nationwide radio networks, mass-circulation newspapers and magazines. However, some forms of mass media such as books and manuscripts had already been in use for centuries.

Mass media includes Internet media (like blogs, message boards, podcasts, and video sharing) because individuals now have a means to exposure that is comparable in scale to that previously restricted to a select group of mass media producers. The communications audience has been viewed by some commentators as forming a mass society with special characteristics, notably atomization or lack of social connections, which render it especially susceptible to the influence of modern mass-media techniques such as advertising and propaganda.

Marshall McLuhan, one of the biggest critics in media's history, brought up the idea that "the medium is the message."

History

Types of drama in numerous cultures were probably the first mass-media, going back into the Ancient World.

The first dated printed book known is the "Diamond Sutra", printed in China in 868 AD, although it is clear that books were printed earlier. Movable clay type was invented in 1041 in China. However, due to the slow spread of literacy to the masses in China, and the relatively high cost of paper there, the earliest printed mass-medium was probably European popular prints from about 1400. Although these were produced in huge numbers, very few early examples survive, and even most known to be printed before about 1600 have not survived. Johannes Gutenberg printed the first book on a printing press with movable type in 1453. This invention transformed the way the world received printed materials, although books remained too expensive really to be called a mass-medium for at least a century after that. Newspapers developed from about 1612, with the first example in English in 1620 ; but they took until the nineteenth century to reach a mass-audience directly.

During the 20th century, the growth of mass media was driven by technology, including that which allowed much duplication of material. Physical duplication technologies such as printing, record pressing and film duplication allowed the duplication of books, newspapers and movies at low prices to huge audiences. Radio and television allowed the electronic duplication of information for the first time.

Mass media had the economics of linear replication: a single work could make money. An example of Riel and Neil's theory. proportional to the number of copies sold, and as volumes went up, unit costs went down, increasing profit margins further. Vast fortunes were to be made in mass media. In a democratic society, the media can serve the electorate about issues regarding government and corporate entities. Some consider the concentration of media ownership to be a grave threat to democracy.

Purposes

Mass media can be used for various purposes:

- Advocacy, both for business and social concerns. This can include advertising, marketing, propaganda, public relations, and political communication.
- Entertainment, traditionally through performances of acting, music, and sports, along with light reading; since the late 20th century also through video and computer games.
- Public service announcements.

JOURNALISM

Journalism is the discipline of collecting, analyzing, verifying and presenting information regarding current events, trends, issues and people. Those who practice journalism are known as journalists. News-oriented journalism is sometimes described as the "first rough draft of history" (attributed to Phil Graham), because journalists often record important events, producing news articles on short deadlines. While under pressure to be first with their stories, news media organizations usually edit and proofread their reports prior to publication, adhering to each organization's standards of accuracy, quality and style. Many news organizations claim proud traditions of holding government officials and institutions accountable to the public, while media critics have raised questions about holding the press itself accountable.

Public relations

Public relations is the art and science of managing communication between an organization and its key publics to build, manage and sustain its positive image. Examples include:

- Corporations use marketing public relations to convey information about the products they manufacture or services they provide to potential customers to support their direct sales efforts. Typically, they support sales in the short and long term, establishing and burnishing the corporation's branding for a strong, ongoing market.
- Corporations also use public relations as a vehicle to reach legislators and other politicians, seeking favorable tax, regulatory, and other treatment, and they may use public relations to portray themselves as enlightened employers, in support of human-resources recruiting programs.
- Nonprofit organizations, including schools and universities, hospitals, and human and social service agencies, use public relations in support of awareness programs, fund-raising programs, staff recruiting, and to increase patronage of their services.
- Politicians use public relations to attract votes and raise money, and, when successful at the ballot box, to promote and defend their service in office, with an eye to the next election or, at career's end, to their legacy.

Forms

Electronic media and print media include:

- Broadcasting, in the narrow sense, for radio and television.
- Many instances of various types of recorded discs or tapes. In the 20th century, these were mainly used for music. Video and computer uses followed.
- Film, most often used for entertainment, but also for documentaries.
- The Internet, which has many uses and presents both opportunities and challenges. Examples can include Blogs and podcasts (such as news, music, pre-recorded speech, and video)
- Mobile phones, which can be used for rapid breaking news and short clips of entertainment like jokes, horoscopes, alerts, games, music, and advertising
- Publishing, including electronic publishing
- Video games, which have developed into a mass form of media since cutting-edge devices such as the PlayStation 3, XBox 360, and Wii broadened their use.

Audio Recording and Reproduction

Sound recording and reproduction is the electrical or mechanical re-creation and/or amplification of sound, often as music. This involves the use of audio equipment such as microphones, recording devices and loudspeakers. From early beginnings with the invention of the phonograph using purely mechanical techniques, the field has advanced with the invention of electrical recording, the mass production of the 78 record, the magnetic wire recorder followed by the tape recorder, the vinyl LP record. The invention of the compact cassette in the 1960s, followed by Sony's Walkman, gave a major boost to the mass distribution of music recordings, and the invention of digital recording and the compact disc in 1983 brought massive improvements in ruggedness and quality. The most recent developments have been in digital audio players.

An album is a collection of related audio recordings, released together to the public, usually commercially.

The term record album originated from the fact that 78 RPM Phonograph disc records were kept together in a book resembling a photo album. The first collection of records to be called an "album" was Tchaikovsky's *Nutcracker Suite*, release in April 1909 as a four-disc set by Odeon records. It retailed for 16 shillings — about £15 in modern currency.

A music video (also promo) is a short film or video that accompanies a complete piece of music, most commonly a song. Modern music videos were primarily made and used as a marketing device intended to promote the sale of music recordings. Although the origins of music videos go back much further, they came into their own in the 1980s, when Music Television's format was based around them. In the 1980s, the term "rock video" was often used to describe this form of entertainment, although the term has fallen into disuse.

Music videos can accommodate all styles of filmmaking, including animation, live action films, documentaries, and non-narrative, abstract film.

Broadcast

The sequencing of content in a broadcast is called a schedule. With all technological endeavours a number of technical terms and slang are developed please see the list of broadcasting terms for a glossary of terms used.

Television and radio programs are distributed through radio broadcasting over frequency bands that are highly regulated by the Federal Communications Commission. Such regulation includes determination of the width of the bands, range, licencing, types of receivers and transmitters used, and acceptable content.

Cable programs are often broadcast simultaneously with radio and television programs, but have a more limited audience. By coding signals and having decoding equipment in homes, cable also enables subscription-based channels and pay-per-view services.

A broadcasting organisation may broadcast several programs at the same time, through several channels (frequencies), for example BBC One and Two. On the other hand, two or more organisations may share a channel and each use it during a fixed part of the day. Digital radio and digital television may also transmit multiplexed programming, with several channels compressed into one ensemble.

When broadcasting is done via the Internet the term webcasting is often used. In 2004 a new phenomenon occurred when a number of technologies combined to produce podcasting. Podcasting is an asynchronous broadcast/narrowcast medium, with one of the main proponents being Adam Curry and his associates the Podshow.

Film

'Film' encompasses motion pictures as individual projects, as well as the field in general. The name comes from the photographic film (also called filmstock), historically the primary medium for recording and displaying motion pictures. Many other terms exist — *motion pictures* (or just *pictures* and "picture"), *the silver screen*, *photoplays*, *the cinema*, *picture shows*, *flicks* — and commonly *movies*.

Films are produced by recording people and objects with cameras, or by creating them using animation techniques and/ or special effects. They comprise a series of individual frames, but when these images are shown rapidly in succession, the illusion of motion is given to the viewer. Flickering between frames is not seen due to an effect known as persistence of vision — whereby the eye retains a visual image for a fraction of a second after the source has been removed. Also of relevance is what causes the perception of motion; a psychological effect identified as beta movement.

Film is considered by many to be an important art form; films entertain, educate, enlighten and inspire audiences. Any film can become a worldwide attraction, especially with the addition of dubbing or subtitles that translate the film message. Films are also artifacts created by specific cultures, which reflect those cultures, and, in turn, affect them.

Internet

The Internet (also known simply as "the Net" or less precisely as "the Web") is a more interactive medium of mass media, and can be briefly described as "a network of networks". Specifically, it is the worldwide, publicly accessible network of interconnected computer networks that transmit data by packet switching using the standard Internet Protocol (IP). It consists of millions of smaller domestic, academic, business, and governmental networks, which together carry various information and services, such as electronic mail, online chat, file transfer, and the interlinked Web pages and other documents of the World Wide Web.

Contrary to some common usage, the Internet and the World Wide Web are not synonymous: the Internet is the system of interconnected *computer networks*, linked by copper wires, fiber-optic cables, wireless connections etc.; the Web is the contents, or the interconnected *documents*, linked by hyperlinks and URLs. The World Wide Web is accessible through the Internet, along with many other services including e-mail, file sharing and others described below.

Toward the end of the 20th century, the advent of the World Wide Web marked the first era in which most individuals could have a means of exposure on a scale comparable to that of mass media. Anyone with a web site has the potential to address a global audience, although serving to high levels of web traffic is still relatively expensive. It is possible that the rise of peer-to-peer technologies may have begun the process of making the cost of bandwidth manageable. Although a vast amount of information, imagery, and commentary (i.e. "content") has been made available, it is often difficult to determine the authenticity and reliability of information contained in web pages (in many cases, self-published). The invention of the Internet has also allowed breaking news stories to reach around the globe within minutes. This rapid growth of instantaneous, decentralized communication is often deemed likely to change mass media and its relationship to society.

"Cross-media" means the idea of distributing the same message through different media channels. A similar idea is expressed in the news industry as "convergence". Many authors understand cross-media publishing to be the ability to publish in both print and on the web without manual conversion effort. An increasing number of wireless devices with mutually incompatible data and screen formats make it even more difficult to achieve the objective "create once, publish many".

The internet is quickly becoming the center of mass media. Everything is becoming accessible via the internet. Instead of picking up a newspaper, or watching the 10 o'clock news, people will log onto the internet to get the news they want, when they want it. Many workers listen to the radio through the internet while sitting at their desk. Games are played through the internet.

The Internet and Education: Findings of the Pew Internet & American Life Project. Even the education system relies on the internet. Teachers can contact the entire class by sending one e-mail. They have web pages where students can get another copy of the class outline or assignments. Some classes even have class blogs where students must post weekly, and are graded on their contributions. The internet thus far has become an extremely dominant form of media.

Blogs (Web Logs)

Blogging has become a huge form of media. A blog is a website, usually maintained by an individual, with regular entries of commentary, descriptions of events, or other material such as graphics or video. Entries are commonly displayed in reverse chronological order. Many blogs provide commentary or news on a particular subject; others function as more personal online diaries. A typical blog combines text, images, and links to other blogs, web pages, and other media related to its topic. The ability for readers to leave comments in an interactive format is an important part of many blogs. Most blogs are primarily textual, although some focus on art (artlog), photographs (photoblog), sketchblog, videos (vlog), music (MP3 blog), audio (podcasting) are part of a wider network of social media. Micro-blogging is another type of blogging which consists of blogs with very short posts.

RSS Feeds

RSS is a format for syndicating news and the content of news-like sites, including major news sites like Wired, news-oriented community sites like Slashdot, and personal blogs. It is a family of Web feed formats used to publish frequently updated content such as blog entries, news headlines, and podcasts. An RSS document (which is called a "feed" or "web feed" or "channel") contains either a summary of content from an associated web site or the full text. RSS makes it possible for people to keep up with web sites in an automated manner that can be piped into special programs or filtered displays.

Podcast

A podcast is a series of digital-media files which are distributed over the Internet using syndication feeds for playback on portable media players and computers. The term podcast, like broadcast, can refer either to the series of content itself or to the method by which it is syndicated; the latter is also called podcasting. The host or author of a podcast is often called a podcaster.

Mobile

Mobile phones were introduced in Japan in 1979 but became a mass media only in 1998 when the first downloadable ringing tones were introduced in Finland. Soon most forms of media content were introduced on mobile phones, and today the total value of media consumed on mobile towers over that of internet content, and was worth over 31 billion dollars in 2007 (source Informa). The mobile media content includes over 8 billion dollars worth of mobile music (ringing tones, ringback tones, truetones, MP3 files, karaoke, music videos, music streaming services etc); over 5 billion dollars worth of mobile gaming; and various news, entertainment and advertising services. In Japan mobile phone books are so popular that five of the ten best-selling printed books were originally released as mobile phone books.

Similar to the internet, mobile is also an interactive media, but has far wider reach, with 3.3 billion mobile phone users at the end of 2007 to 1.3 billion internet users (source ITU). Like email on the internet, the top application on mobile is also a personal messaging service, but SMS text messaging is used by over 2.4 billion people. Practically all internet services and applications exist or have similar cousins on mobile, from search to multiplayer games to virtual worlds to blogs. Mobile has several unique benefits which many mobile media pundits claim make mobile a more powerful media than either TV or the internet, starting with mobile being permanently carried and always connected. Mobile has the best audience accuracy and is the only mass media with a built-in payment channel available to every user without any credit cards or paypal accounts or even an age limit. Mobile is often called the 7th Mass Medium and either the fourth screen (if counting cinema,

TV and PC screens) or the third screen (counting only TV and PC).

Publishing

Publishing is the industry concerned with the production of literature or information – the activity of making information available for public view. In some cases, authors may be their own publishers.

Traditionally, the term refers to the distribution of printed works such as books and newspapers. With the advent of digital information systems and the Internet, the scope of publishing has expanded to include websites, blogs, and the like.

As a business, publishing includes the development, marketing, production, and distribution of newspapers, magazines, books, literary works, musical works, software, other works dealing with information.

Publication is also important as a legal concept; (1) as the process of giving formal notice to the world of a significant intention, for example, to marry or enter bankruptcy, and; (2) as the essential precondition of being able to claim defamation; that is, the alleged libel must have been published.

Book

A book is a collection of sheets of paper, parchment or other material with a piece of text written on them, bound together along one edge within covers. A book is also a literary work or a main division of such a work. A book produced in electronic format is known as an e-book.

Magazine

A magazine is a periodical publication containing a variety of articles, generally financed by advertising and/or purchase by readers.

Magazines are typically published weekly, biweekly, monthly, bimonthly or quarterly, with a date on the cover that is in advance of the date it is actually published. They are often printed in color on coated paper, and are bound with a soft cover. Magazines fall into two broad categories: consumer magazines and business magazines. In practice, magazines are a subset of periodicals, distinct from those periodicals produced by scientific, artistic, academic or special interest publishers which are subscription-only, more expensive, narrowly limited in circulation, and often have little or no advertising.

Magazines can be classified as:

- General interest magazines (e.g. Frontline, India Today, The Week, The Sunday Indian etc)
- Special interest magazines (women's, sports, business, scuba diving, etc)

Newspaper

A newspaper is a publication containing news and information and advertising, usually printed on low-cost paper called newsprint. It may be general or special interest, most often published daily or weekly. The first printed newspaper was published in 1605, and the form has thrived even in the face of competition from technologies such as radio and television. Recent developments on the Internet are posing major threats to its business model, however. Paid circulation is declining in most countries, and advertising revenue, which makes up the bulk of a newspaper's income, is shifting from print to online; some commentators, nevertheless, point out that historically new media such as radio and television did not entirely supplant existing.

Software Publishing

A software publisher is a publishing company in the software industry between the developer and the distributor. In some companies, two or all three of these roles may be combined (and indeed, may reside in a single person, especially in the case of shareware).

Software publishers often license software from developers with specific limitations, such as a time limit or geographical region. The terms of licensing vary enormously, and are typically secret.

Developers may use publishers to reach larger or foreign markets, or to avoid focussing on marketing. Or publishers may use developers to create software to meet a market need that the publisher has identified.

Video Games

A video game is a computer-controlled game where a video display such as a monitor or television is the primary feedback device. The term "computer game" also includes games which display only text (and which can therefore theoretically be played on a teletypewriter) or which use other methods, such as sound or vibration, as their primary feedback device, but there are very few new games in these categories. There always must also be some sort of input device, usually in the form of button/joystick combinations (on arcade games), a keyboard & mouse/trackball combination (computer games), or a controller (console games), or a combination of any of the above. Also, more esoteric devices have been used for input. Usually there are rules and goals, but in more open-ended games the player may be free to do whatever they like within the confines of the virtual universe.

In common usage, a "computer game" or a "PC game" refers to a game that is played on a personal computer. "Console game" refers to one that is played on a device specifically designed for the use of such, while interfacing with a standard television set. "Arcade game" refers to a game designed to be played in an establishment in which patrons pay to play on a per-use basis. "Video game" (or "videogame") has evolved into a catchall phrase that encompasses the aforementioned along with any game made for any other device, including, but not limited to, mobile phones, PDAs, advanced calculators, etc.

NEW MEDIA ART

New media art is a genre that encompasses artworks created with new media technologies, including digital art, computer graphics, computer animation, virtual art, Internet art, interactive art technologies, computer robotics, and art as biotechnology. The term differentiates itself by its resulting cultural objects and social events, which can be seen in opposition to those deriving from old visual arts (i.e. traditional painting, sculpture, etc.) This concern with medium is a key feature of much contemporary art and indeed many art schools and major Universities now offer majors in "New Genres" or "New Media". New Media Art often involves interaction between artist and observer.

New Media concerns are often derived from the telecommunications, mass media and digital modes of delivery the artworks involve, with practices ranging from conceptual to virtual art, performance to installation.

History

The origins of new media art can be traced to the moving photographic inventions of the late 19th Century such as the zoetrope (1834), the praxinoscope (1877) and Eadweard Muybridge's zoopraxiscope (1879).

During the 1960s the development of then new technologies of video produced the new media art experiments of Nam June Paik and Wolf Vostell, and multimedia performances of Fluxus. At the end of the 1980s the development of computer graphics, combined with real time technologies then in the 1990s with the spreading of the Web and the Internet favorished the emerging of new and various forms of interactivity Lynn Hershman Leeson, David Rokeby, Perry Hoberman, telematic art Roy Ascott, Internet Vuk Æosiæ, Jodi, virtual and immersive art Jeffrey Shaw, Maurice Benayoun and large scale urban installation Rafael Lozano-Hemmer.

Simultaneously advances in biotechnology have also allowed artists like Eduardo Kac to begin exploring DNA and genetics as a new art medium.

Contemporary New Media Art influences on new media art have been the theories developed around hypertext, databases, and networks. Important thinkers in this regard have been Vannevar Bush and Theodor Nelson with important contributions from the literary works of Jorge Luis Borges, Italo Calvino, Julio Cortázar, Lev Manovich, and Douglas Cooper. These elements have been especially revolutionary for the field of narrative and anti-narrative studies, leading explorations into areas such as non-linear and interactive narratives. A contemporary timeline of media art can be found here.

Themes

In the book *New Media Art*, Mark Tribe and Reena Jana named several themes that contemporary new media art addresses, including computer art, collaboration, identity, appropriation, open sourcing, telepresence, surveillance, corporate parody, as well as intervention and hacktivism. (Tribe, Mark; Jana, Reena (2007-02-22).

Non-linearity can be seen as an important topic to new media art by artists like Bill Viola who explores the term as an approach to looking at varying forms of digital projects. This is a key concept since people acquired the notion that they were conditioned to view everything in a linear and clear-cut fashion. Now, art is stepping out of that form and allowing for people to build their own experiences with the piece.

People always ask, "What is the difference between non-linearity and randomness?"

Non-linearity describes a project that has freedom with certain parameters, whereas randomness has freedom and no boundaries whatsoever. Non-linear art usually requires the participation of an audience to reveal its non-linearity while random art, more-or-less, acts on its own. When looking at Public Secrets, one can see this piece as non-linear due to ideas stressed by people like Viola. In doing so, viewers can understand another theme in the many forms of new media art.

The inter-connectivity and interactivity of the internet, as well as the fight between corporate interests, governmental interests, and public interests that gave birth to the web today, fascinate and inspire a lot of current New Media Art.

Many new media art projects also work with themes like politics and social consciousness, allowing for social activism through the interactive nature of the media.

Some examples include Sharon Daniel's Public Secrets, a site that shows oppression and struggles behind the prison system in America; Applied Autonomy's Terminal Air, a site that demonstrates the practices of United States Central Intelligence Agency's extraordinary rendition program; Beyondmedia Education, a non-profit organization that collaborates with under-served women, youth, and communities to create and distribute media arts on social justice topics including gender violence and school safety; and Michael Mandiberg's The Oil Standard, a Firefox plugin that shows all prices of online products in the cost of barrels of crude oil.

Presentation & Preservation

As the technologies used to deliver works of new media art such as film, tapes, web browsers, software and operating systems become obsolete, New Media art faces serious issues around the challenge to preserve artwork beyond the time of its contemporary production. Currently, research projects into New media art preservation are underway to improve the preservation and documentation of the fragile media arts heritage.

Methods of preservation exist, including the translation of a work from an obsolete medium into a related new medium, the digital archiving of media, and the use of emulators to preserve work dependent on obsolete software or operating system environments.

NEW MEDIA ARTIST

A New Media artist may use the following media to create works of art: The Internet, computer hardware, computer software-servers, routers, personal computers, database applications, scripts and computer files. These artists use the aforementioned technologies in conjunction with video and computer games, surveillance cameras, wireless phones, hand-held computers, Apache Web server, Hypertext Markup Language and Global Positioning System devices (GPS). The Dada and Pop art movements greatly influence New Media artists and provide a foundation from which to borrow and reinvent conceptual and aesthetic ideas.

Examples and Influences

Pop art and Dada influence the conceptual and aesthetic roots of New Media art. (Tribe2007 p. 7) The photomontage and readymade occur multiple times throughout various New Media works.

In the genres of corporate parody and hacktivism, influences from Pop artists play a highly influential role for New Media artists. Claes Oldenburg designed in a collaborative effort the Second American Revolution monument for Yale's school of architecture in the 1960s. A caterpillar tractor of painted steel, aluminum, and fiberglass tip which subverts the warlike reference by casting a large tube of lipstick in place of a missile, in protest of the Vietnam war. both humor and critical approach were used to drive home a definitive anti-war statement and sentiment.

New Media artists approach differs in that the audience must interact and come to find their own conclusion. The message is straightforward but arriving there requires thought and investigation into the deeper message. An example of this is seen in CarnivorePE, a parody of FBI surveillance activity. CarnivorePE was designed by the Radical Software Group, founded by Alex Galloway in 2000 with a team of artists. What comes into question is the whether the use of technologically sophisticated devices on everyday citizens is reasonable, and what is the rationale behind the practice. CarnivorePE was in response to a digital wiretapping software called Carnivore which the FBI used to surveil internet traffic in the 1990s. Agents could listen into chat room conversations and emails. The software uses an open source tool called a packet sniffer to listen in on the network on which it was installed. This detects the packets of data that make up emails sent and received, text and images posted online and websites browsed by individuals on the network. The data harvested is then used to develop clients: which is raw material for artistic interfaces. These clients are produced by New Media artists who then used an animated Flash interface to create brightly hued translucent circles to represent each active user. Each is represented with a different color; deep green, for example, represents someone using AOL. The intent of these artists is to observe the utilitarian definition of surveillance, examine the use of it, and then to construct an artistic spectacle which demonstrates perhaps that wiretapping on ordinary citizens can be a spectacle in of itself. Software is then transformed into a colorful work of art with moving images and a powerful message.

Pop artists' main goal was to expose the power of commercial culture interestingly, while both embracing and parodying popular culture. In contrast to Pop art, New Media artists commonly employ a level of absurdity or purposeless.

Vuk Cosic, a Slovanian artist trained in archaeology, is among one of the pioneering New Media artists. He also coined the term *net art*. For his piece, he uses ASCII characters to construct images. It is not a new practice for artists prior to the 90s to construct images using this method, and these images can be made manually or by using software that converts images into ASCII characters. Cosic then incorporates the use of films and television programs to convert these images into animation with a retro-futuristic aesthetic..

History

Vera Molnar a pioneer in computer art used geometric and mathematical abstraction to aid her artistic expression. In 1968 she began working with a computer to create images with the aid of a computer and terminals like a plotter and a cathode-ray tube screen. Early works of computer art include *(Des)orders* (1969).

Manfred Mohr influenced by German philosopher Max Bense and French composer Pierre Barbaud, created hypercubes founded on a constructivist, algorithmic aesthetic. In 1969 he used a computer to superimpose multiple rules and found that this was the only way possible to superimpose multiple rules without losing track of the general concept. This strategy made the information become deeply buried and a certain participation is demanded from the viewer. Each work is based in a subset of a defined structure, ranging from cubes to 6-dimensional hypercubes.

NEW MEDIA CAUCUS

The New Media Caucus is a non-profit, international membership organization formed to advance the conceptual and artistic use of digital media, and it is an affiliated society of the College Art Association. The Caucus represents academics and artists whose media are expanding with developments in digital technology and artists working in newly emerging media such as robotics, virtual reality, interactive and installation environments as well as artists working in established digital areas of video, sound and graphics. By providing a forum for the critical review of new media practice, the Caucus increases the visibility and presence of new media practitioners. The Caucus has 450+ members, many of whom are based in North America. It organizes panels, exhibitions, forums, and maintains a peer-reviewed journal, *media-N*.

History

The New Media Caucus was founded in 2003 by Doreen Maloney, Associate Professor of New Media at the University of Kentucky. At the time, panels and exhibitions focusing on new media art were rare at academic conferences despite significant growth of the field in galleries, museums, and universities. Professor Maloney served as President of the New Media Caucus from 2003 – 2006 and was followed from 2006-2009 by Gwyan Rhabyt, Associate Professor of Multimedia at California State University, East Bay. The current president (2009 – 2012) is Paul Catanese, Assistant Professor of Interdisciplinary Arts at Columbia College Chicago.

Conferences

The New Media Caucus organizes discussion panels and exhibitions in association with each conference of the College Art Association. These have expanded to venues beyond the conference itself.

- At the 2010 CAA Conference in Chicago, in addition to one panel onsite at the conference hotel, the NMC organized three additional panels, two professional development roundtables and a unique 6-hour Live-Cinema performance hosted at Columbia College Chicago. Additionally, the NMC organized an artist colloquium/meet & greet event was hosted at the Illinois State Museum in Chicago.
- During the 2009 CAA Conference in Los Angeles, in addition to one panel onsite at the conference center, three panels and an exhibition were co-sponsored by the Southern California Institute of Architecture
- For the 2008 Conference in Dallas, four panels and an exhibition were held, largely in association with the Dallas Contemporary.
- In 2007, panels were hosted at the New York conference center and by the New School's Vera List Center for Art and Politics.
- In 2006, three panels were hosted at the Boston conference center, including one, *Asia Effects*, in association with the 6th Gwangju Bianniale 2006.

Another was offered at Art Interactive, a prominent Cambridge gallery, where there was also an exhibition, *New Media, New Work*.

- In 2005, the NMC hosted two panels as part of the CAA conference in Atlanta.

In addition to CAA related events, the New Media Caucus has also organized panels at SIGGRAPH and the International Symposium for Electronic Arts

NEW MEDIA STUDIES

New media studies is a fairly recent academic discipline that explores the intersections of computing, science, the humanities, and the visual and performing arts. Janet Murray, a prominent researcher in the discipline, describes this intersection as "a single new medium of representation, the digital medium, formed by the braided interplay of technical invention and cultural expression at the end of the 20th century...."

In a course on New Media Studies, students are exposed to ideas and insights on media from communication theorists, programmers, educators, and technologists. Among others, the work of Marshall McLuhan is viewed as one of the cornerstones of the study of media theory. McLuhan's slogan, "the medium is the message" (elaborated on his 1964 book, *Understanding Media: The Extensions of Man*), calls attention to the intrinsic effect of communications media.

A program in New Media Studies may incorporate lessons, classes, and topics within Communication, Journalism, Computer Science, Programming, Graphic Design, Web design, Human-computer interaction, Media theory, English, and other related fields.

9

Investigative and Political Journalism

INVESTIGATIVE JOURNALISM

Investigative journalism is a form of journalism in which reporters deeply investigate a single topic of interest, often involving crime, political corruption, or a scandal. An investigative journalist may spend months or years researching and preparing a report, which often takes the form of an exposé. Most investigative journalism is done by newspapers, wire services and freelance journalists. As part of an investigation, journalists make use of:

- surveillance techniques
- analysis of documents
- investigation of technical issues, including scrutiny of equipment and its performance
- research into social and legal issues
- studying sources: archives, phone records, address books, tax records and license records
- talking to neighbours or other parties
- using subscription research sources such as LexisNexis
- anonymous sources
- going undercover.

Investigations at times can take on the appearance of conspiracy theories. For example, Gary Webb's 1996 San Jose Mercury News expose linking the CIA to Nicaraguan contras organizing the distribution of cocaine into the United States led to its widespread condemnation by the mainstream media as "groundless speculation of government conspiracies". However today, journalists and researchers alike agree that the reporting was "neither false nor fantastic" and historical consensus is that the basic outline of the story was correct.

Professional Definitions

In *The Reporter's Handbook: An Investigator's Guide to Documents and Techniques*, Steve Weinberg defined investigative journalism as:

Reporting, through one's own initiative and work product, matters of importance to readers, viewers or listeners. In many cases, the subjects of the reporting wish the matters under scrutiny to remain undisclosed. There are currently university departments for teaching investigative journalism. Conferences are conducted presenting peer reviewed research into investigative journalism.

De Burgh (2000) states that: "An investigative journalist is a man or woman whose profession it is to discover the truth and to identify lapses from it in whatever media may be available. The act of doing this generally is called investigative journalism and is distinct from apparently similar work done by police, lawyers, auditors and regulatory bodies in that it is not limited as to target, not legally founded and closely connected to publicity."

TO CATCH A PREDATOR

To Catch a Predator is an American reality television show that features hidden camera investigations by the television news-magazine *Dateline NBC*. It focuses on identifying and detaining would be pedophiles, each of whom have made plans via internet chat to enter into relations with a minor. These men are lured to meet with the "minor"—who is actually a decoy—under the pretense of sexual contact. The investigations, many of which have been reported by self-assured *Dateline* correspondent Chris Hansen and producer Lynn Keller, are conducted as an undercover sting operation with the help of online watchdog group Perverted-Justice. Since the third installment, law enforcement and other officials have also been involved in the operation, leading to the arrests of most individuals caught in the sting. In an interview with NPR's Neal Conan on Talk of the Nation, Chris Hansen emphasizes that the subjects of his program should be labelled as sexual predators: "We don't label these guys as pedophiles. Pedophiles have a very specific definition, people who are interested in prepubescent sex. What we're talking about here are potential predators."

Several other NBC affiliates, such as WTMJ in Milwaukee (which was the first news media to conduct a sting operation in cooperation with Perverted-Justice) and Kansas City's KSHB have also done local versions of *To Catch a Predator*, as well as Scranton/Wilkes-Barre NBC affiliate WBRE. A spin-off called *To Catch a Con Man* was developed in early 2007 using similar methods in order to catch con men performing advance fee fraud scams. Further spin-offs have included *To Catch an ID Thief*, *To Catch a Car Thief*, and *To Catch an i-Jacker* (featuring iPod thieves). *To Catch a Car Thief* and *To Catch a Baby Broker* are the only spinoffs that do not include Chris Hansen, but Victoria Corderi instead.

Method

The method that was used to catch would-be sex offenders is derived from that normally used by Perverted-Justice. Perverted-Justice volunteers build profiles of clearly underage individuals on social networking websites, and enter chatrooms as decoys. They wait for an adult to message or email the decoy and begin a dialogue. If the conversation turns sexual in nature (the content in question preferably initiated by the adult), the decoy will not discourage this, nor outright encourage it. This also can help the Perverted-Justice team in collecting incriminating evidence against the alleged offender. Such evidence could include engaging in sexual conversations, sending the decoy pornography or child pornography, and committing other acts. The visitors are, eventually, subsequently led to believe that the supposed minor is home alone, and come inside the house in question seeking sexual activity from the decoy. Soon after meeting the decoy, they are confronted by Hansen when the decoy leaves the room.

Hansen attempts to interview each one at length about their intentions, whereupon the predators in question are free to make the choice to refuse to respond. Some exit the home immediately upon seeing Hansen, because they recognize that he is clearly not a teenager, or they have seen him in previous *Dateline* investigations. Hansen, without initially identifying himself, interviews the predators about their intentions, and also reads aloud some of the graphic portions of the chat to inform the predators that the logs were indeed recorded. Those who have not seen Hansen's *Dateline* investigations before often assume that he is either the child's father or a member of a law enforcement agency. After a few minutes of questioning, Hansen identifies himself as a *Dateline NBC* correspondent and informs the visitor that the entire interview has been recorded on hidden camera as part of the *Dateline NBC* story. Then, *Dateline* crew members with large cameras and microphones reveal themselves, and the predator is offered a chance to make a final statement before being asked to leave.

The first two investigations did not include law enforcement officers on site, and individuals caught in the sting were allowed to leave voluntarily, though *Dateline* would provide all video and transcripts to law enforcement and suspects would eventually be arrested. Arrests are sometimes made in a dramatic fashion by multiple officers who, with tasers drawn, ambush the suspect and command him to lie face-down on the ground before being handcuffed. In the Fort Myers investigation, a police officer in camouflage sometimes arrested the predators as they left the sting house. Tasers are sometimes shown being used to subdue fleeing or unresponsive individuals.

During interviews, suspects often claim not to have any idea how old the supposed minor is, even when confronted by Hansen with chat logs showing the decoy clearly identifying him or herself as a minor. In many jurisdictions, online solicitation with the belief that the other person is a minor is a crime, regardless of whether the other person actually is a minor.

Criticism

The series has been accused of making news rather than reporting news, blurring the line between being a news organization vs. an agency of law enforcement, and having its host impersonating a police officer.

Among the more prominent critics of the series has been Brian Montopoli of the CBS News Public Eye blog and formerly of the *Columbia Journalism Review*. Montopoli argues that although *Dateline NBC* leaves legal punishment up to police and prosecutors, broadcasting the suspects on national television, in the context of exposing criminal behaviour, is already a form of punishment which the media has no right to inflict. Montopoli also suggests that NBC News is more concerned about ratings than actually bringing online predators to justice:

But NBC is first and foremost a business, and the producers' motives are not simply altruistic. Perhaps I'm being cynical, but I find it telling that this program has been remade and rerun so often. You could argue that NBC is just making sure as many people as possible are aware predators are out there, but is it too much to think that a little thing called "ratings" might play a part as well?

In May 2007, a former executive producer for *Dateline* named Marsha Bartel filed a lawsuit against NBC and made assertions about *To Catch a Predator* that contradicted what the show purports to be about. She commented on the relationship the show has with the different police organizations and the group Perverted-Justice. The lawsuit was dismissed by the New York Supreme Court in October 2007, citing that NBC has the right to legally dismiss employees without notification. NBC commented on the dismissal: "We believed from the beginning that this case was without merit and we are pleased with the judge's decision."

Entrapment claims

Montopoli also suggests that *To Catch a Predator* may not be as immune from the defence of entrapment as the show claims. Although Perverted-Justice volunteers wait for the suspect to initiate contact, former *Dateline* anchor Stone Phillips concedes that "... in many cases, the decoy is the first to bring up the subject of sex." (Phillips defends this, saying that "... once the hook is baited, the fish jump and run with it like you wouldn't believe.") Montopoli contends that this alone may render *Predator*-related cases vulnerable to the defence of entrapment. This situation, however, may fail the "reasonable person" test of entrapment, as there is no persuasion or coercion involved, but simply an opportunity is offered. The March 2007 issue of *Law Enforcement* magazine, a publication of Officer.com, addressed the entrapment issue from a law enforcement perspective. "Though defendants raised the entrapment issue in Riverside, a judge's ruling later threw it out. The judge ruled it differs from a police officer presenting a handful of drugs to a subject and asking if he wants to buy some. In this scenario, the person's being invited to make a snap decision. In contrast, driving to a meeting location afforded these Internet offenders plenty of time to change their minds." The article continued:

"Even so, Perverted Justice plunks precautions in place to thwart the entrapment issue. Volunteers never initiate contact with the person; all communication begins with thc offender. Later, contributors never instigate lewd conversations or talks of sexual meetings. "

Charges Dropped

In June 2007, Perverted-Justice was criticized following a sting operation in Collin County, Texas, that resulted in the charges against 23 suspected online sex predators being dropped. Collin County Assistant District Attorney Greg Davis said the cases were dropped after Perverted-Justice failed to provide enough usable evidence.

Conflict of Interest

Beginning with the fourth investigation, *Dateline* began paying Perverted-Justice a consultant's fee to do its regular work; the fee was reported to have been over $100,000 for that operation. It was suggested that this payment created a potential conflict of interest for Perverted-Justice, an organization run largely on the efforts of volunteers, and furthermore, that for *Dateline* to pay this fee would be tantamount to paying news sources, widely frowned upon in the journalism industry. In their FAQ, Perverted-Justice defends this consulting fee, citing, among other things, the costs of keeping its website running and the fact that "... everyone except [themselves] and the predators are being compensated for this massive amount of effort."

This claim was also addressed by the March 2007 issue of

Law Enforcement Technology magazine. A judge also dismissed motions to throw out indictments against seven of the 18 men arrested in the Ohio sex sting. To date, 16 pled guilty and two were convicted at trial. Defence attorneys contended the sting violated state law because of *Dateline*'s involvement with Perverted-Justice and petitioned to have related videos, statements and photos suppressed. A judge ruled against the potential conflict of interest, noting department officials that had partnered with Perverted-Justice were unaware NBC had paid the organization for consultation services.

The department kept itself separate from *Dateline* staff during the sting as well, to avoid legal hassles later on, says Burns. Officials were positioned in a location near but not inside the house where offenders arrived for meetings. Communications and video equipment permitted authorities to keep tabs on what transpired, and all chats were transmitted directly to officials as they took place. "We didn't want to blur the line of ethics between law enforcement and the media," Burns explains. "We didn't even speak to Dateline officials during the operations."

The potential for conflict of interest was one of several concerns that lead to the non-prosecution of 23 cases in Collin County, Texas. District Attorney John Roach questioned circumstances of the May 2007 sting, "What is exactly the deal between the City of Murphy and NBC? What is the deal between NBC and Perverted Justice? Who's getting paid what? Who has an axe to grind?"

Investigative journalist Byron Harris explains, "John Roach knew the money issue would come up in court as part of the required disclosure of benefits received by possible witnesses."

Investigation by 20/20

On September 7, 2007, the ABC newsmagazine *20/20* aired an investigative report into the *To Catch a Predator* series by ABC News investigative reporter Brian Ross. The report critiqued certain aspects of the specials, and also investigated the controversy over the suicide of prosecutor Louis Conradt, Jr. In the report, two former police detectives with the Murphy, Texas Police Department, Sam Love and Walter Weiss, claimed that the decision to arrest Conradt at his home was made by

Chris Hansen, a charge NBC has denied. Both Love and Weiss claimed that the NBC News crew had every intention to confront Conradt, and the attorney for Conradt's family charged that *Dateline* chose to stop at nothing to get Conradt. Love and Weiss claimed that Conradt's death was shrugged off by many in Murphy's police force, and the two of them left the department in disgust.

Neither NBC News nor Perverted Justice cooperated with Ross' report. NBC News accused ABC News of using the *20/20* report as a hit-piece on the rival newsmagazine *Dateline NBC*. "I chalk this up to the usual network silly competitiveness, in a territory of a much more serious handling," NBC News president Steve Capus told *USA Today*. "The competitive wars [for ratings] right now are at a very high level...That's fuelling this." The allegations were denied by Ross, who is a former reporter of NBC News.

Investigations

Bethpage, Long Island (Outside New York City)

The first in the series aired in November 2004 as a *Dateline NBC* segment called *Dangerous Web*. The operation was set up in a home in Long Island, NY, to which 18 men came over two-and-a-half days after making an appointment for sex with a minor. One of the men in the investigation was a New York City firefighter, who was later fired by the FDNY.

Herndon, Fairfax County, Virginia (Suburban Washington, D.C.)

The sequel to the first story was an hour-long special airing in November 2005. The operation was located in Fairfax County, Virginia, in the suburbs of Washington, D.C., and saw 19 men arrive over three days. Among the men caught were David Kaye, a rabbi, and Steven Bennoff, an elementary school teacher, both of whom lost their jobs after taping.

Mira Loma, Riverside County, California (Outside Los Angeles)

The third installment of the series was a two hour special aired in February 2006. The operation was located in Riverside, California, and was the first done in cooperation with local law enforcement officials. During this sting, 50 men were arrested over three days and charged with felonies — so many that three arrived almost simultaneously, and law enforcement, at one point, ran out of personnel. One other person arrested was charged with a misdemeanor. The men arrested included a criminal investigator working for the Department of Homeland Security who was later fired and, for the first time, two men who claimed to have seen previous *Dateline* investigations of online sexual predators.

Greenville, Ohio

The fourth investigation aired in two one-hour-long parts during April and May 2006 as the first half of a month-long series of *To Catch a Predator* specials. The operation was based in Greenville, Ohio. The small-town location of the undercover house meant that potential predators from the larger surrounding cities of Indianapolis, Columbus, and Cincinnati had to drive upwards of an hour and a half to reach the operation. Among the men caught were one who had been slated to start a prison sentence for a different charge of solicitation in four days and a 6th grade school teacher who had also been chatting with an Indiana police officer posing as a teenage girl. Three Perverted-Justice members were temporarily deputized for the length of the operation. It was also the first *Dateline* investigation in which Perverted-Justice was paid a consulting fee. All arrests resulted in convictions.

Fort Myers, Florida

As with the Ohio investigation, the fifth investigation was aired in two one-hour-long parts in May 2006, forming the second half of the month-long series of *To Catch a Predator* specials. The operation was based in Fort Myers, Florida and saw 24 men arrested in three days. Among the more notable moments in the investigation was the arrest of a man who had brought along his five-year-old son to the house, creating a challenge for arresting officers as well as Hansen who did not want to traumatize the boy. Hansen told him immediately that he was on Dateline without attempting to interview him, and police had the difficult task of arresting the father and removing the child without exposing him to the arrest. One man, upon seeing Hansen, said that he knew that he was walking into a setup because of the way that the decoy was talking online, but came anyway. Another man had asked a decoy posing as a 14-year-old if she was willing to have oral sex with a cat and perform sex acts involving Cool Whip. She replied that she would do so on the condition that he would strip naked after entering the house. He did so and was immediately confronted by Hansen. He was the second featured predator to strip naked in the house to date. Another man arrived at almost 4am, but refused to enter the house, trying to talk the girl into getting in his car with him. After pleading with her for over 30 minutes, he gave up and walked to his car where he was arrested. Another man confessed that he was "guilty of whatever's there" (the transcript) and said that he should receive the death penalty. Another duped his sister into driving him to the sting house and waiting for him in the car while he intended to have sex with a 14-year-old girl. This segment resulted in 20 convictions.

On June 30, 2009, all the cases made it through the court system. 20 of the 24 men were convicted of using the internet to solicit a child for sex and some were also convicted of sending harmful material to a child, as some of them emailed pornographic pictures to the decoys. Because these are sex crimes, the 20 convicted men had to register as sex offenders for the rest of their lives. Most of them were also put on sex offender probation.

Fortson, Georgia

In August 2006, Perverted-Justice announced that the sheriff's department in Harris County, Georgia had arrested 20 men over four-and-a-half days in another sting operation. The investigation aired on *Dateline NBC* in two parts on September 13 and September 22, and showed a growing awareness of the television series among potential predators; *Dateline* itself was referenced by name several times. Notable arrests included a military staff sergeant who on his knees pleaded with Hansen "not to ruin my life", a devout Christian man whose MySpace page claimed "Jesus Rocks" and that God was his hero, and one man who had said that he had seen the show "about three times on TV already", and in another case a man who confessed that "he has interest in younger girls, It has just been a fantasy of mine" and also that the "cleanest best pleasure" would be to have sex with a 13-year-old girl. Several months later, that man was rearrested when he exposed himself to a young girl at a public pool.

Shortly after the first half of this investigation aired, the Georgia Governor's office announced a new Child Safety Initiative which would triple the number of special agents in the Georgia Bureau of Investigation dedicated to catching Internet predators and double the number of forensic computer specialists dedicated to helping prosecute computer crimes.

Petaluma, California (Outside San Francisco)

From August 25 to August 27, Like Perverted-Justice and *Dateline* worked with law enforcement in Petaluma, California to arrest 29 men in three days. One suspect was later released due to lack of evidence. The resulting investigation aired on *Dateline NBC* on September 29 and October 6. The confrontations took place in the backyard, the first time they were taped outdoors. All of the previous interviews took place in a kitchen or living room.

Petaluma was the hometown of kidnap and murder victim Polly Klaas, and was also a former home of John Mark Karr, who made a false confession to the murder of JonBenét Ramsey. The last segment of the Petaluma investigation focused in part on the Mark Foley scandal, which broke just days before the investigation went to air. Several political cartoons published in the wake of the scandal explicitly referenced *To Catch a Predator* by name.

Given the proximity of the sting house to Silicon Valley, the investigation saw several computer engineers arrested, one of whom declared to the police that he was a well-respected man in society with a Ph.D. in computer engineering. Among the more notable arrests was that of a medical doctor who was the vice-president of a major cancer research corporation. Another claimed to be an active-duty Marine Corps sniper who, in his chat, said: "I carry a gun everywhere I go". The individual was actually a member of the Marine Corps infantry, and not a sniper. Police intervened immediately before any confrontation with Hansen and found a shotgun in the individual's truck.

This segment resulted in 26 convictions.

Long Beach, California

In September 2006, Perverted-Justice and *Dateline* once again worked with law enforcement in California, this time in Long Beach, to arrest 38 men over three days. The Long Beach investigation featured a man who had previously been encountered in the Riverside operation nearly a year earlier, a post-production video editor for Nickelodeon, a software engineer who worked for the United States Department of Defence, and a man soliciting a decoy posing as an 11-year-old (*Dateline's* youngest fictitious age for a decoy to date). This installment also featured a man who met his decoy at a public park after refusing to meet her at the house. This man had brought the decoy an MP4 player to give her after they had sex and got pulled over for speeding on the way to the meeting. Some predators were ushered out through the back door when it appeared that another predator was on his way to the house, in order to avoid tipping off the next visitor. During some of the encounters in Long Beach, there appeared to be security breaches involving the decoy playing the part of the young teen: one predator was allowed to shake her hand and lean in to kiss her before Hansen walked in, and another was allowed to hug the decoy before being confronted by Hansen. Typically, the decoy is instructed not to have any physical contact with predators, and Hansen usually walks right in when they make a sudden move or request any physical contact such as a hug or a kiss. During this investigation, the presence of the *Dateline* sting operation in town was leaked online through a Craigslist internet posting. Nonetheless, 32 convictions resulted from this segment, which aired on January 30 and February 6, 2007.

Murphy, Texas

In November 2006, Perverted-Justice announced that another *To Catch a Predator* sting had been conducted with law enforcement in Murphy, Texas. There were 25 men who arrived at the filming location over four days, with law enforcement investigating additional suspects. The predators included a former church music director and a former police officer in his 60s. Most notably, these additional suspects, who conducted chats but did not arrive at the undercover house, included Kaufman County assistant district attorney Louis W.

Conradt Jr., who shot and killed himself on November 5, 2006 at his home when police attempted to serve him with a search warrant. An NBC camera crew was waiting outside the house to film the scene when the fatal shot was fired. His estate, managed by his sister Patricia Conradt, filed suit against Dateline for US$105 million The case was eventually settled out of court.

This sting was also notable because it prompted protests from local residents, who were opposed to law enforcement officials purposefully attracting sexual predators to their neighborhood. Others countered that these predators were already in the area (or close by) and that this sting revealed them to be sex offenders. This investigation aired on February 13 and February 20, 2007. Prior to the settlement of Patricia Conradt's lawsuit against NBC Universal Inc, acts from the aired 20 February 2007 episode of *To Catch A Predator* were intended to be introduced in civil court.

On June 1, 2007, all 23 cases brought up against those arrested on this installment of the show were declined to be prosecuted by the Collin County prosecutor's office due to insufficient evidence. The cases were not expected to be considered again. This marks the first segment in which local law enforcement has declined an invitation to prosecute suspects involved in the show. However, one of the cases was successfully prosecuted by the Harris County District Attorney's office after it was determined that one suspect was using computers in Harris County to communicate.

On September 5, 2007, *Dateline* aired the results of the forensic report on Conradt's computer. According to the report, Conradt's "CDs, laptop computers and cell phone all contained pornographic material — some included child pornography."

Flagler Beach, Florida

In December 2006, Perverted-Justice worked with the police department in Flagler Beach, Florida to arrest 21 men over four days, and the sting was filmed again by *Dateline*. Aware that potential predators might be reluctant to show up at a house primarily due to repeated *Dateline* investigations, the crew set up a second location at the beach directly across the street from the house. This second location was also rigged

the publishing of photos, creating what is called a photoblog. Photo sharing sites like Buzznet and Flickr have integrated the typical photo gallery service with photo sharing, blogging and syndication to create a new kind of social software.

Video

In January 2005 the first VloggerCon was held, catering for a new breed of bloggers, the video blogger. A vlog or videoblog is the use of video as a blog post.

Common Terms

Blogging, like any hobby, has developed something of a specialised vocabulary. The following is an attempt to explain a few of the more common phrases and words, including etymologies when not obvious.

Audio Blog

A blog where the posts consist mainly of voice recordings sent by mobile phone, sometimes with some short text message added for metadata purposes.

Blog Feed

The XML-based file in which the blog hosting software places a machine-readable version of the blog so that it may be "syndicated" for further distribution on the web. Formats such as RSS and Atom are used to structure the XML file.

Blogfoo

Statements written with an air of generality while obviously pointed at a specific person or group of people.

Blog Hopping

To follow links from one blog entry to another, with related side-trips to various articles, sites, discussion forums, and more.

Blogorrhoea

A portmanteau of "blog" and "logorrhoea", meaning excessive and/or incoherent talkativeness in a weblog.

Blogroll

A list of blogs. Usually a blogger features a list of his favorite blogs in the sidebar of his blog. These lists can be made dynamic using services like BlogRolling.

Blog Site

The web location (URL) of a blog, which may be either a dedicated domain, a sub-domain, or embedded within a web site.

Blogsite

Sometimes confused with a simple blog or blog site, but a blogsite is a web site which combines blog feeds from a variety of sources, as well as non-blog sources, and adds significant value over the raw blog feeds.

Blogsnob

A person who refuses to respond to comments on their blog from people outside their circle of friends.

Moblog

A portmanteau of "mobile" and "blog". A blog featuring posts sent mainly by mobile phone, using SMS or MMS messages. They are often photoblogs.

Permalink

Permanent link. The unique URL of a single post. Use this when you want to link to a post somewhere.

Ping

The alert in the Track Back system that notifies the original poster of a blog post when someone else writes an entry concerning the original post.

Track Back

A system that allows a blogger to see who has seen the original post and has written another entry concerning it. The system works by sending a 'ping' between the blogs, and therefore providing the alert.

We are entering a new age of information access and dissemination. Tools that make it easy to publish to the Internet have given millions of people the equivalent of a printing press on their desks, and increasingly, in their pockets. Unless we understand the difference between amateur reporting and personal publishing —and recognize weblogs as just one form these activities might take —we will not be able to fully understand the implications they have for culture, journalism, and society.

Let's start with the weblog —a frequently updated website, with posts arranged in reverse chronological order, so new entries are always on top. Early webloggers linked to selected news articles and webpages, usually with a concise description or comment. The creation of software that allowed users to quickly post entries into pre-designed templates led to an explosion of short-form diaries, but the reverse-chronological format has remained constant. It is this format that determines whether a webpage is a weblog.

Note that the form preceded the software. Easy-to-use software has fueled the fast adoption of the form, but weblogs may be created without it. The weblog is arguably the first form native to the Web. Its basic unit is the post, not the article or the page. Bloggers write as much or as little as they choose on a topic, and although entries are presented together on the page, each post is given a permalink, so that individual entries can be referenced separately.

Hypertext is fundamental to the practice of weblogging. When bloggers refer to material that exists online, they invariably link to it. Hypertext allows writers to summarize and contextualize complex stories with links out to numerous primary sources. Most importantly, the link provides a transparency that is impossible with paper. The link allows writers to directly reference any online resource, enabling readers to determine for themselves whether the writer has accurately represented or even understood the referenced piece. Bloggers who reference but do not link material that might, in its entirety, undermine their conclusions, are intellectually dishonest.

ARE WEBLOGS A FORM OF JOURNALISM?

The early claim 'weblogs are a new form of journalism' has been gradually revised to 'some weblogs are doing journalism, at least part of the time.' As even the enthusiasts now concede, weblogs used to record memories, plan weddings, or coordinate workgroups can't be classified as journalism by any definition. So in any discussion about weblogs and journalism, the first question to ask is: Which weblogs?

The four weblog types most frequently cited are:

- Those written by journalists.
- Those written by professionals about their industry.
- Those written by individuals at the scene of a major event.
- Those that link primarily to news about current events.

Weblogs maintained for respected news organizations will certainly qualify as journalism if they uphold the same standards as the entire organization. But some argue that independent sites maintained by journalists automatically constitute journalism, simply because their authors are journalists. A weblog written by a journalist does not necessarily qualify as journalism for the same reason a novel written by a journalist does not: it is the practice that defines the practitioner, not the other way around. The case of Jayson Blair, recently fired from 'The New York Times' for fabricating stories, illustrates that whatever the journalist's reputation or affiliation, journalism is characterized by strict adherence to accepted principles and standards, not by title or professional standing.

Some advocates of weblogs as journalism point to the weblogs produced by industry insiders as the future of trade journalism. They argue that, while reporters tend to rely on only a few sources even when reporting very complex stories, weblogs written by the people working in a field will naturally convey a more complete version of the news about their profession. But those with a stake in the public perception of an issue —as working professionals invariably have —are those we can rely upon least for an unbiased perspective. Their commentary, done with integrity, can be a great source of accurate information and nuanced, informed analysis, but it will never replace the journalist's mandate to assemble a fair, accurate, and complete story that can be understood by a general audience.

Personal accounts are more problematic: Is an eyewitness account journalism, and if so, when? Depending on the event? Depending on the inability of another individual to compile a more complete version of the story? Depending on the skill or training of the person writing the account? The standards used to determine when a personal recollection becomes a journalistic report are likely to vary from case to case. This leaves link-driven sites about current events. There are certainly similarities between the practices behind these weblogs and some of the activities required to produce a newspaper or news broadcast. Just as a newspaper editor chooses which wire stories to run, the weblog editor chooses which stories to link. But bloggers are never in a position to determine which events will be reported. And just as opinion columnists use news accounts as a springboard to present their interpretation of events, bloggers are usually very happy to tell you what they think of what they link.

But is this a New form of Journalism?

Frankly, no. I'm not practicing journalism when I link to a news article reported by someone else and state what I think —I've been doing something similar around the water cooler for years. I'm engaged in research, not journalism, when I search the Web for supplementary information in order to make a point. Reporters might do identical research while writing, but research alone does not qualify an activity as journalism. Bloggers may point to reader comments as sources of information about the items they post, but these are equivalent to letters to the editor, not reporting. Publishing unsubstantiated (and sometimes anonymous) emails from readers is not journalism, even when it's done by someone with journalistic credentials. Credible journalists make a point of speaking directly to witnesses and experts, an activity so rare among bloggers as to be, for all practical purposes, non-existent.

Instead of inflating the term 'journalism' to include everyone who writes anything about current events, I prefer the term 'participatory media' for the blogger's practice of actively highlighting and framing the news that is reported by journalists, a practice potentially as important as —but different from —journalism.

WEBLOGS AS PARTICIPATORY MEDIA

So, when I say weblogs and journalism are fundamentally different, one thing I mean is that the vast majority of weblogs do not provide original reporting —for me, the heart of all journalism. But Joan Connell, former executive producer for opinion and communities at MSNBC, has said that she believes weblogs are journalism only when they are edited. This will be poorly received by those journalists who have embraced the form for its freedom from professional standards and processes. Of course, bloggers unaffiliated with news organizations may state their opinions quite frankly, unworried about placating editors, offending advertisers, or poisoning relationships with sources, since they have none of these.

When bloggers do report the news, the form is usually incidental to the practice. When policy analyst David Steven decided to document the 2002 World Summit on Sustainable Development, he set up a weblog [The Daily Summit] so that he could easily post reports on each day's events. He attended news conferences. He interviewed conference speakers. He summarized the proceedings. But this was not a triumph of the weblog form. It was made possible by the free availability of easy-to-use publishing software. That the end-product was a weblog was irrelevant to Mr. Steven's purposes —and to those of his readers. For two weeks, Mr. Steven was on the front line, reporting, editing, and publishing news from the Summit. Journalism? I believe so, though Ms. Connell might disagree.

Perhaps the biggest reason millions of amateur writers produce weblogs is that the easiest-to-use Web publishing tools produce only that format. Blogs have become the default choice for personal Web publishing to such a degree that the two ideas have become conjoined. When commentators talk about weblogs as the future of journalism, they sometimes seem to mean 'personal publishing is the future of journalism', or 'amateur reporting is the future of journalism' —but neither of these need manifest in the weblog form.

Whether personal publishing and amateur reporting begin to appear in different forms will depend on the availability of tools that allow non-professionals to create and contribute to other kinds of publications. A Korean website called 'OhMyNews' employs more than 26,000 'citizen reporters' who submit articles on everything from birthday celebrations to political events. The publication is credited with helping to elect South Korean President Roh Moo-hyun, who granted his first postelection interview to the site. This is amateur reporting, but it is not blogging.

The wide adoption of weblogs as just the first wave of an age of online personal publishing. As weblog software evolves into content management software, look for a surge of other kinds of online publications, many of which will be updated periodically instead of continually. If these publications employ a weblog, it will be as an annotated table of contents rather than as the focus of the site. Amateur reporting will become more widespread, particularly with the proliferation of mobile devices that can upload photos and text. These devices will be pervasive, but little of this content will be widely seen, partly because there will be so much to pick through. Such content will be widely distributed only when it has the import of the Rodney King video.

Weblogs will be used in mainstream journalism, without question. But the vast majority of bloggers will continue to have a very different mandate from journalists. It is unrealistic to apply the standards of journalism to bloggers who rarely have the time or resources to actually report the news. In my book, The Weblog Handbook, I deliberately reject the journalistic standards of fairness and accuracy in favor of transparency as the touchstone for ethical blogging. As media participants, we are stronger and more valuable working outside mainstream media, rather than attempting to mirror the purposes of the institution we should seek to analyse and supplement.

11

Forms of Participatory Journalism

Online discussion groups are the oldest and still the most popular forms for participation. Discussion groups run the gamut from bulletin boards and forums to mailing lists and chat rooms. Participants might engage a discussion group to answer tech support questions, to trade stock-trading tips, to argue about a favourite sports team, to share experiences about a health care issue, or to join a collaborative work project.

Mailing lists, newsgroups, bulletin boards, and forums are methods of asynchronous communication, meaning that all participants do not have to be online at the same time to communicate. Sometimes this leads to more thoughtful contributions, because participants have more time to refine their responses. Chat rooms, on the other hand, are synchronous, where all participants must be online at the same time to communicate. This has the benefit of providing immediacy and can be used effectively for business services such as customer support. But for the most part, chat rooms are more like virtual cafes or hangouts, with live, unfiltered discussion.

Forum discussions are probably the most familiar discussion group form to the average Internet user. Forums are typically arranged into threads in which an initial message or post appears at the beginning of a discussion and responses are attached in a branching manner. When forums are viewed in threads, it's easy to recognize the branching of conversation that occurs, some of which might not be entirely related to the original post. Some forums permit the audience to sort messages by various means — popularity, date, ranking. Many forums are archived, turning them into a searchable knowledge base of community conversation. Here's a look at the strengths and weaknesses of various forms of online participation, together with a description of how they work.

Self-correcting process: In a discussion group, moderators police the content and actions of participants, sometimes removing and editing parts of the conversations that violate the standards of the community. These moderators are sometimes appointed by the community; in other cases they are appointed by the host or owner of the forums. However, in many discussion communities, the participants police each other, sharing their views of when particular behaviours or actions are inappropriate.

Strengths: Most discussion forms have a relatively low barrier to entry (just create an user account), with an especially low level of commitment. For example, a participant can engage a forum only once, or few times, and still have a meaningful experience.

Weaknesses: Sometimes forums are too open, easily garnering flip, reactive comments. Active, large forums can get noisy, with so many posts from so many members, it's hard to determine what information is meaningful or useful. In addition, some moderated forums require each post to be pre-approved before it appears online, slowing down and smothering the conversation. Many online media outlets have abandoned discussion forums in the past few years, citing legal problems as well as lack of sufficient staff to moderate and maintain forums. Ultimately, some media outlets think forums provide little value to the audience and to the bottom line (ROI). One barrier to effective advertising on these pages is the lack of content control by either the advertiser or publisher.

Examples

- Lawrence Journal World-Reader Reaction
- About.com-Voices of Hysterectomy Forum

User-generated Content

Many news sites provide a vehicle — through Web-based forms or email — designed to collect content from the audience and redistribute it. This vehicle can collect full-length articles, advice/tips, journals, reviews, calendar events, useful links, photos and more. The content is usually text-based, but increasingly we are seeing the contribution of audio, video and photographs. After submission, the content appears online with or without editorial review, depending on the nature of content and the host policy.

Ranking is another popular and easy way for the audience to participate. Examples include rating a story, a reporter and other users. Ranking systems typically provide the best benefit when a sufficient number of users have participated, for example, "4,202 readers give this movie 4 out of 5 stars." Internet users also provide content through feedback systems, such as polls or mini-forums attached to story pages.

Self-correcting process: Usually, audience submissions go to a traditional editor at the host site, undergo an editing or approval process, and then are posted to the Web. Ranking and feedback mechanisms, however, are typically posted live immediately. Communities often police the submissions, and strong agreement or disagreement with a submission may prompt members to submit their own comments. This commonly occurs with reviews of products, movies and restaurants.

Strengths: Like forums, audience submissions have a relatively low barrier to entry, with a low level of commitment. A participant can submit (usually on topics that meet a special interest) only once, or few times, and still have a meaningful experience. Those who post repeatedly may build up over time a reputation among their peers as an expert on the subject.

Weaknesses: The quality of user-generated content can be uneven, with participants who are not trained writers or fact-checkers. As a result, some content can require extensive editing. Generally, this type of content relies on the good will of the audience to not exploit the system. It's easy, in some cases, to skew polls and other feedback systems, by voting multiple times. Also, a low volume of participation can limit the value of feedback systems.

Weblogs

Among the newest forms of participatory journalism to gain popularity is the weblog. A weblog is a web page made up of usually short, frequently updated text blocks or entries that are arranged in reverse chronological order (most recent to oldest). The content and purpose of weblogs vary greatly, ranging from personal diary to journalistic community news to collaborative discussion groups in a corporate setting. Weblogs can provide links and commentary about content on other Web sites. They can be a form of "latest news" page. Or they can consist of project diaries, photos, poetry, mini-essays, project updates, even fiction. The quick, short posts on weblogs have been likened to "instant messages to the Web." On other weblogs, the content can be longer, such as excerpts from a research paper in progress, with the author seeking comment from peers.

Weblogs fall into the one-to-many (individual blogs) or many-to-many (group blogs) model of media, with some allowing no or little discussion by users and others generating robust reader responses. Either way, weblogs inevitably become part of what is now called the "blogosphere." This is the name given to the intercast of weblogs — the linking to and discussion of what others have written or linked to, in essence a distributed discussion. The blogosphere is facilitated by several technologies. First, it is supported by TrackBack — a mechanism that automatically finds other comments about a blog post on a weblog, and provides excerpts and links to the comments alongside the post. It's like having an editorial page of commentary on the Web, automatically generated to appear alongside a story.

Second, the blogosphere is fuelled by meta-sites such as Daypop, MIT's Blogdex, Technorati and others. Theses sites track what items weblogs are linking to and talking about — news stories, weblog posts, new products, whatever subject is catching their attention. Meta-sites provides a popularity ranking of the most linked-to items, and then indexes all links to those items. The blogosphere is also supported by a third technology, XML or RSS syndication. This allows weblogs to syndicate their content to anyone using a "news reader," a downloadable program that creates a peer-to-peer distribution model. With content so easily exchanged, it's easy to know what others in your peer group are talking about. Weblogs are a powerful draw in that they enable the individual participant to play multiple roles simultaneously – publisher, commentator, moderator, writer, documentarian. Weblogs have also proven to be effective collaborative communication tools. They help small groups (and in a few cases, large) communicate in a way that is simpler and easier to follow than email lists or discussion forums.

For example, a project team can collaboratively produce a weblog, where many individuals can post information (related Web site links, files, quotes, meeting notes or commentary) that might be useful or interesting to the group or to inform others outside the group. A collaborative weblog can help keep everyone in the loop, promoting cohesiveness in the group.

***Self-correcting process*:** Weblogs rely on audience feedback, through weblog commenting forms, email or remarks made on other weblogs, as a method of correction. Typically, webloggers are reliable about correcting their mistakes, and a great many frequently link to dissenting viewpoints on the Web.

***Strengths*:** Weblogs are easy to set up, operate and maintain. The technology is relatively inexpensive, sometimes even free. This allows just about anyone to simultaneously become a publisher, creator and distributor of content.

***Weaknesses*:** This type of publishing requires a higher level of commitment and time from the creator than other forms. Also, it is difficult for weblogs to attract readers, other than through word of mouth and weblog aggregation and search engines. Weblogs have also been judged as being too self-referential, with critics likening them more to the "Daily Me" than the "Daily We."

COLLABORATIVE PUBLISHING

The technology behind many online communities is open source and free. In addition, Web publishing tools and content management systems are becoming easier to install, deploy and manage. As a result, thousands of Web-based collaborative publishing communities have appeared in the past five years.

As open-source tools for forums, weblogs and content management systems (CMS) have evolved, they have begun to blur into each other. This has led to the development of groupware, Web-or desktop-based applications designed for the collaborative creation and distribution of news and information, file-sharing and communication. Weblogs are considered to be groupware, because they can be collaboratively created. But in this section, we are addressing systems that are somewhat more complex.

A collaborative publishing environment is designed to enable a group of participants (large or small) to play multiple roles: content creators, moderators, editors, advertisers and readers. While the environment may be owned by an individual creator or host organization, the goal of these systems is distributed ownership and deep involvement from its community of users. Forums, mailing lists and weblogs can be effective collaborative publishing environments. But what distinguishes this group from other forms is the self-correcting process and the rules that govern participation.

Forums use moderators and community feedback. Weblogs usually have a feedback feature or, more often, other weblogs link back and discuss posts. However, in complex collaborative publishing environments, the self-correcting processes are more akin to peer review, traditional editing oversight and meta-moderators, individuals who police moderators to make sure the conversation doesn't get skewed or diluted. The most well-known of these environments is Slashdot.org, which resembles a cross between a large-scale forum and a collaborative weblog. Slashdot is driven by a combination of editorial oversight by its owners, submissions by users, and moderation and meta-moderation by the community of users. The site attracts more than 10 million unique readers each month, with roughly a half million audience members (5 percent) participating by submitting articles, moderating, ranking and posting comments. The open-source technology behind Slashdot now runs thousands of similar communities on the Web.

Extending the Slashdot model in a different direction, Kuro5hin.org passed on editorial oversight to its members. Every story is written by a member and then submitted for peer review. Next, the story is edited, discussed and ranked before it even appears on the site. Finally, the audience reacts, comments and extends the story. The open-source technology that runs Kuro5hin, called Scoop, is a "collaborative media application" according to its creator, Rusty Foster. "It empowers your visitors to be the producers of the site, to contribute news and discussion, and to make sure the signal remains high."

One measure of the success of these two collaboration systems is that Google News includes Slashdot and Kuro5hin as two of the 4,500 sources for its news search index. A somewhat less-structured approach to collaborative publishing is the Wiki model. Wiki technology, depending on how its deployed, is used for writing, discussion, storage, email and collaboration. In this discussion, we will narrow our focus to collaborative examples, such as Wikipedia. Wikipedia is an international, open content, collaboratively developed encyclopedia. In just over two years, it has amassed more than 120,000 articles in English as well as more than 75,000 articles in other languages.

At first glance, a Wiki appears to be somewhat chaotic, allowing any member the ability to create public domain articles and edit just about any piece of text within the environment. The central component is that every change is tracked, and can be reviewed, challenged or restored — an omnipotent version history. As evidence to the ever-blurring lines of these forms, there are now experiments in Wiki-style weblogs. Another interesting example of a collaborative publishing is Zaplet technology, where discussion forums, polling and group decision-making tools are exchanged inside dynamic emails.

Among the most advanced and ambitious groupware desktop applications is Groove, created by Ray Ozzie, who also created one of the best-known collaboration tools, Lotus Notes. Groove is a peer-to-peer program that allows large or small groups to collaboratively write, surf, exchange files, chat, create forums and invite outsiders to participate. It even supports voice-over-IP communications.

Self-correcting process: Collaborative systems usually have a detailed workflow for built-in correction, such as Slashdot's system, where the audience ranks other audience members and their comments, moderators police discussions, and moderators are monitored by meta-moderators. In the case of Kuro5hin, the audience acts as editor before and after publishing.

Strengths: Participants can engage multiple roles, or earn the privilege of new roles. A greater level of involvement and ownership from the audience usually yields greater reward (better discussion and content) than in other forms.

Weaknesses: These systems are more difficult to launch and maintain than others, due to technical complexity. Depending on the number of participants in the environment, the speed at which membership grows, and how active the membership is in creating content, collaborative systems become increasingly unwieldy and complex to manage.

Peer-to-Peer

Peer-to-peer (P2P) describes applications in which people can use the Internet to communicate or share and distribute digital files with each other directly or through a mediating Web server.

P2P communication: Instant Messaging (IM) and Short Message Service (SMS) are the most pervasive forms of peer-to-peer communication. These forms constitute types of social media, where personal, informal conversation occurs in a "one-to-one" or "one-to-few" model.

While the content of IM and SMS is difficult to categorize or analyse, its appeal and usefulness as a communications medium is unquestionable. Surveys from the Pew Internet and American Life Project reveal that more than 50 million Americans (about 46 percent of all Internet users) have send instant messages, and about 7 million (11 percent) of all these users send instant messages daily. AOL, one of the most popular of instant messaging providers, transmits almost 1.4 billion instant messages each day.

SMS, short text messages that are sent between cell phones, is pervasive in Europe and Asia but hasn't yet gained traction in the United States due to the lack of support for a key industry technology (GSM). In the past decade, as American culture has embraced mobile technologies, instant messaging has become a powerful means of distributing news and information to computers, cell phones, pagers and PDAs. Now, everything from news headlines and stories, sports scores, stock quotes, airline flight schedules and eBay bids are regularly sent directly to mobile devices, through instant messages or SMS. In addition, parents keep in closer contact with their teen children through IM. Reuters explored the business prospects for instant messaging of news, sports and financial information with an ActiveBuddy tool. Audience members who added this intelligent news agent as a IM buddy could ask for news on demand based on keywords. In Hong Kong, the Chinese government sent a blanket of 6 million SMS messages to spread the word and avert panic about the outbreak of the SARS respiratory illness. As cell phones and mobile devices have integrated digital camera technology, instant messaging is now expanding outside of text communications to include still photography and video. This is already being used in a peer-to-peer fashion among friends or colleagues, but it is also being used as a vehicle to submit photography and video directly to a Web site or weblog. During worldwide protests against the war in Iraq, the BBCNews.com asked its readers to submit photos from their digital cameras and cell phones.

Microsoft's ThreeDegrees application is an interesting experiment in peer-to-peer communication. Participants form groups with this software to chat, share pictures and music to the group, without permanently sharing the files. Music and images are streamed to the group members on the fly.

***P2P Distribution*:** Peer-to-peer forms excel when it comes to the distribution and dissemination of digital files, which may carry valuable news and information. Instant messaging users can exchange digital files on the fly in the middle of a conversation. But the heart of P2P file sharing was born with Napster, the controversial desktop software program designed to enable participants to share any digital music file on their hard drives.

At its zenith, 70 million users were trading 2.7 billion files per month. Since Napster was shut down, other file-sharing programs (called Gnutella clients) such as Morpheus and Kazaa have stepped in, allowing billions of movies, songs, ebooks, software and other digital files to be exchanged among the masses.

From a participatory journalism perspective, P2P has enormous potential to distribute the content created by digital amateurs. One example is the recent emergence of P2P photo-sharing software programs. Such programs let you define a list of friends and mark photos that you want to share with your with cameras and microphones and had police hiding in a bunker below the deck. Some of the men arrested included a retired truck driver who claimed that he lied during his chat log about wanting to have sex with the underage girl because he is no longer able to achieve an erection, a Taekwondo instructor who masturbated on webcam for the decoy with whom he chatted, and a sheriff's deputy from Alabama who was arrested in a vehicle containing an arsenal of weapons. In one case, two potential predators arrived within five minutes of each other, resulting in Hansen conducting the first dual interview of predators who had each made separate appointments for sex. This investigation aired on February 27 and March 6, 2007, and resulted in 21 guilty pleas.

Ocean County, New Jersey

From March 28 to April 1, 2007, Perverted-Justice worked with the Ocean County Prosecutor's Office in Ocean County, New Jersey to arrest 28 men who showed up at *Dateline*'s undercover house. The arrests spanned several Northeast states, including Pennsylvania, New York, New Jersey, and Connecticut. The investigation was covered by *Dateline NBC* for a two-show edition of *To Catch a Predator* that aired on July 18 and July 25, 2007. As in the Flagler Beach investigation, a second meeting location was also set up at a nearby beach for those who were reluctant to show up at the sting house.

The female decoy assuming the role of the young teen was played by the 18-year-old daughter of the homeowner who rented out the beachfront house to *Dateline*. (It should be noted that this property is strictly used as a summer rental, and neither the decoy nor her father actually live in the home.) She was more interactive in speaking with the predators than in shows past, doing a pre-interview with featured predators before Hansen conducted the main interview. For the first time in the *TCAP* series, "Casey" gave an on-camera interview on what it is like to play a decoy.

Those arrested included a school bus driver, a court administrator, a senior web developer, a bodybuilder, a United States Air Force mechanic, a former firefighter, unemployed man from Staten Island, and a registered sex offender from Pennsylvania who once molested a young girl he had met online. As in previous episodes, most of the men denied an intent to have sex with the teen, yet brought gifts, condoms, and lubricants with them.

This installment of *To Catch A Predator* featured a man who became so ill while being interviewed by Chris Hansen that he passed out and crashed head-first into the bottom section of a counter. After being treated for his injuries, which were not serious, he was arrested. Another man seemed pleasantly surprised at meeting Hansen, shaking his hand before leaving, knowing that he would be arrested immediately afterward. In addition, a man caught in the sting mentioned on-air that he was a religious watcher of To Catch A Predator. He had heard Chris Hansen on the Opie and Anthony radio talk show. He went on to mention he was "really funny." Opie and Anthony commented about the incident on their show the next day.

Bowling Green, Kentucky

On October 22, 2007, the Warren County District Attorney's Office announced that 29 men were arrested in an internet child sex sting conducted by local police in conjunction with Perverted Justice and *Dateline NBC*. Footage of this sting operation aired in an installment of the *To Catch a Predator* series on December 28, 2007. This is the twelfth investigation covered by *Dateline* and host Chris Hansen since the series began in 2004. Perverted Justice partnered with the Kentucky Bureau of Investigation as well as the Attorney General's office in three separate sting operations in three cities in Kentucky, but *Dateline NBC* was only involved in the Bowling Green portion of the operation. The female decoy used by *Dateline* in this operation was the same decoy they had used in the New Jersey operation though her hairstyle was different in order to avoid the possibility of being recognized by one of the predators who had watched the New Jersey investigation. Only seven men showed up to the house during *Dateline*'s portion of the investigation, a sharp decline from previous *Dateline* investigations. One man arrested claimed to be a police officer in Indiana, although he was only a cadet and was fired before he graduated from the police academy. Kentucky police attempted to taser him when he ran, screaming, back into the house as police confronted him. Another arrestee was a man with cerebral palsy who walked with a cane and admitted to chatting inappropriately with underage girls before. All men arrested face 5-10 years in prison if convicted.

Cancellation

NBC News canceled production of future episodes in December 2008. The original episodes continue to air occasionally on MSNBC, which also shows a series called *Predator Raw: The Unseen Tapes* which feature Hansen in a studio providing his later reflections and extra information on the original encounters, as well as some additional footage related to production of the episodes that had not previously aired.

However, on July 8, 2009, Chris Hansen mentioned the possibility of *To Catch A Predator* returning on his Facebook status, stating that, "Right now we're focused on a number of other topics and once we get those stories done we'll circle around and take a look at some more Predator investigations."

Parody

South Park did a parody of the show by having Chris Hansen tell Eric Cartman to "Take a seat right there" numerous times. Despite his objections, Cartman is ultimately compelled to sit down and comments "how does he do that?"

The Insane Clown Posse have a song called "To Catch a Predator" on the album "Bang! Pow! Boom!" that use voice clips from the show.

There is also a flash movie parody of the show titled "To Catch a Super Predator", made by Chris Crazy House productions, in which various super heroes, such as Batman or Mario, are put on the show as would be predators.

SOME ORGANISATION RELATED TO INVESTIGATIVE JOURNALISM

Centre for Investigative Reporting (Bosnia-Herzegovina)

The Centre for Investigative Reporting (Centar istragivacko novinarstvo or CIN) is a non-profit investigative centre that writes about problems in BiH especially corruption and organized crime. It is based in Sarajevo but covers much of the Balkan region. Its stories appear in local media including, Vecernji list, Euro Blic, Dnevni Avaz, Start Magazin, and other publications. It also operates an online publication called "Izvor" or The Source and distributes an English language newsletter.

CIN was formed in 2004 under a grant by USAID and is funded by various government and non-profit sources as well as some commercial revenues. CIN stories use international standards for investigative reporting and it tries to avoid unnamed sources and other practices common in regional media. CIN stories are rigorously fact checked.

Its staff of 10 reporters have reported on corrupt energy traders, prime ministers who get almost free apartments, stolen privatizations, cigarette and drug smugglers, diploma mill universities and other corrupt practices. CIN's work has led to arrests, firings, investigations and even tailings.

One of CIN's better known stories looked at how then BiH Federation Prime Minister Nedzad Brankoviæ got an almost free apartment. CIN detailed each step of the process with records showing how the Prime Minister selected the apartment, the government bought it, moved it into an inventory of excess apartments and then allowed the Prime Minister to privatize it for nearly worthless privatization script—all in the matter of a few weeks.

CIN's work, which involved finding a second sources of documents that had been removed from the official records, led to two investigations of Brankovic and then an indictment by cantonal prosecutors. A citizens group plastered the town with graffiti and later billboards protesting Brankovic's windfall. He resigned in June 2009 after he lost power in his own political party.

The centre also was a founding member of the Organized Crime and Corruption Reporting Project (OCCRP), a regional consortium of investigative centres, journalists and news organizations who report on transnational organized crime.

Awards

CIN has won a number of awards including the 2007 Online Journalism Award for investigative reporting at a small website for its work on food safety. In 2007 it also won the BiH Transparency International award for journalism integrity. It won the Media Plaque for Excellence in Reporting in the 2007 Vecernji list awards.

CIN and its OCCRP partners along with SCOOP won the first Global Shining Light Award in 2006 for reporting under duress for its stories on energy traders. CIN, along with its partners in Romania, Bulgaria and Albania showed that while energy traders were getting sweatheart deals from the government and making tens of millions of dollars and adding very little to the economy, pensioners and the working poor were barely able to pay their energy bills and were often living in darkness. In 2009, CIN was part of a team led by the International Consortium of Investigative Reporters that won both the Overseas Press Club Award and the Tom Renner Award for crime reporting from Investigative Reporters and Editors for their work on tobacco smuggling.

CIN's OCCRP partners include the Centrul Roman Pentru Jurnalism Investigatie, the Bulgarian Investigative Journalism Centre, the Centar za istrazivacko novinarstvo-Serbia, Investigative Journalists of Armenia (HEQT) and others.

10

Weblogs and Journalism

A weblog, web log or simply a blog, is a web application which contains periodic time-stamped posts on a common webpage. These posts are often but not necessarily in reverse chronological order. Such a website would typically be accessible to any Internet user. "Weblog" is a portmanteau of "web" and "log". The term "blog" came into common use as a way of avoiding confusion with the term server log.

Blogs run from individual diaries to arms of political campaigns, media programs and corporations, and from the writing of one occasional author to the collaboration of a large community of writers. Many weblogs enable visitors to leave public comments, which can lead to a community of readers centered around the blog; others are *non-interactive*. The totality of weblogs or blog-related websites is usually called the blogosphere. When a large amount of activity, information and opinion erupts around a particular subject or controversy in the blogosphere, it is commonly called a blogstorm or blog swarm.

The format of weblogs varies, from simple bullet lists of hyperlinks, to article summaries with user-provided comments and ratings. Individual weblog entries are almost always date and time-stamped, with the newest post at the top of the page. Because links are so important to weblogs, most blogs have a way of archiving older entries and generating a static address for individual entries; this static link is referred to as a permalink. The latest headlines, with hyperlinks and summaries, are offered in weblogs in the RSS or Atom XML format to be read with a feed reader. A weblog is edited, organized and published often through a content management system or *CMS*.

HISTORY

Precursors

- Electronic communities existed before internetworking. For example the AP wire was, in effect, similar to a large chat room where there were "wire fights" and electronic conversations. Another pre-digital electronic community Amateur (or "ham") radio allowed individuals who set up their own broadcast equipment to communicate with others directly. Ham radio also had logs called "glogs" that were personal diaries made using wearable computers in the early 1980s.
- Before blogging became popular, digital communities took many forms, including Usenet, email lists and bulletin boards. In the 1990s Internet forum software, such as WebX, created running conversations with threads. Many of the terms from weblogging were created in these earlier media.
- Diarists kept journals on the internet: some called themselves escribitionists.

For example, "troll," a term for a person who disrupts a discussion by posting messages to trick other users into reacting in hostility or aggravation, dates back to Usenet. "Thread," in reference to consecutive messages on one specific topic of discussion, comes from email lists and Usenet as well, and "to post" from electronic bulletin boards, borrowing usage directly from their corkboard predecessors.

Blogging Begins

Blogging combined the personal web page with tools to make linking to other pages easier, specifically blogrolls and TrackBacks, as well as comments. This way, instead of a few people being in control of threads on a forum, or anyone able to start threads on a list, there was a moderating effect that was the personality of the weblog's owner.

The term "weblog" was coined by Jorn Barger in December

1997. The shorter version, "blog," was coined by Peter Merholz, who, in April or May of 1999, broke the word weblog into the phrase "we blog" in the sidebar of his weblog. This was interpreted as a short form of the noun and also as a verb, to blog, meaning "to edit one's weblog or a post to one's weblog." Usage spread during 1999, with the word being further popularized by the near-simultaneous arrival of the first hosted weblog tools: Evan Williams and Meg Hourihan's company Pyra Labs launched Blogger (which was purchased by Google in 2004) and Paul Kedrosky's GrokSoup. As of March 2003, the Oxford English Dictionary included the terms weblog, weblogging and weblogger in their dictionary.

One of the pioneers of the tools that make blogging more than merely websites that scroll is Dave Winer. One of his most important contributions was the creation of servers which weblogs would ping to show that they had updated. Blog reading utilities, such as Blogrolling, use the aggregated update data to show a user when their favorite blogs have new posts.

Blogging's Rise to Influence

After the September 11, 2001 attacks, many blogs which supported the U.S. "War On Terrorism" quickly gained readership among a public searching for information to understand that event; many new blogs in the same genre sprang up in this environment. By 2002, many of these were supporting the policy of an invasion of Iraq to remove Saddam Hussein from power (based on U.S. policy since 1998) and eliminate supposed stockpiles of WMDs. These "war bloggers" came primarily, though not exclusively, from the right side of the political spectrum, and included Instapundit. The term was later broadened to include all bloggers whose focus was the war in Iraq, which spread representation across the political spectrum. By the spring of 2003, *Forbes Magazine* used "war blogger" in this larger sense when listing the "best warblogs."

The first blog-driven controversy was probably the fall of Trent Lott, who had made apparently racist remarks at a party honoring Strom Thurmond. In the aftermath, bloggers such as Josh Marshall strove to demonstrate that his remarks were not an isolated misstatement, by finding evidence including quotes from other previous speeches of Lott's which were taken to be racist—their efforts kept the story "alive" in the press until a critical mass of disapproval forced Lott to resign his position as Senate Majority Leader.

By this point blogging was enough of a phenomenon that how-to manuals had begun to appear, primarily focusing on using the tools, or creating content. But the importance of a blog as a way of building an electronic community had also been written on, as had the potential for blogs as a means of publicizing other projects. Established schools of journalism began researching the blogging phenomenon, and noting the differences between current practice of journalism and blogging.

Since 2003, weblogs have gained increasing notice and coverage for their role in breaking, shaping or spinning news stories. One of the most significant events was the sudden emergence of an interest in the Iraq war, which saw both left-wing and right-wing bloggers taking measured and passionate points of view that did not reflect the traditional left-right divide. The blogs which gathered news on Iraq, both left and right, exploded in popularity, and *Forbes magazine* covered the phenomenon. The use of blogs by established politicians and political candidates—particularly Howard Dean and Wesley Clark—to express opinions on the war and other issues of the day, cemented their role as a news source. Meanwhile, the increasing number of experts who blogged, such as Daniel Drezner and J. Bradford DeLong, gave blogs a built-in source of in-depth analysis.

The Iraq war was the first "blog war" in another way: bloggers in Baghdad gained wider readership, and one (Salam Pax) published a book of his blog. Blogs also arose amongst soldiers serving in the Iraq war. Such milblogs have given readers a new perspective on the realities of war. Reading the thoughts of people who were "on the spot" provided a counterpoint, if not a counterweight, to official news sources. Blogs were often used to draw attention to obscure news sources, for example posting links to the traffic cameras in Madrid as a huge anti-terrorism demonstration filled the streets in the wake of the M11 attacks. Bloggers would often provide nearly instant commentary on televised events, which became a secondary meaning of the word "blogging," such as "I am blogging Rice's testimony," i.e., "I am posting my reactions to Rice's testimony to my blog as I watch it." By the end of 2003 top rated blogs Instapundit, Daily Kos and Atrios were receiving over 75,000 unique visitors per day.

BLOGGING GOES MAINSTREAM

In 2004, the role of blogs became increasingly mainstream, as political consultants, news services and candidates began using them as tools for outreach and opinion formation. Even politicians not actively involved in a campaign such as Tom Watson, a UK Labour Party MP, began to use blogging as a means for creating a bond with constituents and creating a channel for their ideas and opinions. Minnesota Public Radio broadcast a program by Christopher Lydon and Matt Stoller called "The Blogging of the President," which covered the transformation in politics that blogging seemed to presage. The *Columbia Journalism Review* began regular coverage of blogs and blogging. Anthologies of blog pieces began to reach print, and blogging personalities began appearing on radio and television. In the summer of that year both the Democratic and Republican National Conventions credentialed bloggers, and blogs became a standard part of the publicity arsenal, with mainstream programs, such as Chris Matthews' *Hardball*, forming their own blogs. Merriam-Webster's Dictionary declared "Blog" as the word of the year in 2004.

Blogs were some of the driving forces behind the "Rathergate" scandal involving Dan Rather of CBS and some memos used on the show *60 Minutes II*. Within 72 hours a coordinated group of bloggers had built a case that they were likely forgeries. The evidence presented eventually created such concern over the issue that CBS was forced to address the situation and make an apology for their inadequate reporting techniques. This is viewed by many bloggers as the point of blogs' acceptance by the mass media as a source of news. It also showed how blogs could keep the pressure on an established news source, forcing defenses and then a retraction of the original story.

Blogging is also used now to break consumer complaints and vulnerabilities of products, in the way that Usenet and email lists once were. One such example is the vulnerability of Kryptonite 2000 locks.

Bloggers have also moved over to other media. Atrios, Glenn Reynolds and Markos Moulitsas Zúniga appear on the radio, and Ana Marie Cox, better known as Wonkette, appears on television. Hugh Hewitt is an example of a media personality who has moved in the other direction, adding to his reach in "old media" by being an influential blogger.

In January of 2005, *Fortune* magazine listed Xeni Jardin, Ben Trott and Mena Trott, Jonathan Schwartz, Jason Goldman, Robert Scoble, and Jason Calacanis as 8 Bloggers that business people "could not ignore".

Blogging and Culture

Blogging however, was as much about technology as politics, and the proliferation of tools to run blogs and the communities around them connected blogging with the Open Source movement. Writers such as Larry Lessig and David Weinberger used their blogs to promote not just blogging in specific, but different social models in general. One of the running discussions within journalism and blogging is what "blogging" means for the way news "happens" and is covered. This leads to questions over intellectual property and the role of the mass media in society. Many bloggers differentiate themselves from the mainstream media, while others are members of that media working through a different channel.

Many bloggers have large agendas, and see blogging as part of Open Source Politics, or the ability of people to participate more directly in politics, helping to frame the debate. Whereas institutions see blogging as a means of "getting around the filter" and pushing message directly to the public.

CREATING AND PUBLISHING WEBLOGS

Since their introduction, a number of software packages have appeared to allow people to create their own weblog. Blog hosting sites and Web services to provide editing via the Web have proliferated. Common examples include GreatestJournal, Pitas, Blogger, Live Journal and Xanga.

Many more advanced bloggers prefer to generate their blogs by using server-side software tools such as Nucleus CMS, Movable Type, Blog, WordPress, evolution and Serendipity to publish on their own Web site or a third party site, or to host a group of blogs for a company or school. Such programs provide greater flexibility and power, but require more knowledge. If they provide a Web interface for editing, server-based systems make it easy for travelers to create and edit text; many travelers like to produce their travelblogs from Internet cafes while they travel around the globe.

In addition, some people program their own blogs from scratch by using PHP, CGI, or other server side software. While these are much more difficult to create, they add a maximum potential for creativity.

Two features which are common to blogging are "blogrolls" and "commenting" or "feedback." A blogroll is a list of other blogs that are linked separately from any article. This is one means by which a blogger creates a context for his blog, by listing other blogs that are similar to his/her own, or blogs the blogger thinks may be of relevance to users. It is also used as measure of the number of citations a blog has, and is used to rank "blog authority" in a manner similar to the way that Google uses hard coded HTML linking to create "page rank." Still another use of the "blogroll" is reciprocal linking: bloggers agree to link to each other, or link to another blog in hopes of getting a link in return.

Another central, and sometimes controversial, aspect of blogging is the use of a feedback comment systems. A comment system allows users to post their own comments on an article or "thread." Some blogs do not have comments, or have a closed commenting system which requires approval from those running the blog. For other bloggers, including several very prominent ones, comments are the crucial feature which distinguishes a "true" blog from other kinds of blogs. Commenting can either be built into the software, or added by using a service such as Halo Scan. If a blog has regular commenters, this is referred to as the blog's *community*.

Tools such as Ecto allow users to maintain their Web hosted blog without the need to be online while composing or editing posts. Enhancements to weblog technology continue to be developed, such as the Track Back feature introduced by Movable Type in 2002 and subsequently adopted by other software companies to enable automatic notification between websites of related content—such as a post on a particular topic or one which responds to a post on another blog. Blog has gone as far as implementing threaded track backs on comments, and comments on track backs. Blogs with features such as Track Back are credited with complicating search engine page ranking techniques. Integrating these into search engines has proven to be a challenge, and has been used to deliberately "push" page rankings. However, as one Google executive remarked, it is the search engine's job to find the ways that a website represents a "vote" for another website.

Web hosting companies and online publications also provide blog creation tools, such as Salon and America Online, which calls its subscriber blogs "journals."

TYPES OF WEBLOGS

Personal

Often, the word *blog* is used to describe an online diary or journal, such as Live Journal. The weblog format of an online diary makes it possible for users without much experience to create, format, and post entries with ease. People write their day-to-day experiences, complaints, poems, prose, illicit thoughts and more, often allowing others to contribute, fulfilling to a certain extent Tim Berners-Lee's original view of the World Wide Web as a collaborative medium. In 2001, mainstream awareness of online diaries began to increase dramatically.

Online diaries are integrated into the daily lives of many teenagers and college students, with communications between friends playing out over their blogs. Even fights may be posted in the diaries, with not-so-veiled insults of each other easily readable by all their friends, enemies, and complete strangers.

Thoughtful

Where a personal weblog is primarily concerned with daily life and events, and many topical weblogs focus on some technical topic, weblogs in the "thoughtful" category present an individual's (or a small group's) thoughts on whatever subject comes to hand; not necessarily the latest computer technology or the latest political scandal, but typically less contingent and more philosophical subjects. Thoughtful weblogs of course blur into personal weblogs on one side and topical or political ones on the other, but are distinct enough to constitute a category of their own.

Friend Blog

A Friend Blog is a distributed networked journal on the web, composed of short, frequently updated posts written by friends connected through their similar interests. The author allows his Friend Blog to connect to other FriendBlogs, belonging to friends and acquaintances, and by doing so, their posts also appears in his.

Topical

Topical blogs focus on a specific niche, often a technical one. An example is Google Blog, covering nothing but Google news. Another example is a soldier blog. Many blogs now allow categories, which means a general blog can be reshuffled to become a topical blog at the user's need.

News

Many weblogs provide a news digest on a certain topic e.g. "Internet in China" or Baseball, with short abstracts/summaries and links to interesting articles in the press.

Collaborative

Many weblogs are written by more than one person about a specific topic. Collaborative weblogs can be open to everyone or limited to a group of people. Meta Filter is an example of this type of weblog. Slashdot, whose status as a blog has been debated, nevertheless has a team of editors who approve and post links to technology news stories throughout the day. Although Slashdot does not refer to itself as a weblog, it shares some characteristics with weblogs.

A new form of blog involves cooperation between bloggers and traditional media sources, allowing for topics discussed on the air to find legs on the Web, and vice-versa. The first and most prominent example of this form is Lone Star Times, which is affiliated with Houston talk-radio station KSEV.

Political

Another common kind of blog is a political blog. Often an individual will link to articles from news web sites and post their own comments as well. Many of these blogs comment on whatever interests the author. Some of them are more specialized. One subspecies is the watch blog, a blog which sets out to criticize what the author considers systematic errors or bias in an online newspaper or news site — or perhaps even by a more popular blogger.

Political blogs attracted attention because of their use by two political candidates in 2003: Howard Dean and Wesley Clark. Both gained political buzz on the internet, and particularly among bloggers, before they were taken seriously by the establishment media as candidates. Joe Trippi, Dean's campaign manager, made the internet a particular focus of the campaign. Both candidates stumbled in the end, but were, at one time or another, thought of as front runners for the Democratic Nomination. In 2004, the Democrats took political blogging a major step forward by creating Blog Swarm to coordinate the hypertext links of progressive blogs. This allowed one blog to drive traffic by harnessing the power of a full blog array.

Legal

Blogs that discuss law and legal affairs are often referred to as blawgs.

Directory

Directory weblogs are useful for web-surfers because they often collect numerous web sites with interesting content in an easy to use and constantly updated format. News-related weblogs can fall into this category or the previous one (political blogs).

Corporate

Increasingly, employees of corporations are posting official or semi-official blogs about their work. The employers however, do not always appreciate the endeavor. In January 2005 Joe Gordon was fired from Waterstone's bookshop in Edinburgh, Scotland, because he referred to his boss as an "as shole in sandals." In 2004 Ellen Simonetti, a Delta Air Lines flight attendant, was fired for posing in uniform on her blog. Perhaps the most famous case of all occurred when "Troutgirl" Joyce Park was fired from Friendster because she discussed the rationale behind the website's technology conversion from J2EE to PHP on her blog. Other employers have reacted differently. For instance, when Power Line bloggers were attacked by a Minneapolis Star Tribune columnist, one of the bloggers' employers came to his defence.

With the rise in popularity of blogs in 2004 senior management caught on to the trend and by January 2005 several types of organizations, including universities, had started using blogs to communicate with their stakeholders. Many believe this corporate takeover of a tool that was used primarily by Internet enthusiasts will lead to a decrease in the popularity of the medium. Others believe that the use of blogs by organizations will add new voices and vitality to the medium. At any rate, there is little evidence that the growth rate of the blogosphere has slowed. In 2005 the Electronic Frontier Foundation (EFF) published a guide to blog anonymously and safely about work or anything else.

Advice

Many weblogs provide expert advice, such as Microsoft technical knowledge or fiction publishing for women.

Formats

Some weblogs specialise in particular forms of presentation, such as images, or videos, or on a particular theme, and acronyms have been developed for some of these, such as moblogs.

Audio

One of the types of blog that has undergone rapid expansion since the year 2000 is the MP3 blog, which make audio files available to the user. MP3 blogs are normally targeted at highly specialized musical genres, such as late 60s soul music or early 90s hip-hop or even the latest stuff in electronic dance music genres like grime. However, personal audioblogs are also on the rise.

Photography

The increasing ubiquity of digital cameras and broadband connections has made it ever easier to post and share photos on the web. Bloggers have adapted their software to facilitate

them. The program watches for your friends to log on and then automatically makes the images available for downloading or real-time viewing.

***Self-correcting process*:** Peer-to-peer file sharing doesn't necessarily need correction, but ranking and filtering mechanisms can increase the signal-to-noise ratio. Peer-to-peer communication such as instant messaging doesn't need correction either, any more than a conversation with a friend would. However, chat rooms sometimes benefit from moderation.

***Strengths*:** Synchronous communication is a powerful vehicle for immediate news and information. SMS has the advantage of being both synchronous and asynchronous, because if a participant isn't online, the message is stored for later retrieval.

***Weaknesses*:** Instant messaging requires participants to be online in order to communicate. The lack of interoperability between software programs, conflicting messaging standards and closed devices are sources of continual frustration, creating islands of users who are unable communicate with others. For example, an AOL instant messaging user cannot communicate with an MSN user.

XML Syndication

The content on many of these forms, especially blogs and collaborative systems, can be syndicated through the use of an XML specification called RSS, Rich Site Summary. An RSS file typically contains a list of headlines, summaries and links recently published by a given site. Using news reader applications such as NewzCrawler, AmphetaDesk or NetNewsWire, Web readers can browse these RSS files, sorting through large amounts of news content at a rapid rate. When a reader finds an item of interest, she clicks on the headline and it takes her to the story on the source's site.

RSS syndication seems to be making an impact in several ways. Content creators, from mainstream media to the average blogger, can easily syndicate their content to RSS reader applications, creating a peer-to-peer distribution model. In many cases, the user doesn't have to do a thing. "It's all part of the democratization effect of the Web," says entrepreneur Dave Winer, who incorporated an early version of RSS in Userland blogging software in 1999. "It puts bloggers on the same field as the big news corporations, and that's great."

News readers can be trained to go out and refresh content based on a time schedule. This allows readers to be up to date without having to search for recent news on their own. "Most people, once they start using RSS to check the news, just don't go back (to surfing Web pages)," says Tim Bray, co-editor of the World Wide Web Consortium's XML specification. "The amount of time and irritation saved is totally, completely addictive."

According to columnist J.D. Lasica, this virtue can motivate users into an immediate online dialogue, whether through e-mails, discussion boards or blog entries. "Interactivity is much more vibrant when the news is fresh." "News readers help to build community," adds Matthew Gifford, a Web developer in Bloomingdale, Ill. "You can see the ebb and flow of ideas around the network much better now." The XML structure of RSS feeds also allows other sites to easily integrate a headline and summary feed into other products, redistributing content in a viral fashion.

Open vs. Closed

The scale of these forms, the technology behind them and type of participation that occurs varies greatly. However, the nature of participation can be affected by one additional key factor that should be considered: Is the environment public or private? We have identified four categories of openness that these forms usually fall within:

1. *Open Communal*: While there typically is a single host, facilitator or architect of the community, almost all activity within it — membership, editing, filtering, moderation, content contribution, etc. — is managed and governed by the community it serves.
2. *Open Exclusive*: A group of privileged members, usually the owners of the site, is allowed to post primary content to the site, while the audience creates secondary content through commentary. This is typical of weblogs. Sometimes exclusivity can be assigned to audience members. For example, MetaFilter limits the number of new members that can join each day.

3. *Closed*: Only a group of privileged members can read, post, edit and comment on content. The system, which can take the form of a weblog or forum, exists in a private Web environment, such as a company intranet. Instant messaging and email are private, and thus closed.
4. *Partially Closed*: In this case, some portion of the information created by a closed community is exposed to a public Web space.

Function of Participation

This section attempts to categorize participatory journalism by the function the audience serves.

Commentary

The most pervasive, and perhaps fundamental, level of participation is commentary. During the past three decades, forums, newsgroups, chat rooms and instant messaging have enabled online discussion on just about any subject of interest imaginable. Summing up the ubiquity and popularity of this activity, a Pew Research report noted that in the days following the Sept. 11 attacks, nearly one-third of all American Internet users "read or posted material in chat rooms, bulletin boards or online forums."

In the past five years, weblogs have increased the signal of this activity, with some advocating the blog form as the next generation of newspaper op/ed page. "Though webloggers do actual reporting from time to time, most of what they bring to the table is opinion and analysis — punditry," says Glenn Reynolds, a law professor at the University of Tennessee and author of the popular weblog InstaPundit.

Filtering and Editing

With the flood of information available, as well as competing demands of media attention, the door has opened for alternative forms of editing — filtering, sorting, ranking and linking. This process is akin to "editing" in the sense of editorial judgment and selection. The online participants "guide and direct" their community, large or small, to valued news and information.

Filtering and ranking can be based on explicit singular or

collective participation. For example, Gizmodo, "the Gadgets Weblog," is a well-edited, "best-of" list of links to news and information about cutting-edge consumer electronics. Gizmodo is produced by one person. The search engine Daypop, also run by one person, has a collection of the Top 40 most linked-to news and information Web pages within the blogging community.

Many news sites, such as MSNBC.com and CNN.com, employ a similar "Most Read Top 10," where all site visitors' choices are accumulated into a popularity ranking. Other interesting examples of filtering systems include Google's Page Rank algorithms, Yahoo's Buzz — based on popular searches — and The New York Times' "most e-mailed stories."

Filtering, however, doesn't have to come from explicit activities, such as linking or favourite lists. It can also have implicit origins, such as Amazon's well-known "People who bought this item also bought..." feature. This is an example of collaborative filtering, in which Amazon uses information about previous sales and browsing to suggest potentially relevant products to returning customers.

Fact-Checking

In discussion forums and weblogs, the act of verification is a frequent activity. The initial post in either form begins with a link to a story, followed by a statement questioning the validity of certain facts. What ensues is a community effort to uncover the truth. Sometimes journalists enter the fray in an effort to uncover the truth in traditional media. One example of this occurred when the Slashdot community and an Associated Press reporter uncovered a fraudulent ad campaign by Microsoft.

"This is tomorrow's journalism," says blogger and journalist Dan Gillmor, "a partnership of sorts between professionals and the legions of gifted amateurs out there who can help us — all of us — figure things out. It's a positive development, and we're still figuring out how it works."

Grassroots Reporting

Taking the form of eyewitness or first-hand accounts, Internet users are participating in the fact-gathering and reporting process, sometimes even conveying breaking news.

Weblogs and forums brought compelling first-hand accounts and photography to the events of September 11. The terrorist attacks were the watershed event for grassroots reporting in weblogs, says John Hiler, co-founder of WebCrimson, a software consulting firm based in Manhattan, and Xanga.com, one of the largest weblog community sites. "Eyewitness reporting comes in large part from people's desire to share their stories and publish the truth. These are key features in blog-based grassroots reporting, and a big reason that weblogs have exploded in popularity since September 11th."

"There are so many post 9-11 weblogs that they've gotten their own name: warblogs," Hiler says. Warblogs continue to dissect and analyse the news from the war on terrorism. The scope of blog journalism has expanded to other areas of interest. "[A]lternative internet sources are gaining a reputation for breaking important news stories more quickly than traditional media sources," says Chris Sherman, associate editor of SearchEngineWatch.com. "For example, The New York Times reported that the first hint of problems that doomed the space shuttle Columbia appeared on an online discussion eleven minutes before the Associated Press issued its first wire-service alert."

Fact-gathering and grassroots reporting also come from professional or amateur subject matter experts who publish a weblog or participate in a collaborative community, such as Slashdot. These participants tend to produce a wealth of original content as well as opinion, links and original databases of resources on their expertise. This is particularly successful on a subject or theme that is not covered well by mainstream media.

An excellent example of such niche amateurs is the Web site Digital Photography Review. This news and reviews site is written and produced by UK photography consultant Phil Askey and his wife Joanna. The nearly 4-year-old site features a weblog on digital photography news, plus in-depth equipment reviews and original coverage of trade shows. It also has a active discussion forum. From its modest beginnings in late 1998, it now attracts almost 7 million unique visitors and 40 million page views each month.

Annotative Reporting

Another way to characterize the fact-checking, grassroots reporting and commentary in weblogs and related forms is to view the activity as an extension of traditional reportage. Adding to, or supplementing, the information in a given story is the goal of many participants who believe that a particular point of view, angle or piece of information is missing from coverage in the mainstream media.

Reporters have also used participatory forms on the web to annotate themselves, calling it "transparent journalism," by publishing the complete text of their interviews on their weblogs. For example, Online Journalism Review's senior editor J.D. Lasica sometimes uses his weblog to print the complete text of interviews he conducts for an OJR article. Lasica explains why he did this earlier this year on a story about RSS syndication, "I'm posting the comments of my interview subjects here, since I had so little room to include them in my column. I suspect most journalists don't do this because (a) it's a hell of a lot of work, and (b) it could call into question the decision-making process on which quotes the writer selected for his or her story."

When taking the role of a source, Lasica also posts transcripts of when he's been interviewed by media outlets about subjects like the state of online news media. This could have tremendous impact if sources such as politicians, celebrities, athletes and others begin to post transcripts of interviews by the media.

Open-Source Reporting and Peer Review

Some media are allowing their readers to evaluate and react to content online before its official publication in the traditional product. Journalism researcher Mark Deuze suggests that this type of journalism, similar to a peer review process, is best suited to "specialized niche markets" whose audience has comparably specialized interests and needs. Considering the fluidity and connectivity of the Internet, it is within reason to suggest that a community of interested peers could quickly be assembled on any given subject.

The most frequently documented case of open-source journalism, is the story of Slashdot and Jane's Intelligence

Review. Dan Gillmor recounts what happened: "In 1999, Jane's Intelligence Review, the journal widely followed in national security circles, wondered whether it was on the right track with an article about computer security and cyberterrorism. The editors went straight to some experts — the denizens of Slashdot, a tech-oriented Web site — and published a draft. In hundreds of postings on the site's message system, the technically adept members of that community promptly tore apart the draft and gave, often in colourful language, a variety of perspectives and suggestions. Jane's went back to the drawing board, and rewrote the article from scratch. The community had helped create something, and Jane's gratefully noted the contribution in the article it ultimately published."

Audio/Video Broadcasting

While not nearly as widespread due to cost barriers and technological know-how, the Web has empowered the audience to the play the role of audio or video broadcaster. Internet radio and television stations use streaming servers or straight file downloads to deliver content. These bandwidth-intensive sites can be expensive to operate and require donations or some type of revenue stream to survive. Yet thousands of these sites continue to thrive, like many audience-driven sites, by providing alternative/niche content.

As broadband adoption increases, creation tools get cheaper and more simple, and the entertainment centre of the home (TV) gets connected to the Web, we should see a significant proliferation of audio and video content created and distributed by the audience.

Buying, Selling and Advertising

The egalitarian ethos driving participatory journalism is not restricted merely to the dissemination of news and information but also encompasses commerce and advertising. "The web has created an unprecedented opportunity for consumers to openly discuss the products that fill their lives," says Derek Powazek in his book Design for Community. "From email to web sites to Usenet, there are millions of conversations on anything and everything you can buy, rent, or do."

Commerce communities began to develop in the mid-'90s

with sites such as Amazon, which include reviews by users on its product pages. Sites like Edmunds.com provide discussion and advice about purchasing cars. The participation in commerce communities includes commentary, grassroots reporting and fact-checking. At the same time, in the mid-'90s, consumer to consumer (C2C) environments began to establish the notion of the audience owning all aspects of the business chain — buying and selling to each other. Examples range from the monolithic auction site eBay, with more than 12 million items for sale, to the intimate, down-to-earth classifieds of craigslist.org.

Easy-to-use systems such as PayPal, Amazon zShops and Yahoo Stores enable any Internet user to put up a storefront in a few hours. Affiliate programs, like those set up by Amazon, allow anyone to share in the profits when an item sells. Donation engines, like Amazon's Honour System, enable small-scale publishers like webloggers to collect an income ranging from the modest to respectable. During a one-week pledge drive in December 2002, weblogger and New Republic senior editor Andrew Sullivan generated $79,020 in donations from 3,339 of his weblog readers.

In the past few years, following the lead of Google and collaborative weblogs such as MetaFilter and Kuro5hin, we have begun to see the proliferation of text-based advertising. Depending on how the system is designed and priced, audience members can compete with large companies for the same ad space.

Kuro5shin's community text ads offers a key twist — any community member can publicly comment on an advertisement.

"The idea behind ad comments is twofold," explains Foster, Kuro5hin's founder. "For the advertiser, the benefit is that potential customers can meet you on 'neutral ground,' ask questions and get more information in a place they're already comfortable. And for the users, the benefit is that they can see what others have said abut the product, whether it's good or bad, and how the advertiser has dealt with other people."

Knowledge Management

Some people are taking weblogs and using them as a tool for personal and corporate knowledge management, in what's become known as "klogging." Weblogs have proven to be a great enabler of knowledge collecting and sharing. A strong emphasis on hypertext linking, simple content publishing and syndication helps creators amass a searchable and distributable knowledge base related to personal interests, academic research or the workplace.

Weblogging also encourages interaction and refinement of ideas, enabling a group of peers to add to the knowledge through feedback or comment. Group weblogging has become an effective tool for knowledge management in the workplace. The authors of We Blog: Publishing Online with Weblogs explain one scenario of how weblogs build and capture knowledge: "By integrating the weblog publishing process into how inter-office communication happens, it becomes possible for weblogs to function simultaneously as informal knowledge management systems. An e-mail exchange between two technical support reps outlining a fix to a common problem can be copied to the department weblog. Now that fix, that knowledge, is stored in a centralized location, and is available to everyone else in the group."

THE RULES OF PARTICIPATION

The abundance and proliferation of virtual communities and collaboration environments provide the opportunity for anyone to play just about any role in the journalistic process. The audience has taken on the roles of publisher, broadcaster, editor, content creator, commentator, documentarian, knowledge manager (librarian), journaler and advertiser (buyer and seller).

For media organizations and businesses to understand how to engage their empowered audience, we must consider what motivates the audience to take on their new roles and what kinds of rules yield the most fruitful participation. Finally, we look at reputation systems and the balance of trust that's struck between buyers and sellers or content creators and their online peers.

Why we Participate

Through these emerging electronic communities, the Web has enabled its users to create, increase or renew their social capital. These communities are not merely trading grounds for information but a powerful extension of our social networks.

And as in any social system, looking at our motivations helps us understand and trust the system as well as find our place in it.

The Hierarchy of Needs was the brainchild of Abraham Maslow, one of the founding fathers of humanistic psychology. He believed that people are motivated by the urge to satisfy needs ranging from basic survival to self-fulfilment, and that they don't fill the higher-level needs until the lower-level ones are satisfied.

In her book Community Building on the Web, online community expert Amy Jo Kim mapped Maslow's offline needs to online community equivalents. Viewed in this context, we can assume that people are motivated to participate in order to achieve a sense of belonging to a group; to build self-esteem through contributions and to garner recognition for contributing; and to develop new skills and opportunities for ego building and self-actualization.

Through our interviews and research on participatory journalism, we have compiled a list of reasons why audience members are becoming participants. While reading this list, consider that an individual may be motivated by multiple reasons.

To gain Status or Build Reputation in a Given Community

Social recognition is one of the biggest motivators, intoxicating participants with instant gratification and approval. This ego-driven motivation to enhance social capital is best captured by the advice Web sites and review engines rampant in the late 1990s, which enabled anyone to showcase his or her expertise and recommendations on just about any subject imaginable.

"People with expertise contributed answers, tidbits, essays, pages of software code, lore of astonishing variety," Howard Rheingold writes in Smart Mobs. "A few contributors earned the kind of currency banks accept. Most contributed for the social recognition that came with being a top-ranked reviewer. The 'reputation managers' that enabled users and other recommenders to rate each other made possible opinion markets that traded almost entirely on ego gratification." For some, the ego-driven surface of this motivation is more practical underneath — people want to establish themselves as an authority on a subject. For example, one the primary reasons people write a blog is that they aspire to become "legitimate" writers in mainstream media. The weblog becomes a place to hone their craft and showcase their skills.

In general, this is viewed as a benefit to the individual. Small business proprietors, consultants and budding writers can quickly gain an audience and build a positive reputation that they can parlay into real-world business opportunities. But organizations can benefit as well because individual reputation can be transferred to some extent. For example, if a reporter begins to gain an involved audience through a weblog, that good will and trust could be transferred to the media organization that he or she works for.

These new forms also allow people who haven't had a voice — because of educational, economic, social or cultural barriers — to enter the dialogue by building a personal reputation. Online communities have also empowered those with physical or emotional impediments to blossom in a virtual space.

To create connections with others who have similar interests, online and off. An oft-read claim is that the majority of the billions of Web pages on the Internet today are junk. The trouble with this criticism is that the wheat — the relevant 2 percent — is different for every person. What many dismiss as "junk" is made by junkies – people who are fanatical or passionate about a subject. People want to feed their obsessions and share them with like-minded individuals. This is what fuels, in large part, many social connections on the Internet. Whether it's a fan page for '50s and '60s jazz pianist and vocalist Buddy Greco, or a database of airfoils used in the wing design of aircraft, people are using online communities to share passions, beliefs, hobbies and lifestyles.

Stuart Golgoff, from the University of Arizona's Office of Distributed Learning, says that "while chat rooms, newsgroups, forums and message boards continue to play a role in computer-mediated communication, the Web has assumed a prominent place in forging relationships among people with common interests." According to a study by the Pew Internet & American

Life Project, about 45 million participants in online communities say the Internet has "helped them connect with groups or people who share their interests." Participation in an online community, the study says, has helped them get to know people they otherwise would not have met.

The same Pew study revealed that these virtual relationships are transferring to offline interaction. "In addition to helping users participate in communities of interest that often have no geographical boundaries, the Internet is a tool for those who are involved with local groups, particularly church groups (28 million). Internet users have employed the Internet to contact or get information about local groups."

Sociologist Barry Wellman argues that a good deal of new social capital is being formed through "glocalization" — the capacity of the Internet to expand users' social worlds to faraway people and simultaneously to connect them more deeply to the place where they live. According to the Pew study, "glocalization" is widespread. "The Internet helps many people find others who share their interests no matter how distant they are, and it also helps them increase their contact with groups and people they already know and it helps them feel more connected to them."

Sense-Making and Understanding

Faced with an overwhelming flow of information from a massive number of media sources, people are increasingly going to online communities to learn how to make sense of things. Moreover, the conglomeration and corporatization of media and the sophisticated means by which sources (such as politicians and business executives) "spin" media leaves the mass audience often grasping to make sense of the news and wondering what information to trust.

Witness the increasing number of experts on TV news trying to explain market fluctuations, political maneuvers and medical advancements. But that doesn't completely satisfy the audience, write Bill Kovach and Tom Rosenstiel in their book The Elements of Journalism, because "a journalism that focuses on the expert elite — the special interests — may be in part responsible for public disillusionment. Such a press does not reflect the world as most people live and experience it." Weblogs, forums, usenets and other online social forms have become real-time wellsprings of sense-making from their peers on just about any subject. They also function as archives of perspective.

According to a study by the Pew Internet & American Life Project, "The pull of online communities in the aftermath of the September 11 attacks shows how Americans have integrated online communities into their lives. In the days following the attacks, 33 percent of American Internet users read or posted material in chat rooms, bulletin boards, or other online forums. Although many early posts reflected outrage at the events, online discussions soon migrated to grieving, discussion and debate on how to respond, and information queries about the suspects and those who sponsored them."

To Inform and be Informed

Participants in discussion forums, weblogs and collaborative publishing communities also play the role of "thin media" publishers, inexpensively providing news, information and advice not normally found in mainstream media. Everyone on the Internet is a potential expert on some subject — from Pez dispensers to digital photography techniques to wormholes — and these participatory forms are great places to find and share not only obscure or rare information, but commentary that might be too controversial for mainstream media.

"Thin media publishers are far nimbler and will feed happily on new niches that are far too obscure for traditional media to notice and too thin for traditional media to profitably mine," says Henry Copeland, founder of the Web consultancy Pressflex and author of the weblog Blogads. "And, because they are small and nimble, thin media can help discover and invent the Next Big Thing much easier than their big peers who are busy looking for huge revenues from huge services." The social network created by Internet virally spreads information extremely quickly among their participants. This may be because participatory forms attract "mavens" and "connectors." These types of individuals, whom Malcolm Gladwell identified in his book The Tipping Point, are crucial to the spread of information, online and off.

Mavens are information brokers, sharing and trading what they know. They are aggressive collectors of information but are socially motivated to share it as well. Connectors are people who know a lot of people in diverse settings. They have their feet in many different worlds and are socially motivated to bring them together. Participatory forms offer an excellent outlet for mavens to satisfy their need to share and acquire information, and provides connectors the ability to help information seekers find mavens. (It also provides the opportunity to position themselves as an authority on a subject.)

In a foreword to Seth Godin's book on marketing, Unleashing the Ideavirus, Gladwell explains the potential power of what's happening in participatory forms: "(The) most successful ideas are those that spread and grow because of the customer's relationship to other customers — not the marketer's to the customer." Later in the book, Godin adds: "The future belongs to marketers who establish a foundation and process where interested people can market to each other. Ignite consumer networks and then get out of the way and let them talk."

To Entertain and be Entertained

Just about anything will suffice as entertainment, as long as it can serve as a distraction from the day-to-day grind. To get people to pay for this diversion, it usually must be compelling or "fun." And there are seemingly no limits to what we will pay for fun. But, as anyone in the entertainment business will testify, fun can be one of the most difficult experiences to satisfy. What seems to resonate with an audience of thousands one month falls into relative obscurity the next month. Factors such as novelty, trend and cultural status weigh heavily in the success of entertainment. The result is a large target that is hard to hit. According to the authors of The Cluetrain Manifesto, the Web is not a natural vehicle for prepackaged entertainment. "Unlike the lockstep conformity imposed by television, advertising and corporate propaganda, the Net has given new legitimacy — and freedom — to play. Many of those drawn into this world find themselves exploring a freedom never before imagined: to indulge their curiosity, to debate, to disagree, to laugh at themselves, to compare visions, to learn, to create new art, new knowledge."

Online participation is simply fun — whether a political riff by a deeply committed weblogger, a casual forum discussion, or a one-off album review posted on Amazon. As futurist Paul

Saffo notes, "In the end, much of what passes for communications actually has a high entertainment component. The most powerful hybrid of communications and entertainment is 'particitainment' — entertaining communications that connects us with some larger purpose or enterprise."

To Create

Those who participate online usually create content to inform and entertain others. But creating also builds self-esteem and, in Maslow's view, it's an act of self-actualization. We derive fulfilment from the act of creation. "Five percent of the populace (probably even less) can create. The others watch, listen, read, consume," says Marc Canter, one of the founders of Macromedia and now chairman and founder of Broadband Mechanics. "I think one of the destinies of digital technology is to enable the other 95 percent to express their creativity somehow. That's the gestalt view." "Digital cameras, storytelling, assembling stuff from existing content, annotating, reviews, conversations, linking topics together — are all forms of creativity," Canter says. "(Weblogging is) at the core of creativity — expressing your feelings, opinions and showing everyone else what you think is important." Traditional media tend to understate the value of participation journalism, holding that comments, reviews and content created by "amateurs" provide little value to their mass audience. As such, they are missing the inherent psychological value of the creative process to the individual.

For the most part, our list contains motivations that are positive or fairly benign. An egalitarian/for-the-common-good ethic tends to permeate most of these forms. Yet, anyone that has participated in online communities knows that not all participants play fairly. People will abuse these forms by performing pranks, manipulating the rules, spreading false information and rumors, engaging in flaming — indeed, just about any mischief imaginable — and the results can serious.

According to a CNET article in 1996, "Several stocks have seen meteoric rises, or dramatic falls, in their valuation because of information posted to Internet newsgroups and online services. The Securities and Exchange Commission and other federal regulatory agencies are concerned that unscrupulous insiders or stock promoters could disseminate false or misleading information to manipulate securities prices." Regulatory agencies have policed Internet postings aimed at manipulating stock prices, but they need to tread carefully lest they infringe on free speech rights. Conflict is a key component of any social environment, from a party to a chat room, so we have learned to develop rules designed to guide the experience in a positive direction. "Social interaction creates tension between the individual and the group," explains Clay Shirky, a consultant and teacher who writes frequently on the social and economic effects of Internet technologies. "This is true of all social interaction, not just online. Any system that supports groups addresses this tension by enacting a simple constitution — a set of rules governing the relationship between individuals and the groups. These constitutions usually work by encouraging or requiring certain kinds of interaction, and discouraging or forbidding others."

Rules Governing Participation

In broadcast models, the rules of participation are strict and limited. The media organization has supreme control as the informed intermediary of the news and it only allows the audience to participate through limited means, e.g., submitting letters to the editor or phoning a talk show. Mainstream media are comfortable with this level of participation because it's relatively easy to authenticate the credibility of these participants (though occasional pranks do occur). Because not all participatory journalism is collaborative, We Media can follow the same model as broadcast models. For example, reviews are submitted by the audience to a product recommendation site, authenticated by editors, and broadcast out to a mass audience. Likewise, many webloggers have little interaction or open discussion with their audience. It's simply push media.

But collaborative forms of participatory journalism — forums, newsgroups, chat rooms, group weblogs and publishing systems — are more complex because they must balance the tension between the group and the individual. Even more challenging are the dynamically forming groups that come together briefly to achieve goals through Internet-connected mobile devices (dubbed "smart mobs" by Rheingold). In the past few decades, the Internet has become highly successful in giving the consumer a voice, but author Stephen Johnson says "... systems like Slashdot force us to accept a more radical proposition. To understand how these new media experiences work, you have to analyse the message, the medium and the rules. What's interesting here is not just the medium, but rather the rules that govern what gets selected and what doesn't." When we talk about rules, we really are describing control — the governance of how participants assume roles, how they are allowed to interact with others, and the ownership of the social system. The rules of participation come from a few places. First, they come from technology — rules that are built into the social software that runs the community or participatory form. These rules are then configured by the host (whoever creates the environment). A basic rule of most systems, for example, is that you have to become a registered member to participate. A host would define whether registration is necessary and the criteria that a registrant must meet. Second, rules come from the community of members. This can come from moderators — appointed community members who police the ebb and flow of communication based on the established rules of the environment. For example, in chat rooms or discussion forums, it's common to have a moderator that disciplines or kicks out users who are behaving improperly.

Even those who are not appointed as moderators will police the activity of the system. Much as in any social situation, individuals draw boundaries about what's appropriate and what's not. As the community grows and evolves, members push back against the rules of the host to the point where the system becomes co-owned and operated. In this regard, many of these environments are highly democratic in the way they operate. Various technologies have evolved over the past 40 years to enable us to establish rules, monitor behaviour and to tune out the unwanted voices. As online community expert Rheingold says, "Hiding the crap is the easy part. The real achievement is finding quality."

To increase the signal-to-noise ratio of online communities, emerging technologies called "reputation systems" are helping participants define which information is credible, reliable and trustworthy.

12

Broadcasting Laws in India

Media was under complete monopoly of the Government of India. Private organizations were involved only in commercial advertising and sponsorships of programmes. However, in *Secretary, Ministry of I&B* v. *CAB* 1, the Supreme Court clearly differed from the aforementioned monopolistic approach and emphasized that, every citizen has a right to telecast and broadcast to the viewers/listeners any important event through electronic media, television or radio and also provided that the Government had no monopoly over such electronic media as such monopolistic power of the Government was not mentioned anywhere in the Constitution or in any other law prevailing in the country.

This judgment, thus, brought about a great change in the position prevailing in the broadcast media, and such sector became open to the citizens. The Broadcasting Code, adopted by the Fourth Asian Broadcasting Conference in 1962 listing certain cardinal principles to be followed buy the electronic media, is of prime importance so far as laws governing broadcast medium are concerned. Although, the Broadcast Code was chiefly set up to govern the All India Radio, the following cardinal principles have ideally been practiced by all Broadcasting and Television Organization; viz:-

- To ensure the objective presentation of news and fair and unbiased comment
- To promote the advancement of education and culture
- To raise and maintain high standards of decency and decorum in all programmes

- To provide programmes for the young which, by variety and content, will inculcate the principles of good citizenship
- To promote communal harmony, religious tolerance and international understanding
- To treat controversial public issues in an impartial and dispassionate manner
- To respect human rights and dignity

Cable Television Networks (Regulation) Act, 1995 basically regulates the operation of Cable Television in the territory of India and regulates the subscription rates and the total number of total subscribers receiving programmes transmitted in the basic tier. In pursuance of the Cable Television Network (Regulation) (Amendment) Bill, 2002, the Central Government may make it obligatory for every cable operator to transmit or retransmit programme of any pay channel through an addressable system as and when the Central Government so notifies. Such notification may also specify the number of free to air channels to be included in the package of channels forming the basic service tier.

CABLE TELEVISION NETWORKS (REGULATION) ACT, 1995

Chapter 1: Preliminary

1. Short title, extent and commencement:
   (1) This Act may be called the Cable Television Networks (Regulation) Act,1995.
   (2) It extends to the whole of India.
   (3) It shall be deemed to have come into force on the 29th day of September, 1994.
2. Definitions : In this Act, unless the context otherwise requires,-
   (a) "authorised officer" means, within his local limits of jurisdiction;-
      (i) a District Magistrate, or
      (ii) a Sub-divisional Magistrate, or
      (iii) a Commissioner of Police, and includes any other officer notified in the Official Gazette, by

the Central Government or the State Government, to be an authorised officer for such local limits of jurisdiction as may be determined by that Government;

(aa) "cable operator' means any person who provides cable service through a cable television network or otherwise controls or is responsible for the management and operation of a cable television network;

(b) "cable service" means the transmission by cables of programmes including re-transmission by cable of anybroadcast television signals;

(c) "cable television network" means any system consisting of a set of closed transmission paths and associated signal generation, control and distribution equipment, designed to provide cable service for reception by multiple subscribers;

(d) "company" means a company as defined in section 3 of the Companies Act, 1956 (1 of 1956);

(e) "person" means-

(i) an individual who is a citizen of India;

(ii) an association of individuals or body of individuals, whether incorporated or not, whose members are citizen of India;

(iii) a company in which not less than fifty-one percent of the paid up share capital is held by the citizens of India;

(f) "prescribed" means prescribed by rules made under this Act;

(g) "programme" means any television broadcast and includes-

(i) exhibition of films, features, dramas, advertisement and serials through video cassette recorders or video cassette players;

(ii) any audio or visual or audio-visual live performance or presentation, and the expression "programme service" shall be construed accordingly;

(h) "registering authority" means such authority as the Central Government may, by notification in the Official Gazette, specify to perform the functions of the registering authority under this Act;

(i) "subscriber" means a person who receives the signals of cable television network at a place indicated by him to the cable operator, without further transmitting it to any other person.

Chapter II: Regulation of Cable Television Network

Cable television network not to be operated except after Registration:-No person shall operate a cable television network unless he is registered as a cable operator under this Act:

Provided that a person operating a cable television network, immediately before the commencement of this act, may continue to do so for a period of ninety days from such commencement; and if he has made an application for registration as a cable operator under section 4 within the said period, till he is registered under that section or the registering authority refuses to grant registration to him under that section.

Registration as cable operator :-

(1) Any person who is operating or is desirous of operating a cable television network may apply for registration as a cable operator to the registering authority.

(2) An application under sub-section (1) shall be made in such form and be accompanied by such fees as may be prescribed.

(3) On receipt of the application, the registering authority shall satisfy itself that the applicant has furnished all the required information and on being so satisfied, register the applicant as a cable operator and grant to him a certificate of such registration:

Provided that the registering authority may, for reasons to be recorded in writing and communicated to the applicant, refuse to grant registration to him if it is satisfied that he does not fulfil the conditions specified in clause (e) of section 2.

Transmission of programmes through addressable systems:-

(1) Where the Central Government is satisfied that it is necessary in the public interest so to do, it may, by

notification in the Official Gazette, make it obligatory for every cable operator to transmit or retransmit programme of any pay channel through an addressable system with effect from such date as may be specified in the notification and different dates may be specified for different States, cities, towns or areas, as the case may be.

(2) If the Central Government is satisfied that it is necessary in the public interest so to do, it may, by notification in the Official Gazette, specify one or more free-to-air channels to be included in the package of channels forming basic service tier and any or more such channels may be specified, in the notification, *genre-wise* for providing a programme mix of entertainment, information, education and such other programmes.

(3) The Central Government may specify in the notification referred to in sub-section (2), the number of free-to-air channels to be included in the package of channels forming basic service tier for the purposes of that sub-section and different numbers may be specified for different States, cities, towns or areas, as the case may be.

(4) If the Central Government is satisfied that it is necessary in the public interest so to do, it may, by notification in the Official Gazette, specify the maximum amount which a cable operator may demand from the subscriber for receiving the programmes transmitted in the basic service tier provided by such cable operator.

(5) Notwithstanding anything-contained in sub-section (4), the Central Government may, for the purposes of that sub-section, specify in the notification referred to in that sub-section different maximum amounts for different States, cities, towns or areas, as the case may be.

(6) Notwithstanding anything contained in this section, programmes of basic service tier shall be receivable by any subscriber on the receiver set of a type existing immediately before the commencement of the Cable Television Networks (Regulation) Amendment Act, 2002 without any addressable system attached with such

receiver set in any manner. (7) Every cable operator shall publicise, in the prescribed manner, to the subscribers the subscription rates and the periodic intervals at which such subscriptions are payable for receiving each pay channel provided by such cable operator.

(8) The cable operator shall not require any subscriber to have a receiver set of a particular type to receive signals of cable television network; Provided that the subscriber shall use an addressable system to be attached to his receiver set for receiving programmes transmitted on pay channel.

(9) Every cable operator shall submit a report to the Central Government in the prescribed form and manner containing the information regarding-

(i) the number of total subscribers;

(ii) subscription rates;

(iii) number of subscribers receiving programmes transmitted in basic service tier or particular programme or set of programmes transmitted on pay channel, in respect of cable services provided by such cable operator through a cable television network, and such report shall be submitted periodically at such intervals as may be prescribed and shall also contain the rate of amount, if any, payable by the cable operator to any broadcaster.

Explanation.-For the purposes of this section,-

(a) "addressable system" means an electronic device or more than one electronic devices put in an integrated system through which signals of cable television network can be sent in encrypted or unencrypted form, which can be decoded by the device or devices at the premises of the subscriber within the limits of authorisation made, on the choice and request of such subscriber, by the cable operator to the subscriber;

(b) "basic service tier" means a package of free-to-air channels provided by a cable operator, for a single price to the subscribers of the area in which his cable television network is providing service and such channels are receivable for viewing by the subscribers on the receiver set of a type existing immediately before the commencement of the Cable Television Networks (Regulation) Amendment Act, 2002 without any addressable system attached to such receiver set in any manner;

(c) "channel" means a set of frequencies used for transmission of a programme;

(d) "encrypted", in respect of a signal of cable television network, means the changing of such signal in a systematic way so that the signal would be unintelligible without a suitable receiving equipment and the expression "unencrypted" shall be construed accordingly;

(e) "free-to-air channel", in respect of a cable television network, means a channel, the reception of which would not require the use of any addressable system, to be attached with the receiver set of a subscriber;

(f) "pay channel", in respect of a cable television network, means a channel, the reception of which by the subscriber would require the use of an addressable system, to be attached to his receiver set;

Programme code : No person shall transmit or re-transmit through a cable service any programme unless such programme is in conformity with the prescribed programme code:

Advertisement code : No person shall transmit or re-transmit through a cable service any advertisement unless such advertisement is in conformity with the prescribed advertisement code:

Maintenance of register : Every cable operator shall maintain a register in the prescribed form indicating therein in brief the programmes transmitted or retransmitted through the cable service during a month and such register shall be maintained by the cable operator for a period of one year after the actual transmission or re-transmission of the said programmes.

Compulsory transmission of two Doordarshan channels :

(1) Every cable operator shall retransmit,-

(i) channels operated by or on behalf of Parliament in the manner and name as may be specified by the Central Government by notification in the Official Gazette;

(ii) at least two Doordarshan terrestrial Channels and one regional language channel of a State in the Prime band, in satellite mode on frequencies other than those carrying terrestrial frequencies

(2) The channels referred to in sub-section (1) shall be retransmitted without any deletion or alteration of any programme transmitted on such channels.

(3) The Prasar Bharti (Broadcasting Corporation of India) established under sub-section (1) of section 3 of the Prasar Bharti (Broadcasting Corporation of India) act, 1990 (25 of 1990) may, by notification in the Official Gazette, specify the number and name of every Doordarshan channel to be retransmitted by cable operators in their cable service and the manner of reception and retransmission of such channels.

Use of standard equipment in cable Television network : No cable operator shall, on and from the date of the expiry of a period of three years from the date of the establishment and publication of the Indian Standard by the Bureau of Indian Standards in accordance with the provisions of the Bureau of Indian Standards Act, 1986 (63 of 1986), use any equipment in his cable television network unlesssuch equipment conforms to the said Indian Standard.

Provided that the equipment required for the proposes of section 4A shall be installed by cable operator in his cable television network within six months from the date, specified in the notification issued under sub-section (1) of that section, in accordance with the provisions of the said Act for said purposes.

Cable Television network not to interfere with any telecommunication system :- Every cable operator shall ensure that the cable Television network being operated by him does not interfere, in any way, with the functioning of the authorised telecommunication systems.

Chapter III : Seizure and Confiscation of Certain Equipment

Power to seize equipment used for operating the cable television network :-

(1) If any authorised officer has reason to believe that the provisions of section 3, 4A, 5, 6 or 8 have been or are being contravened by any cable operator, he may seize the equipment being used by such cable operator for operating the cable television network.

(2) No such equipment shall be retained by the authorised officer for a period exceeding ten days from the date of its seizure unless the approval of the District Judge, within the local limits of whose jurisdiction such seizure has been made, has been obtained for such retention.

Confiscation :-The equipment seized under sub-section (1) of section 11 shall be liable to confiscation unless the cable operator from whom the equipment has been seized registers himself as a cable operator under section 4 within a period of thirty days from the date of seizure of the said equipment.

Seizure or confiscation of equipment not to interfere with the other punishment :l-No seizure or confiscation of equipment referred to in section 11 or section 12 shall prevent the infliction of any punishment to which the person affected thereby is liable under the provisions of this Act. Giving of opportunity to the cable operator of seized equipment:-

(1) No order adjudicating confiscation of the equipment referred to in section 12 shall be made unless the cable operator has been given a notice in writing informing him of the grounds on which it is proposed to confiscate such equipment and giving him a reasonable opportunity of making a representation in writing, within such reasonable time as may be specified in the notice against the confiscation and if he so desires of being heard in the matter:

Provided that where no such notice is given within a period of ten days from the days of the seizure of the equipment, such equipment shall be returned after the expiry of that period to the cable operator from whose possession it was seized.

(2) Save as otherwise provided in sub-section (1), the provisions of the Code of Civil Procedure, 1908 (5 of 1908) shall, so far as may be, apply to every proceeding referred to in sub-section (1).

Appeal

(1) Any person aggrieved by any decision of the court adjudicating a confiscation of the equipment may prefer an appeal to the court to which an appeal lies from the decision of such court.

(2) The appellate court may, after giving the appellant an opportunity of being heard, pass such order as it thinks fit confirming, modifying or revising the decision appealed against or may send back the case with such directions as it may think fit for a fresh decision or adjudication, as the case may be, after taking additional evidence if necessary.

(3) No further appeal shall lie against the order of the court made under sub-section (2).

Chapter IV: Offences and Penalties

Punishment for contravention of provisions of this Act :-

(1) Whoever contravenes any of the provisions of this Act shall be punishable,-

  (a) for the first offence, with imprisonment for a term which may extend to two years or with fine which may extend to one thousand rupees or with both;

  (b) for every subsequent offence, with imprisonment for a term which may extend to five years and with fine which may extend to five thousand rupees.

(2) Notwithstanding anything contained in the Code of Criminal Procedure, 1973(2 of 1974), the contravention of section 4A shall be a cognizable offence under this section

Offences by companies :-

(1) Where an offence under this Act has been committed

by a company, every person who, at the time the offence was committed, was incharge of and was responsible to the company for the conduct of the business of the company, as well as the company, shall be deemed to be guilty of the offence and shall be liable to be proceeded against and punished accordingly:

Provided that nothing contained in this sub-section shall render any such person liable to any punishment, if he proves that the offence was committed without his knowledge or that he had exercised all due diligence to prevent the commission of such offence.

(2) Notwithstanding anything contained in sub-section (1), where any offence under this Act has been committed by a company and it is proved that the offence has been committed with the consent or connivance of, or is attributable to any negligence on the part of, any director, manager, secretary or other officer of the company, such director, manager, secretary or the officer shall also be deemed to be guilty of that offence and shall be liable to be proceeded against and punished accordingly.

Explanation : For the purposes of this section,-

(a) "company" means any body corporate and includes a firm or other association of individuals; and

(b) "director" in relation to a firm, means a partner in the firm.

Cognizance of offences :-No court shall take cognizance of any offence punishable under this Act except upon a compliant in writing made by any authorized officer.

Chapter V: Miscellaneous

Power to prohibit transmission of certain programmes in public interest:-Where *any authorised officer* thinks it necessary or expedient so to do in public interest, he may, by order, prohibit any cable operator from transmitting or re-transmitting any programme or channel if, it is not in conformity with the prescribed programme code referred to in section 5 and advertisement code referred to in section 6 or if it is likely to promote, on grounds of religion, race, language, caste or community or any other ground whatsoever, disharmony or feelings of enmity, hatred or ill-will between different religious, racial, linguistic or regional groups or castes or communities or which is likely to disturb the public tranquility.

Power to prohibit operation of cable television network in public interest :-

(1) Where the Central Government thinks it necessary or expedient so to do in public interest, it may prohibit the operation of any cable television network in such areas as it may, by notification in the Official Gazette, specify in this behalf.

(2) Where the Central Government thinks it necessary or expedient so to do in the interest of the-

(i) sovereignty or integrity of India; or

(ii) security of India; or

(iii) friendly relations of India with any foreign State; or

(iv) public order, decency or morality, it may, by order, regulate or prohibit the transmission or retransmission of any channel or programme.

(3) Where the Central Government considers that any programmeof any channel is not in conformity with the prescribed programme code referred to in section 5 or the prescribed advertisement code referred to in section 6, it may by order, regulate or prohibit the transmission or re-transmission of such programme.

Application of other laws not barred :-The provisions of this Act shall be in addition to, and not in derogation of, the Drugs and Cosmetics Act, 1940 (23 of 1940), the Pharmacy Act, 1948 (8 of 1948), the Emblems and Names (Prevention of Improper Use) Act, 1950 (12 of 1950), the Drugs (Control) Act, 1950 (26 of 1950), the Cinematograph Act, 1952 (37 of 1952), the Drugs and Magic Remedies (Objectionable Advertisements) Act, 1954 (21 of 1954), the Prevention of Food Adulteration Act, 1954 (37 of 1954), the Prize Competitions Act, 1955 (42 of 1955), the Copyright Act, 1957 (14 of 1957), the Trade and Merchandise Marks Act, 1958 (43 of 1958), the Indecent Representation of

Women (Prohibition) Act, 1986 (60 of 1986) and the Consumer Protection Act, 1986 (68 of 1986)

Power to make rules :-

(1) The Central Government may, by notification in the Official Gazette, make rules to carry out the provisions of this Act.

(2) In particulars, and without prejudice to the generality of theforgoing power, such rules may provide for all or any of the following matters, namely:-

(a) the form of application and the fee payable under subsection (2) of section 4; (aa) the manner of publicising the subscription rates and the periodical intervals at which such subscriptions are payable under sub-section (7) of section 4A; (aaa) the form and manner of submitting report under subsection (9) of section 4A and the interval at which such report shall be submitted periodically under that subsection,

(b) the programme code under section 5;

(c) the advertisement code under section 6;

(d) the form of register to be maintained by a cable operator under section 7;

(e) any other matter which is required to be, or may be, prescribed.

(3) Every rule made under this Act shall be laid, as soon as may be after it is made, before each House of Parliament, while it is in session, for a total period of thirty days which may be comprised in one session or in two or more successive sessions, and if, before the expiry of the session immediately following the session or the successive sessions aforesaid, both Houses agree in making any modification in the rule or both Houses agree that the rule should not be made, the rule shall thereafter have effect only in such modified form or be of no effect, as the case may be; so, however, that any such modification or annulment shall without prejudice to the validity of anything previously done under that rule.

Repeal and saving :- (1) The Cable Television Networks (Regulation) Ordinance, 1995 (3 of 1995) is hereby repealed. (2) Notwithstanding such repeal, anything done or any action taken under the said Ordinance, shall be deemed to have been done or taken under the corresponding provisions of this Act.

DIRECT-TO-HOME BROADCASTING

Direct-to-Home (DTH) Broadcasting Service, refers to distribution of multi-channel TV programmes in Ku Band by using a satellite system and by providing TV signals directly to the subscribers' premises without passing through an intermediary such as a cable operator. The Union Government has decided to permit Direct-to-Home TV service in Ku band in India.

Guidelines For Obtaining License for Providing Direct-to-home (Dth) Broadcasting Service in India

The Union Government has decided to permit Direct-to-Home (DTH) TV service in Ku Band in India. The prohibition on the reception and distribution of television signal in Ku Band has been withdrawn by the Government vide notification No. GSR 18 (E) dated 9th January, 2001 of the Department of Telecommunications. The salient features of eligibility criteria, basic conditions/obligations and procedure for obtaining the license to set up and operate DTH service are briefly described below. For further details, reference should be made to the Ministry of Information & Broadcasting. Following are the eligibility criteria for applicants, conditions which will apply to DTH license and procedural details :

i) Eligibility Criteria:

- Applicant Company to be an Indian Company registered under Indian Company's Act, 1956.
- Total foreign equity holding including FDI/NRI/OCB/FII in the applicant company not to exceed 49%.
- Within the foreign equity, the FDI component not to exceed 20%.
- The quantum represented by that proportion of the paid up equity share capital to the total issued

equity capital of the Indian promoter Company, held or controlled by the foreign investors through FDI/NRI/OCB investments, shall form part of the above said FDI limit of 20%.

- The applicant company must have Indian Management Control with majority representatives on the board as well as the Chief Executive of the company being a resident Indian.
- Broadcasting companies and/or cable network companies shall not be eligible to collectively own more than 20% of the total equity of applicant company at any time during the license period. Similarly, the applicant company not to have more than 20% equity share in a broadcasting and/or cable network company.
- The Licensee shall be required to submit the equity distribution of the Company in the prescribed Proforma once within one month of start of every financial year.

ii) Number of Licensees:

- There will be no restrictions on the total number of DTH licenses and these will be issued to any person who fulfils the necessary terms and conditions and subject to the security and technical clearances by the appropriate authorities of the Govt.

iii) Period of license:

- License will be valid for a period of 10 years from the date of issue of wireless operational license by Wireless planning and Coordination Wing of Ministry of Communicatons. However, the license can be cancelled/suspended by the Licensor at any time in the interest of Union of India.

iv) Basic conditions/obligations:

- The license will be subject to terms and conditions contained in the agreement and its schedule (Form-B)

v) Procedure for application and grant of licenses:

- To apply to the Secretary, Ministry of I&B, in triplicate, in the prescribed proforma (Form-A)
- On the basis of information furnished in the application form, if the applicant is found eligible for setting up of DTH platform in India, the application will be subjected to security clearance of Board of Directors as well as key executives of the company such as CEO etc. in consultation with the Ministry of Home Affairs and for clearance of satellite use with the Department of Space.
- After these clearances are obtained, the applicant would be required to pay an initial non-refundable entry-fee of Rs.10 crores to the Ministry of Information and Broadcasting.
- After such payment of entry-fee, the applicant would be informed of intent of Min. of I & B to issue license and requested to approach WPC for SACFA clearance.
- After obtaining SACFA clearance, within one month of the same, the Licensee will have to submit a Bank guarantee (Form-C) from any Scheduled Bank to the Ministry of Information and Broadcasting for an amount of Rs.40 crores valid for the duration of the license.
- After submission of this Bank Guarantee, the applicant would be required to sign a licensing agreement with the Ministry of Information and Broadcasting as per prescribed proforma (Form-B).
- After signing of such licensing agreement with the Ministry of Information and Broadcasting, the applicant will have to apply to the Wireless Planning & Coordination (WPC) Wing of the Ministry of Communications for seeking Wireless Operational License for establishment, maintenance and operation of DTH platform.
- The Licensee shall pay an annual fee equivalent to 10% of its gross revenue as reflected in the audited accounts of the Company for that particular financial

year, in the manner detailed under Article-3 (License Fee) of the "Schedule to the License Agreement"

- The Licensee shall also, in addition, pay the license fee and royalty for the spectrum used as prescribed by Wireless Planning & Coordination Authority (WPC), under the Department of Telecommunications.

Arbitration Clause: Incase of any dispute, matter will be referred to the sole Arbitration of the Secretary, Department of Legal Affairs, Government of India or his nominee, for adjudication. The award of the Arbitrator shall be binding on the parties. The Arbitration proceedings will be governed by the law of Indian arbitration in force at the point of time. Venue of Arbitration shall be India.

Bibliography

Aggarwal, Vir Bala : *Media and Society: Challenges and Opportunities*, Concept, Delhi, 2002.

Ajay Dash: *Basic Concept of Journalism*, Discovery, Delhi, 2007.

Ajay S. Jasra: *Internet Journalism in India*, Kanishka, Delhi, 2002.

Anil K Rai Ankit: *Understanding Digital Media and Weblog Journalism*, Shree Pub, Allahabad, 2007.

Arvind Rajagopal: *The Indian Public Sphere : Readings in Media History*, Oxford University Press, London, 2009.

Basu, R. N. : *Handbook of Journalism*, Pointer, Delhi, 2005.

Bhagwan Das Gupta: *Contemporary Sources of the Mediaeval and Modern History of Bundelkhand (1531-1857),* S. S. Pub., Banglore, 1999.

Bhatia, Arun : *Theory and Research in Interpersonal and Mass Communication*, Akansha, Delhi, 2005.

Chakravarty, Jaya : *Media and Women's Development*, Sarup, Delhi, 2007.

Datta, K.B. : *Mass Communication : Theory and Practice*, Akansha, Delhi, 2005.

Des Freedman: *War and the Media : Reporting Conflict 24/7*, Vistaar, Allahabad, 2003.

Desai, Amit : *Journalism and Mass Communication*, Reference Press, Mumbai, 2003.

Dixit, S N. : *Introduction to Journalism and Mass Communication*, Pearl Books, Delhi, 2007.

Hemant Tahiliani: *Learning Disability : A Remedial Reading Programme*, Gagan Deep, Mumbai, 2004.

Howard Boone Jacobson: *Cosmo Dictionary of Mass Communication*, Cosmo Pub, Delhi, 2006.

Jagadish Chakravarthy: *Changing Trends in Public Broadcasting Journalism*, Authorspress, Mumbai, 2004.

Jagannath Pati: *Media and Tribal Development*, Concept, Delhi, 2004.

Kapil Desai: *Media Communication in the Twenty First Century*, Swastik Pub, Jammu, 2008.

Kapoor, S. K. : *Library Science Education and Mass Communication*, Cyber Tech Publications, Delhi, 2010.

Kelly Oliver: *Women as Weapons of War : Iraq Sex and the Media*, Seagull Books, Delhi, 2008.

Kewal Anand: *Dynamics of Journalism : In Historical Perspective*, Swastik, Mumbai, 2008.

Khan, Jahangir : *Basics of Electronic Media*, Shipra Pub, Delhi, 2006.

Kulwant Singh Pathania: *Public Distribution System : Status, Challenges and Remedial Strategies*, Kanishka, Delhi, 2005.

Kurchania, A. K. : *Climatic Changes and Remedial Measures*, Shubhi, Delhi, 2004.

Madhusudan, K. : *Traditional Media and Development Communication*, Kanishka, Delhi, 2006.

Mahendra Kumar Goel: *Encyclopaedia of Electronic Media*, Rajat, Delhi, 2010.

Manohar Puri: *Outlines of Mass Communication*, Pragun Pub, Delhi, 2006.

Muntassir Mamoon: *Media and the Liberation War of Bangladesh, Selections from the Frontier*, Centre for Bangladesh Studies, Delhi, 2002.

Narendra Basu: *Mass Media and Contemporary Social Issues*, Commonwealth Pub, Delhi, 2007.

Narendra Ojha: *Mass Media and Communication*, ABD Pub, Delhi, 2006.

Nihar Ghosh: *Islamic Art of Mediaeval Bengal Architectural Embellishments*, Rama Chattopadhyay, Delhi, 2003.

Ninan Thomas: *Strong Religion, Zealous Media : Christian Fundamentalism and Communication in India*, Sage, Delhi, 2008.

Niranjan Dass: *Media and Terrorism*, MD Pub, Delhi, 2008.

Owen Thomas: *Imagi-Nations and Borderless Television : Media, Culture and Politics Across Asia*, Sage, Delhi, 2005.

Own P. Ward: *Biodegradation and Bioremediation*, Springer, Delhi, 2010.

Parthasarathy, G.K. : *Electronic Media and Communication Research Methods*, GNOSIS, Meerat, 2006

Quereshi, P. : *Islamic Media*, MD Pub, Delhi, 2009.

Rabin Khemchand: *Training for Journalism*, Dominant, Delhi, 2001.

Rajsekhar, T. : *Modern Media and Television Journalism*, Sonali Publications, Delhi, 2007.

Ramaswami Harindranath: *Audience—Citizens : The Media, Public Knowledge and Interpretive Practice*, Sage, Delhi, 2009.

Ranjit Makkuni: *Eternal Gandhi : Design of the Multimedia Museum*, Aditya Birla Group, Delhi, 2007.

Ravindranath, P. K. : *Contemporary Issues : For Students of Journalism*, Authorspress, Banglore, 2008.

Ronald M. Atlas: *Handbook of Media for Environmental Microbiology*, CRS Press, Taylor and Francis Group, Delhi, 2010.

Roy, Durgadas : *Financial Intermediation in Economic Development : The Indian Perspective*, Rajat Pub, Meerut, 2009.

Sahib Dineschandra Sen: *The Vaisnava Literature of Mediaeval Bengal*, Sanskrit Book Depot, Meerut, 2003.

Sama, Umar : *Law of Electronic Media*, Deep and Deep, Delhi, 2007.

Sarita Kumari and D. S. Srivastava: *Education : Assessment, Evaluation and Remedial*, Isha Books, Delhi, 2005.

Shamsi, A. N. : *Mass Media in New World Order*, SBS, Delhi, 2006.

Sheela Verma: *Intermediate Level Hindi : A Textbook*, Manohar, Delhi, 2002.

Shukla, A S : *Handbook of Journalism and Mass Communication*, Rajat, Delhi, 2008.

Sikha Sarkar: *Mother Goddess in Pre-Mediaeval Bengal : A Study of the Evolution of Concept and Forms of Female Divinities*, Firma KLM, Delhi, 2001.

Singh, Archana Rakesh : *Mass Communication in Prevention and Control of AIDS*, Concept, Delhi, 2006.

Singh, Dharmendra : *Mass Communication and Social Development*, Adhyayan, Delhi, 2004.

Singh, J K : *Media and Journalism*, APH Pub, Delhi, 2007.

Sinha, Sushil Kumar : *Sociology of Media : Impact of Doordarshan on Tribals*, Raj Publications, Delhi, 2004.

Srinivasan, T. M. : *Use of Computers and Multimedia in Education*, Aavishkar, Delhi, 2002.

Subarno Chattarji: *Tracking the Media : Interpretations of Mass Media Discourses in India and Pakistan*, Routledge, Delhi, 2008.

Subrato Ghosh: *Modern Trends in Journalism and Mass Communication*, Adhyayan Pub, Delhi, 2008.

Sudhakar Rao: *Multiple Media Schooling : Problems and Management*, Deep and Deep, Delhi, 2006.

Syed Bismillah Geelani: *Manufacturing Terrorism : Kashmiri Encounters With Media and the Law*, Promilla and Co, Delhi, 2006.

Trivedi, P.C. : *Phytoremediation and Environmental Biotechnology*, Pointer, Meerut, 2009.

Uday Moray: *Press in India 2002 : 46 Annual Report of the Registrar of Newspapers for India*, Ministry of Information and Broadcasting, Government of India, Delhi, 2002.

Vanita Kohli: *The Indian Media Business*, Response Books, Delhi, 2003.

Verghese, B. G. : *Breaking the Big Story : Great Moments in Indian Journalism*, Penguin Books, Delhi, 2003.

Verma, N. K. : *Emerging Development of Mass Communication*, Sumit, Delhi, 2006.

Verma, T. C. : *Practice of World Journalism*, ABD, Delhi, 2005.

Vermam, D S : *Media and Communication Management*, Pearl Books, Delhi, 2007.

Vidya Bhushna: *A History of Indian Logic : Ancient, Mediaeval and Modern Schools*, Shiv Books International, Delhi, 2005.

Index

A

Audio Recording, 183, 188.

B

Broadcasting Laws, 266.

C

Cable Television Networks, 267, 270, 272, 279.
Citizen Media, 71, 161.
Collaborative Publishing, 244, 245, 246, 261.
Commission, 3, 5, 8, 23, 70, 72, 73, 76, 77, 97, 100, 104, 116, 160, 167, 189, 263, 276.
Communication, 16, 18, 19, 20, 21, 24, 42, 45, 47, 48, 49, 50, 52, 53, 55, 56, 65, 66, 67, 73, 79, 83, 99, 126, 133, 135, 144, 145, 146, 147, 150, 151, 155, 157, 183, 184, 188, 191, 192, 196, 245, 248, 249, 252, 253, 254, 262, 264, 271.
Cultural Politics, 57.
Culture, 13, 20, 21, 29, 45, 53, 56, 57, 61, 67, 68, 76, 87, 88, 139, 140, 141, 142, 145, 147, 148, 149, 150, 154, 155, 156, 157, 162, 163, 179, 184, 200, 227, 235, 247, 266.

D

Data Processing, 178.
Development Journalism, 26, 28, 29, 30, 31, 32, 33.
Developments, 2, 47, 128, 129, 188, 195, 201.
Digital Media, 80, 176, 178, 181, 185, 201.
Distribution, 10, 31, 69, 80, 84, 144, 188, 194, 205, 233, 243, 245, 248, 249, 268, 279, 280.

F

Freedom, 4, 5, 6, 7, 9, 12, 13, 14, 17, 19, 27, 32, 46, 50, 52, 66, 69, 71, 73, 74, 76, 77, 81, 84, 93, 94, 96, 97, 99, 101, 102, 104, 105, 110, 111, 112, 113, 115, 118, 119, 129, 131, 198, 238, 262.
Fundamental Rights, 117, 119, 120, 131, 132, 137, 138.

G

Global Journalism, 83, 84, 85, 87, 88.
Global Media, 81, 83, 146, 174.

I

Interactive Media, 42, 179, 184, 185, 193.

J

Journalistic Ethics, 72.

L

Laws, 6, 10, 11, 12, 13, 44, 48, 58, 61, 72, 116, 119, 120, 131, 141, 161, 266, 277.
Legislative Privileges, 130, 131.

M

Mass Media, 51, 52, 68, 69, 70, 76, 185, 186, 190, 191, 193, 197, 226, 227.
Media Art, 196, 197, 198, 199, 202.
Media Culture, 147, 148, 149.
Media Democracy, 68, 69, 71.
Media Development, 9, 28.
Media Industry, 12, 17, 80, 146, 176.
Media Ownership, 50, 55, 69, 70, 71, 186.
Media Structures, 20, 21, 22, 23, 25.

O

Opportunity, 138, 209, 255, 257, 262, 274, 275.
Organizations, 3, 4, 5, 9, 18, 19, 20, 21, 23, 24, 25, 83, 84, 87, 88, 147, 149, 159, 172, 187, 232, 236, 238, 257, 259, 266.
Ownership, 50, 55, 68, 69, 70, 71, 73, 77, 86, 186, 245, 247, 265.

P

Parliamentary Privileges, 110, 111.
Participatory Media, 237.
Peace Communication, 20.
Policy, 1, 15, 16, 26, 33, 34, 38, 39, 56, 59, 66, 69, 162, 224, 238, 242.
Provisions, 7, 27, 72, 75, 97, 99, 110, 112, 116, 118, 119, 137, 273, 274, 275, 277, 278, 279.
Public Broadcasting, 63, 147, 159, 160, 161, 162, 163, 164, 166, 167, 169, 171, 172, 173.
Public Media, 19, 25, 54, 63, 64, 67.
Public Relations, 56, 57, 122, 186, 187.
Public Sphere, 42, 43, 44, 45, 46, 47, 48, 49, 50, 51, 52, 53, 56, 60, 67, 86, 87.

S

Software Publishing, 195.
Sting Operations, 94, 96, 97, 104, 105, 106, 107, 108, 109.
Sustainable Development, 238.

T

Technology, 12, 16, 42, 45, 49, 53, 71, 80, 81, 82, 83, 84, 86, 94, 95, 97, 105, 148, 150, 166, 176, 178, 179, 186, 201, 210, 227, 228, 229, 230, 232, 243, 244, 245, 246, 247, 248, 250, 263, 265.
Transport Media, 158.
Tsunami Coverage, 30.

V

Video Broadcasting, 255.

❑❑❑